BRADSHAW ON: THE FAMILY

A New Way of Creating Solid Self-Esteem

John Bradshaw

Health Communications, Inc.
Deerfield Beach, Florida

www.hcibooks.com

Library of Congress Cataloging-in-Publication Data

Bradshaw, John, 1933-
    Bradshaw on the family: a new way of creating solid self-esteem/
John Bradshaw. —Rev. ed.
        p.   cm.
    Based on the television program entitled: Bradshaw on—the family.
    Includes bibliographical references.
    ISBN-13: 978-1-55874-427-1 (alk. paper)
    ISBN-10: 1-55874-427-4 (alk. paper)
    1. Family—United States—Psychological aspects. 2. Self-actualization
(Psychology) 3. Family—Religious life—United States. I. Bradshaw
on—the family (Television program)
    II. Title.
HQ536.B72   1996   96-34325
306.8'5—dc20   CIP

© 1988, 1996 John Bradshaw

Published by: Health Communications, Inc.
            3201 S.W. 15th Street
            Deerfield Beach, FL 33442

Cover redesign by José Villavicencio

*To Nancy, who is my friend and
the most gentle person I have ever known.
Together we shared a sometimes difficult
and always exciting journey
of family-making.*

CONTENTS

PREFACE TO THE FIRST EDITION

The material presented here is an amplification of a recent television series entitled *Bradshaw On: The Family*. These programs were recorded ad-lib before a live audience, during which I used no manuscript or Teleprompters. Consequently, the material often lacked detail. In that medium this lack was acceptable, as my goal was to present material not only for content but also for emotional impact on the listener.

This book is for those who want to pursue the material in more depth. It is also for anyone from a dysfunctional family, whether the individual viewed the series or not, and for anyone in our society who is not aware of the potential for emotional numbing, deselfment and addiction embodied in our patriarchal rules for raising children.

The chapters follow the general outline of the television series. I've extended the material on families as systems and made a separate chapter out of it. I've also changed the specific titles of the last three programs.

In this series I offered a new understanding of emotional health and illness, as well as an understanding of the way this health and illness are multi-generationally transmitted. This book offers you a way to recover your lost childhood self, as well as a new way to enrich your self-esteem. It will also help you understand why functional families are absolutely essential if we are to heal our societal wounds.

Much has been written about the family as a system. Most of the writing has been directed toward counselors, therapists and clinicians, the professional practitioners in the field. To my knowledge, little has been directed to the layperson; the nonexpert. But the layperson also needs a bridge of understanding to these innovative and powerful concepts. The most important aspect of this understanding is how each of us may have lost our true self in the family system shuffle, and how our family systems embody and create the addicted society we live in.

While only 45 years old, the concept of families as social systems is a new and effective approach to the understanding not only of ourselves but of major social problems as well.

Ronald David "R. D." Laing, the great existentialist psychotherapist, has suggested that the theory of family systems is in as much dramatic contrast to past theories as the work of Sigmund Freud was to the practice of imprisoning disturbed people in asylums. This may be an exaggerated claim, but I'm convinced that unless I know and understand the family system from which I came, I will have difficulty understanding my true self and the society I live in.

What has been said about cultural history is true of individuals: If we do not know our familial history, we may be doomed to repeat it.

In what follows, I shall draw freely from the work of many pioneers in the field of family systems theory. Men such as Milton H. Erickson, Murray Bowen, Nathan W. Ackerman, Gregory Bateson, Jay Haley and Carl A. Whitaker immediately come to mind as fathers of this movement; and the great mother of the movement, Virginia Satir, has had a tremendous impact on my own work. I also acknowledge my indebtedness to Alice Miller, Renee Fredrickson, Gershen W. Kaufman, Robert W. Firestone, Sharon Wegscheider-Cruse and Bob Subby.

Special thanks go to Terry Kellogg, who appeared on programs 7 and 8 of the television series. Terry's insights have been an important help in clarifying some aspects of my own position. In all cases, unless I quote these sources directly, I take responsibility for my interpretations of the thoughts and ideas of others.

As a theologian I have concern for the spiritual issues involved in our knowing and loving ourselves. These issues, grounded in the family, have a major impact on society. I have underscored this concern by my choice of the subtitle: *A New Way to Enrich Your Self-Esteem and Foster Deep Democracy*.

Spirituality is about wholeness. One source of the wounds that destroy our wholeness can be uncovered by exploring our family systems. My thesis is that there is a crisis in society today that is reflected in our families, a crisis in which we are cut off from our true selves.

Part of the remedy lies in identifying the roots of the crisis in the families our society creates and the society created by our families. The family is the major source of the wars within ourselves, and in a real sense, the wars with others.

One of my great teachers, Gregory Baum, has defined the demonic as "a structure of evil which transcends the malice of men and women." In Baum's sense this book confronts the demonic in human experience and offers some choices as to a way out.

I'd like first to express my gratitude to all of you who watched the PBS series *Bradshaw On: The Family* and read the first edition of this book. Your kind words and testimonials of transformation made the labor more worthwhile than I could have ever dreamed of. Your support and enthusiasm more than allayed my fears relating to the relevance of the material presented in this book.

I am also grateful to those of you who took the time to write me constructive criticisms and suggested ways to expand certain ideas I presented in this book.

I am grateful to the public critics whose sometimes vitriolic attacks forced me to critically think and rethink certain positions I had taken and presented on television and in this book. I am grateful for the opportunity to add new materials and update my ideas in this book.

Bradshaw On: The Family was my first book and has the bold stamp of youthful passion and idealism. I was on fire with almost evangelical zeal when I wrote it. When I made the PBS series in October of 1984, I still felt anger and pain over my own childhood wounds and was in the throes of my own original pain grief work. I had just come to a full awareness of how the theory of family systems applied to my own alcoholic family and had identified with the characteristics relating to Adult Children of Alcoholics (ACoA).

This knowledge was so exciting to me and helped me reduce my toxic shame so much that I embraced family systems thinking like the devotee of a salvational religion. In 1984, the adult child movement and the newly understood discussion of co-dependency were just beginning to gather momentum. I felt that my work would further the recovery movement.

Today, I realize that my own unfinished business and my passionate belief about family systems as a kind of salvation system colored my presentation, which was at times polarized. However, I still believe that the PBS series and this book were needed at that time. If I hadn't done it, someone else would have.

I had no idea of the impact that the TV series and this book would have on people's lives. Almost immediately after airing the PBS series, I received numerous requests (far more than I could begin to handle) from all over the U.S. and Canada for live talks and workshops. Since its publication in January of 1988, this book has sold more than 1,250,000 copies. Some 250,000 people have attended my workshops and lectures.

The early energy of the recovery movement has now subsided. Much of the recovery philosophy has become a way of life for many people. Phrases like "dysfunctional family," "shame-based personality" and "wounded inner-child," which were uncommon when I began this work, are now commonplace, at times even clichés. The reality of these phrases has been taken seriously, and according to the testimonial letters I have received, real healing has taken place.

The recovery movement has been ridiculed, criticized, debated and challenged. I believe it has stood the test of time. Many people now see it as an important part of a larger historical phenomenon. Let me briefly discuss why I think this is so.

Human evolution and human history have been characterized by what the French call *prise de conscience. Prise de conscience* refers to the process of enlightenment and self-understanding that takes place in the growth and maturity of an individual or a group. Once the evolutionary process reached the self-reflecting level of human consciousness, there was a deepening awareness of those elements that constitute human nature. This awareness extends to an understanding of the kinds of environments that allow our essential nature to flourish. Humankind is constituted precisely as human by virtue of our ability to reason, exercise free will, develop moral conscience, be creative and live by the rules of law. There seems to be very little argument that these human activities are enhanced more by democratic forms of human governance than by monarchial, dictatorial (whether patriarchal or matriarchal) forms of political leadership. But monarchy has ruled most of Western history.

A large portion of that history is characterized by the social agreement that allowed powerful kings and/or landlords to have enormous power in exchange for their protection and security. Life during most of human history was far more primitive than any of us can imagine. Until a little more than a century ago, we had no electricity, mass communication, rapid transit, airlines, TV, refrigeration, microwaves, computers, Internet, etc.

It is difficult to imagine what life was like without the products of the *industrial* and *informational* revolutions. I once remember reading that people in colonial times held their evening parties on the night of the full moon because that was when there was more light. Monarchial systems (mostly patriarchal) worked well to organize social life and give people a sense of security.

Religious patriarchy validated the political structure with doctrines like the divine "right" of kings and the belief that all authority (no matter how corrupt) was from God and must be obeyed. Unjust kings and rulers were held accountable to God, and blind obedience was even more virtuous in the face of kingly or princely injustice.

The family naturally took on this monarchial structure. This is where the parenting rules I refer to in this book as poisonous pedagogy come from. Parents were to be obeyed as if they were gods. They were to be *honored*. Children were never allowed to raise their voices or express anger toward their parents. Like the great monarchs, parents were held answerable to God. And within the parental dyad itself, there was hierarchy. Women were subject to and were to obey their husbands. Both father and mother had the right to hit and spank their children. Anger was especially forbidden and punished. It seems clear why monarchs did not want their subjects to have anger. Anger is the feeling that gives us energy to fight those who violate us. Our anger protects our rights. Since subjects had few rights, the monarchs wanted to make sure they did not protest their lowly status. Anger, if allowed, could be the energy that sparked a revolution. As parental authority mirrored kingly authority, anger was forbidden to children. The family hierarchy of power was blatantly nondemocratic.

The French and American Revolutions were direct responses to the abuse of monarchial power. They ushered in representational democracy. But even with representational democracy, the family maintained its authoritarian structure. I personally know men who fought in the wars to make the world safe for democracy, yet rule their families like Nazi dictators.

Hitler's Nazi regime was the extreme social embodiment of monarchial patriarchy. *Vater über alles* (the fatherland over all) was a Nazi slogan endorsing the extreme cruelty of unbridled power that fostered the most heinous and inhuman crimes the world has ever known.

I look upon the defeat of Nazism as the end of Western monarchial patriarchy. Obviously we still have strong remnants of patriarchal/matriarchal systems in current social life. But Nazism magnified the inherent potentiality for abuse and brutality in monarchial-type dictatorships and made it clear that this social structure is far too dangerous and risky to continue to use.

I see the last 50 years as the beginning of a new and *deeper* stage of democracy. Our consciousness has expanded immensely beyond the sexism, racism, homophobia and emotional primitiveness of pre-World War II patriarchy. Our expanded consciousness has also been aided by the 19th-century existentialist movement in philosophy. Prior to this movement, philosophical thinking was dominated by rationalism. The rationalist thinkers believed that everything could be explained logically. Thinkers like Dostoevski, Kierkegaard, Kafka and Nietzsche were prophetic voices. Dostoevski predicted the rise of communism. Kafka and Nietzsche warned about nihilistic wars and the atrocities spawned by them. All of these philosophers were clear about the consequences that follow the repression of will and the emotions. They understood long before modern physics that whatever is repressed in an energy field will ultimately be expressed. A case could be made that our 20th-century wars, social revolutions, acute anxiety and massive addictiveness are the expressions of centuries of monarchial patriarchy and rationalistic repression of affective life—the life of emotion, will and desire. While monarchial patriarchy and rationalism were necessary stages in the evolution of consciousness, we now see that they do not help us reach our highest potential. They keep us emotional primitives.

All these factors—the French and American Revolutions, the catastrophe of Nazism, the existential revolt against rationalism have helped raise our consciousness to a new awareness of the meaning of democracy. We are now seeing that a *deeper* democracy is the way to more fully actualize our essential nature.

In my zeal I desperately wanted people to understand how the new shift in consciousness was exposing the old patriarchal model of child rearing as abusive. One of the patriarchal methods for keeping children in their place was shaming punishment. I saw how this toxic shaming damaged my own self-esteem. Others saw this also. Marilyn Mason, a psychologist in Minnesota, has referred to toxic shame as the most damaging form of domestic violence there is.

I wanted to warn parents that these socially accepted *normal* parenting rules were damaging their children's self-esteem, especially since the parents were doing this unknowingly or unintentionally. I tried to make it clear that it is *not a matter of blame.* Our parents did the best they could within the limits of their own awareness. Monarchial child rearing is seen as abusive *only when our consciousness shifts toward a deeper internalization of democracy.*

The first edition of *Bradshaw On: The Family* served an important function in focusing our collective consciousness on some revolutionary new information explaining the ways that families work. *Never before in history has such a precise knowledge about family dynamics and how families work been available.* And I believe the material in this book is still totally relevant as a resource for revising traditional values and healing our pressing societal wounds.

For the first time in human history we now have a sense of the family's awesome power—how it can shape our primal identity and how it can impact its members' lives for generations. *We are also learning how to enhance the family's health and how to strengthen it over generations.*

Families, like species, can go into extinction. Understanding the dynamics of how this can happen gives us valuable information for strengthening our families for future generations.

This new understanding of how families work gives us added justification for the traditional values that emphasize the importance of strong marriages and mature, efficient parenting. Our new awareness about how families shape our identities forces us to take parental discipline even more seriously and moves us to learn what discipline really means.

The family is the matrix of character—the most likely place for us to develop the foundation for true virtues and to internalize real and abiding values. We need to learn more about these matters, as the family is clearly being threatened and is failing to deliver virtuous people.

The relevance of this book is more urgent in view of the regressive cry for traditional values. We need traditional values. The information in this book makes that clearer than ever before. But the plea for traditional values that we most often hear today is asking us to go back to a monarchial system of hierarchical power and to reinstate the rules of the poisonous pedagogy.

Paradoxical as it might seem, to return to *these* traditional values will cause more divorce, more abusers, more teenage drug abuse, more chaotic undisciplined children, more unthinking people who will become the pawnlike followers of any strong, articulate, opinionated and rigid leader. Dittohead co-dependents are not the virtuous people of character that we need for the new age of deep democracy. As chaotic as modern family life may seem, the high divorce rate and runaway children can actually be seen as expressions of an emerging deeper democracy. Unlike times past, many women and children are expressing their courage and individuality by refusing to live in families where they are beaten and abused.

Let me say more about the reality of *deep* democracy. Deep democracy, as I'm using the phrase, has to do with an internalizing process whereby the democratic revolutions of 200 years ago became part of our very being. *Deep* democracy, as the psychologist Arnold Mindell points out in his book, *The Leader as Martial Artist*, is a timeless feeling of shared compassion for all living beings. It is a sense of the value and importance of the whole, including and especially our own personal reality. Deeply democratic people value every organ in their body as well as their inner feelings, needs, desires, thoughts and dreams. Since we cannot be any more honest or loving with others than we are with ourselves, charity must begin at home. And when we love ourselves in a deeply democratic manner, we will love our children, parents and siblings the same way. Once our families are deeply democratic, we will create a deeply democratic love of nature, society and the world.

It is in the context of the transition to deep democracy in relation to monarchial patriarchy that Virginia Satir, one of the germinal thinkers in family systems theory, made the comment that "96 percent of families are dysfunctional." (This quote has often been attributed to me. I never said it or wrote it.) I actually believe that all families carrying generations of monarchial patriarchal rules have a propensity to be dysfunctional because our new consciousness of deep democracy calls us to a kind of individuality never dreamed of in the past. The past was not bad. It is simply inadequate in the light of our new consciousness of deep democracy.

It is worth noting that our expanded understanding of the dangers of monarchial patriarchy and the poisonous pedagogy has grown most passionately over the last 50 years. The war trials at Nuremberg began a wave of poignant and socially revolutionary anti-patriarchal movements. At the Nuremberg war trials, *conscience* triumphed over monarchial patriarchy's most treasured tenet—*blind obedience*. The Civil Rights movement often engaged in civil disobedience. Other anti-patriarchal movements include the Women's Rights movement, the Gay and Lesbian Rights movement and the recent Men's Rights movement. From my perspective, two other movements are of great significance—the Flower Children's movement of the 1960s and the Adult Children movement in the 1980s. Understanding the historical significance of these social phenomena as anti-patriarchal movements helps me see that *the Recovery movement was part of the collective paradigm shift of consciousness into deep democracy.*

The flower children bore witness to the original innocence and desire for love and peace we all possess as our birthright. During the 1960s, we became acutely conscious of the raw horror of war. We saw clearly how our innocent youth are victimized at the hand of the often power-hungry patriarchal elders who make the wars.

The statement often seen on placards in those days, "Suppose they gave a war and no one came," is a powerful albeit naïve expression of a way to end the exploitation of our youth by wars.

The Adult Child movement in the 1980s attested to the tremendous impact childhood trauma and abuse have on adult life. It showed us clearly that our "normal" parenting rules (the poisonous pedagogy) that worked for past generations cannot work in the age of deep democracy. These rules are undemocratic and likely to cause some degree of low self-esteem and toxic shame. In the past the denial of self (deselfment) was desirable, as was the repression of strong feelings. What was wanted was loyalty to the family system.

Perhaps now for the first time we fully see that childhood abuse is the greatest social problem of our time. Maria Montessori said this years ago. She urged us to see the potential for abuse in monarchial patriarchal rules for rearing children.

The Adult Child movement has made us acutely aware of the dynamics of deselfment. It was unfortunate that the reality of deselfment was described by the Recovery movement with the rather vague term co-dependency. Even though the word co-dependency causes some confusion, I have left it in much of my text. In my later work, *Family Secrets,* I used the word "deselfment" to describe the reality of co-dependency. I prefer that word, but since the early Adult Child movement was identified with co-dependency, I think it is important to leave it.

Whatever we call it, there is a reality that it refers to. That reality is the loss of solid self-esteem and the development of a false self. Children raised by patriarchal parenting rules quickly learn that the way to get love is to give up their authentic self and develop a self that meets the demands of blind obedience and duty. When the core of self is covered up with a false self, true self-love and self-esteem are impossible.

This book focuses on the rebuilding of solid self-esteem—especially in lieu of the damage caused by the poisonous pedagogy.

When I first published this book in 1988, there was confusion and argument about the difference between mental and emotional illness. Early family systems theorists believed that they had found relational patterns in the family that helped explain the formation of schizophrenia and other so-called mental illnesses. The terms mental and emotional illness were often used interchangeably. Today, there is strong agreement that mental illness, like autism and schizophrenia, is biochemically rooted and is not the result of socialization. I have corrected the places where this distinction was not clear in my earlier text.

Wherever possible, I have softened my tendency toward absolutizing. In my canonization of systems thinking, I had a tendency to deify dysfunction. I often implied that families were inherently dysfunctional. From my deeper readings of Dr. Murray Bowen, I now understand that family dysfunction is more dynamic and relative than I made it out to be. Any family *can* become dysfunctional during times of extreme stress and anxiety. Strong families, characterized by high levels of parental maturity, have better and more flexible coping skills. Because such families have better coping strategies, they reduce the duration of distress and limit the time of family dysfunction. Weaker families, characterized by lower levels of parental maturity, tend to use ineffective coping strategies and can remain dysfunctional for long periods of time—even for generations. Healthy families are characterized by the level of solid self-esteem each parent has achieved. High levels of self-esteem result from high degrees of individuality or self-differentiation. Self-differentiation is characterized by the ability to separate thinking from feeling, affording a person the ability to think about feelings and to feel about thinking. Self-differentiation reduces the amount of reactiveness and irrational behavior in a family.

To conclude this preface, let me emphasize my belief that there is still a crisis in our country and in all the countries of the world. The old order, with its monarchial patriarchal and matriarchal cosmology, served a valuable function. It produced a technology that has allowed us to venture into outer space and break the code of DNA. We can now literally *see* that the Earth is a living being and we are now experimenting with genetically engineering life.

As our consciousness emerges, we've come to realize that we are the Earth thinking—we, the whole human family, are the consciousness of the Earth. We realize that all of us are needed to do the job of providing for the future. Our differences are not the source of our problems; they are the source of our solutions. We need the whole family of humans—every culture, every language, every religion, every species of living being—in order to solve our planetary problems.

Our consciousness is not very old. It is technologically smart, but seemingly not very wise. How can we live together as the family of the Earth? What will we choose for our future? These are the weightiest questions we face. Understanding how families work will help us to understand how we got socialized in our original families and how that socialization carries over into our larger world. I hope this book will give us some new awareness as we grope with the many problems we face as we approach the third millennium. I hope you will find the contents of this book a source of hope.

I am primarily a teacher, and I have tried to synthesize the wide variety of new materials on the family as a social system. In order to make matters clear I needed to translate sometimes highly technical clinical language into a more popular form. It is risky to do that, since technical language is technical because of the need for accuracy and precision. I take full responsibility for my presentation and offer my apologies in advance for any misrepresentations to the brilliant clinical thinkers who formulated systems theory.

As a teacher my job is to organize and clarify. That is the reason I created the many mnemonic formulae and summaries at the end of each chapter. I am very pleased that several university professors have chosen to use this book as a text and I hope that they will find this revised edition more precise and useful. I also hope the new material in this revised edition will further aid those who identify themselves as adult children as they continue their internalization process. I hope this material will be helpful to new readers, too.

A PARABLE: THE STORY OF HUGH

Once upon a time a royal person was born. His name was Hugh. Although I'll refer to Hugh as "he," no one actually knew whether Hugh was male or female and it didn't really matter.[1] Hugh was unlike anyone who ever lived before or who would ever live again. Hugh was precious, unrepeatable, incomparable; a trillion-dollar diamond in the rough.

For the first 15 months of life, Hugh only knew himself from the reflections he saw in the eyes of his caretakers. Hugh was terribly unfortunate. His caretakers, although not blind, had glasses over their eyes. Each set of glasses already had an image on it, so that each caretaker only saw Hugh according to the image on his glasses. Thus, even though Hugh's caretakers were physically present, not one of them ever actually saw him. By the time Hugh was grown, he was a mosaic of other people's images of him, none of which was the real Hugh. No one had ever really seen Hugh, so no one ever mirrored back to him what he really looked like. Consequently, Hugh thought he was this mosaic of other people's images. He really did not know who he was.

Sometimes in the dark of the night when he was all alone, Hugh knew that something of profound importance was missing. He experienced this as a gnawing sense of emptiness—a deep void.

Hugh tried to fill the emptiness and void with many things: power, worldly fame, money, possessions, chemical highs, food,

---

[1] For grammatical consistency and clarity, the pronouns "he," "his" and "him" have been used throughout instead of "she or he," "his or her" and "her and him." No sexual bias or insensitivity is intended.

sex, excitement, entertainment, relationships, children, work— even exercise. But no matter what he did, the gnawing emptiness never went away. In the quiet of the night when all the distractions were gone, he heard a still, quiet voice that said: "Don't forget; please don't forget me!" But alas! Hugh did forget and went to his death never knowing who he was.

Overview: The Crisis

*Our very
psychology has
been shaken to its
foundation. . . .
to grasp the meaning
of the world today
we use a language
created to express the
world of yesterday.
The life of the past
seems to us nearer
our true nature, but
only for the reason
that it is nearer
our language.*

ANTOINE
DE SAINT-EXUPÉRY

The last 45 years have ushered in a new awareness about the impact of families on the formation of solid self-esteem. While we've always known that our families influence us, we're now discovering that the influence is beyond what we had imagined. We now understand that families are dynamic social systems, having structural laws, components and rules.

The most important family rules are those that determine what it means to be a human being. These rules embrace the most fundamental beliefs about raising children. What parents believe about human life and human fulfillment governs their way of raising children. The way children are parented forms their core beliefs about themselves. Nothing could be more important. Children are any

1

culture's greatest natural resource. The future of the world depends on our children's conceptions of themselves. All their choices depend on their views of themselves.

But a crisis exists in the family today. This crisis centers on our parenting rules and the multi-generational process by which families perpetuate these rules.

Sickness of the Soul: Shame

The parenting rules I refer to are abusive and shaming. They destroy children's self-esteem, resulting in shame. According to psychologist Gershen Kaufman in his book, *Shame,* shame is

> *. . . a sickness of the soul. It is the most poignant experience of the self by the self, whether felt in humiliation or cowardice, or in a sense of failure to cope successfully with challenge. Shame is a wound felt from the inside, dividing us both from ourselves and from one another.*[1]

According to Kaufman, shame is the source of most of the disturbing inner states that deny full human life. Depression, alienation, self-doubt, isolating loneliness, paranoid and schizoid phenomena, compulsive disorders, splitting of the self, perfectionism, a deep sense of inferiority, inadequacy or failure, the so-called borderline conditions and disorders of narcissism—all result from shame. Shame is a kind of self-murder. Internalized, shame is characterized by a kind of psychic numbness that becomes the foundation for a kind of living death. Forged in the matrix of our source relationships, shame conditions every other relationship in our lives. Shame destroys self-esteem.

Shame and Guilt

Shame is at the heart of our wound and differs greatly from the feeling of guilt. Guilt says I've *done* something wrong; shame says

---

[1] Gershen Kaufman, *Shame: The Power of Caring,* 3rd rev. ed. (Rochester, Vt.: Schenkman Books, 1992), vii-viii.

there *is* something wrong with me. Guilt says I've *made* a mistake; shame says I *am* a mistake. Guilt says what I *did* was not good; shame says I *am* no good. The difference is distinct and profound.

Our parenting rules have not been seriously updated in years. They come from a time when monarchial patriarchy ruled the day rather than democracy. The high divorce rate; violent teenage disorders; massive drug abuse; and epidemic incest, eating disorders and physical battering all are evidence that something is radically wrong. The old rules no longer work. Our consciousness has changed, as has our view of the world.

Shame Through Abandonment

Our parenting rules primarily shame children through varying degrees of abandonment. Parents abandon their children in the following ways:

1. By actually physically leaving them
2. By failing to model their own emotions for their children, and by failing to affirm their children's expressions of emotion
3. By failing to provide for their children's developmental dependency needs
4. By physically, sexually, emotionally and spiritually abusing them
5. By using their children to take care of their own unmet dependency needs
6. By using children to take care of their marriages
7. By hiding and denying their shame secrets to the outside world so that the children have to protect these covert issues in order to keep the family balance
8. By not giving children enough of their time, attention and direction
9. By acting shameless

Children's needs are insatiable in the sense that they need their parents continuously throughout childhood. No five-year-old ever packed his bags and called a family meeting to thank his parents for their support and guidance as he got ready to make his way in the world. It takes 15 years before nature awakens these urges to leave home and parents. Children need their parents to be there for them.

Abandoned children have no one there for them. Children may even have to take care of their parents. The preciousness and uniqueness every human child possesses are destroyed through abandonment. The child is alone and alienated. This abandonment creates a shame-based inner core.

Emergence of the False Self

Once a child's inner self is flawed by shame, the experience of self is painful. To compensate, the child develops a *false self* in order to survive.

The false self forms a defensive mask, distracting the true self from its pain and inner loneliness. After years of acting, perform-ing and pretending, the child loses contact with the true self. That true self is numbed out. The false self cover-up makes it impossible to develop self-esteem.

The crisis is far worse than is generally known because adults who parent their children badly cover up their shame-based inner selves. So the crisis is not just about how we raise our children; it's about a large number of people who look like adults, talk and dress like adults, but who are actually adult children. These adult children often run our schools, our churches and our government. They also create our families. This book is about the crisis in the family today—*the crisis of adult children raising children who will become adult children.*

The Family Rules

The rules about raising children are the most sacred of all rules. They are authenticated by religious teaching and reinforced in our school systems. Seriously questioning them is considered sacrile-gious. This is why the crisis is so dangerous.

Like the story of the emperor with no clothes, we are not sup-posed to look. But in this case, the consequences are far more serious. We share a collective denial and a *cultural no-talk rule.*

This no-talk rule is rooted in the rules governing parenting. Children should speak only when spoken to; children should be seen and not heard; children should obey all adults (any adult) without question. To question is an act of disobedience. And so the rules are carried out by the obedient child in all the adults who are raising families. The hidden child in every adult continues to obey, so that the rules are carried multi-generationally, and "the sins of the fathers" are visited on the children, to the third and fourth generations.

The crisis is cunning and baffling because *one of the rules comprising the sacred rules is that we can't question any of the rules.* We are not supposed to talk about the rules. This would dishonor our parents.

We have no alternative. We must break the sacred rule and question these rules because unless we talk about them, there is no way out. We must evaluate them in the light of our newfound knowledge of families as systems.

We must also examine these rules so that we can come to terms with our compulsiveness. Shame, with its accompanying loneliness and psychic numbness, fuels our compulsive/addictive lifestyle. Since the child in the adult has insatiable needs, we cannot find fulfillment. As grownups we can't go back as children and sit in Mom's lap or have Dad take us fishing. And no matter how hard we try to turn our children, lovers and spouses into Mom and Dad, it never works. We cannot be children again. No matter how many times we fill the cup, we still want more.

Shame fuels compulsivity and compulsivity is the black plague of our time. We are driven. We want more money, more sex, more food, more booze, more drugs, more adrenaline rush, more entertainment, more possessions, more ecstasy. Like a starving person, even more of everything does not satiate us.

Our dis-eases permeate everyday life. Our troubles are focused on what we eat, what we drink, how we work, how we sleep, how we are intimate, how we have orgasm, how we play, how we worship. We stay so busy and distracted that we never feel how lonely, hurt, mad and sad we really are. Our compulsivities cover up a lost city—a place deep inside of us where a child hides in the ruins.

Compulsive/Addictive Behavior

I understand compulsive/addictive behavior as a pathological relationship to any mood-altering experience that has life-damaging consequences. Such a definition helps us move from our stereotypical pictures of the dives and back alleys of drug and alcohol addiction to the respectable corporate and religious lives of work and religion addicts. It also helps us see the effect of the broken relationship with our original caretakers that produced shame. Because our original dependency bridge with our survival figures has been broken, we are set up for problems with dependency and with relationships. In the abandonment relationships that shame us, our compulsivities are set up.

Our families are the places where we have our source relationships. Families are where we first learn about ourselves in the mirroring eyes of our parents; where we see ourselves for the first time. In families we learn about emotional intimacy. We learn what feelings are and how to express them. Our parents model what feelings are acceptable and family-authorized and what feelings are prohibited.

When we are abused in families, we learn to protect ourselves with ego defenses. We repress our feelings; we deny what's going on; we displace our rage onto our lovers, spouses or our friends; we create illusions of love and connectedness; we idealize and minimize; we dissociate so that we no longer feel anything at all; we turn numb.

Our addictions and compulsivities are our mood alterers. They are what we develop when we grow numb. They are our ways of being alive and our ways of managing our feelings. This is most apparent in experiences that are euphoric, like using alcohol and drugs, compulsively having sex, eating sugar, the adrenaline rush that comes with the feelings of ecstasy and righteousness. It is not as obvious in activities that are used to distract from emotions, such as working, buying, gambling, watching television and thinking obsessively. These are mood-altering nonetheless.

Addiction has become our national lifestyle—or deathstyle. It is a deathstyle based on the relinquishment of the self as a worthwhile being to a self who must achieve and perform or use something outside of self in order to be lovable and happy. Addictions are painkilling substitutes for legitimate suffering. To legitimately suffer we have to feel as bad as we feel.

The fastest-growing problem in our country is sexual addiction. Some estimates say that the number of sex addicts is equal to the number of chemical addicts. Grave social consequences have arisen from this problem. The spread of AIDS is certainly fueled by sexual addiction, as are incest and molestation. And while all sex addicts are not child molesters, most child molesters are sex addicts.

Another major factor in family dysfunction is the addiction to power and violence. Battered children and battered wives expose the horror of physically abusing families.

Violence itself can be an addiction. An essential component in any abusing relationship is the addiction to being victimized. Traumatic bonding, a form of learned helplessness, is a true addiction that enslaves and soul-murders.

I stated earlier that the old rules no longer work. What are these old rules?

Poisonous Pedagogy

The Swiss psychiatrist Alice Miller in her book, *For Your Own Good,* groups these parenting rules under the title "poisonous pedagogy." The subtitle of her book is *Hidden Cruelties in Child Rearing and the Roots of Violence.* She argues that the poisonous pedagogy is a form of parenting that violates the rights of children. Such violation is then reenacted when these children become parents.

The "poisonous pedagogy" exalts obedience as its highest value. Following obedience are orderliness, cleanliness and the control of emotions and desires. Children are considered "good" when they think and behave the way they are taught to think and behave. Children are virtuous when they are meek, agreeable, considerate and unselfish. The more a child is "seen and not heard" and "speaks only when spoken to," the better that child is. Miller summarizes the poisonous pedagogy as follows:

1. Adults are the masters of the dependent child.

2. Adults determine in a godlike fashion what is right and wrong.

3. The child is held responsible for the anger of adults.

4. Parents must always be shielded.

5. The child's life-affirming feelings pose a threat to the auto-cratic parent.

6. The child's will must be "broken" as soon as possible.

7. All this must happen at a very early age so the child "won't notice" and will not be able to expose the adults.[2]

If followed, these family system rules result in the absolute control of one group of people (parents) over another group of people (children). Yet in our present society, only in extreme cases of physical or sexual abuse can anyone intervene on a child's behalf.

Abandonment, with its severe emotional abuse, neglect and enmeshment, is a form of violence. Abandonment, in the sense I have defined it, has devastating effects on a child's belief about himself. And yet, no agency or law exists to monitor such abuse. In fact, many of our religious institutions and schools offer authoritarian support for these beliefs. Our legal system enforces them.

Another aspect of poisonous pedagogy imparts to the child from the beginning false information and beliefs that are not only unproven, but in some cases, demonstrably false. These are beliefs passed on from generation to generation, the so-called "sins of the fathers." Again, I refer to Alice Miller, who cites examples of such beliefs:

1. A feeling of duty produces love.

2. Hatred can be done away with by forbidding it.

3. Parents deserve respect because they are parents. (Note: Any 15-year-old can be a parent without any training. We give telephone operators more training than parents. We need telephone operators, but we need good parents more.) *[Emphasis mine.]*

---

[2] Alice Miller, *For Your Own Good: Hidden Cruelties in Child Bearing and the Roots of Violence* (New York: Farrar, Straus, Giroux, 1983), 59.

4. *Children are undeserving of respect simply because they are children.*
5. *Obedience makes a child strong.*
6. *A high degree of self-esteem is harmful.*
7. *A low-degree of self-esteem makes a person altruistic.*
8. *Tenderness (doting) is harmful.*
9. *Responding to a child's needs is wrong.*
10. *Severity and coldness toward a child give him a good preparation for life.*
11. *A pretense of gratitude is better than honest ingratitude.*
12. *The way you behave is more important than the way you really are.*
13. *Neither parents nor God would survive being offended.*
14. *The body is something dirty and disgusting.*
15. *Strong feelings are harmful.*
16. *Parents are creatures free of drives and guilt.*
17. *Parents are always right.*[3]

Probably no modern parents embody all of the above. In fact, some have accepted and imposed the opposite extreme of these beliefs with results just as abusive. But most of these beliefs are carried unconsciously and are activated in times of stress and crisis. *The fact is, parents have little choice about such beliefs until they have worked through and clarified their relationships with their own parents.* I referred to this earlier as the problem of adult children. Let me explain further.

Children's Belief Patterns

The great paradox in child-parent relationships is that *children's beliefs about their parents come from the parents.* Parents teach their children the meaning of the world around them. For the first 10 years of life the parents are the most important part of the child's world. If a child is taught to honor his parents no matter how they behave, why would a child argue with this?

---

[3] Miller, 59-60.

The helpless human infant is the most dependent of all living creatures. And for the first eight years of life, according to the cognitive psychologist Jean Piaget, children think nonlogically, egocentrically and magically. You can better understand nonlogical thinking by asking a four-year-old boy, who has a brother, if he has a brother. He will probably answer "yes." But if you then ask him if his brother has a brother, he will usually either be confused or answer "no."

An example of egocentric thinking is to stand across from a pre-five-year-old child who knows his right hand from his left. Hold your hands out and across from him. Ask him which is your right hand and your left hand. As his right hand will be opposite your left hand, he will say that your left hand is your right hand. His mind is immature and has not yet attained the ability to completely differentiate or separate himself from objects around him. The child projects his own view of the world on everything. His viewpoint is the only viewpoint. Winnie-the-Pooh has exactly the same feelings the child does. Little matter that Pooh is a toy bear. This egocentricity contains a survival value for the child as it relates to self-preservation.

The magical part of the child's thinking *deifies the parents*. They are gods, all-powerful, almighty and all-protecting. No harm can come to the child as long as he has parents. This magical idealization serves to protect the child from the terrors of the night, which are about abandonment and, to the child, death. The protective deification of the parents, this magical idealization, also creates a potential for a shame-binding predicament for the child.

For example, if the parents are abusive and hurt the child through physical, sexual, emotional or mental pain, the child will assume the blame and make himself bad in order to keep the all-powerful parental protection. For a child at this stage, realizing the inadequacies of parents would produce unbearable anxiety.

In essence, children are equipped with an innate ability to defend their conscious awareness against threats and intolerable situations. Freud called this ability an *ego defense*. The earliest defenses are archaic and, once formed, function automatically and unconsciously. It is this unconscious quality of these defenses that potentially makes them so damaging.

In a recent book called *The Fantasy Bond,* psychologist Robert Firestone elaborates on Freud's work. According to the author, the fantasy bond is the core defense in all human psychological systems, ranging from those of psychotics to the systems of fully functioning individuals. The fantasy bond is the illusion of connectedness we create with our major caretaker whenever our emotional needs are not adequately met. The fantasy bond is like a mirage in the desert that enables us to survive.

Since no mother, father or other parenting person is perfect, all humans develop this fantasy bond to some degree. In fact, growing up and leaving home involves the overcoming of this illusion of connection and protection. Growing up means accepting our fundamental aloneness. It means that we face the terrors of the night and grapple with the reality of death on our own. Most of all, it means giving up our parents in their illusory and idealized form.

The more emotionally deprived a person has been, the stronger his fantasy bond. And paradoxical as it sounds, the more a person has been abandoned, the more he tends to cling to and idealize his family and his parents. Idealizing parents also extends to the way they raised you.

Development of the False Self

No child, because of his helplessness, dependency and terror, wants to accept the belief that his parents are inadequate, sick, crazy or otherwise imperfect. Nature protects the child by providing the egocentric, magical and nonlogical mode of cognition I spoke of earlier. To be safe and survive, an abandoned child *must idealize his parents and think of himself as bad, thus splitting himself.* This split-off part is actually the parts of his parents that he has rejected. He projects this split and forbidden self to others, that is, to strangers who are not of his clan or family. He then introjects his parents' voices. This means that the child continues to hear an internal shame dialogue he originally had with the parents.

The child parents himself the way he was parented. If the child got shamed for feeling angry, sad or sexual, he will shame himself each time he feels angry, sad or sexual. All of his feelings, needs and drives become shame-bound. The inner self-rupture is so painful, the child develops a "false self." This false self manifests in a mask or rigid role that is determined both by the culture and by the family system's need for balance. Over time the child identifies with the false self and is largely unconscious of his own true feelings, needs and wants. The shame is internalized. Shame is no longer a feeling; it is an identity. The real self has withdrawn from conscious contact and therefore cannot be the object of his esteem.

Even after the magical period passes, around the age of eight, and the child moves into a more logical way of thinking, nature continues to provide an egocentric idealization of the parents. The youngster now thinks in a concretely logical manner and assumes the point of view of others. He "gets it" that Santa Claus cannot be in six department stores at the same time. At this stage he is more cooperative in games and play. He is less magical (stepping on a crack does not *really* break Mom's back). He now has greater appreciation for rules.

Even so, the logical child will remain egocentric and undifferentiated until early puberty. Only then will he have the capacity for full other-centered love and understanding. Until then, he will make a hypothesis and then cast it in bronze. If new data emerge to refute this hypothesis, the child will revise the data to fit his hypothesis.

One such hypothesis carried by children (because it is taught at the magical age) is that adults—parents especially—are benevolent and totally good.

Parents are good and *no amount of evidence to the contrary* will convince children differently. In addition, the emotional and volitional reasons the child clings to this belief is that children love their parents and are emotionally bonded to them. Abused children are more powerfully bonded. Abuse creates intense bonding because as a child is abused, his self-esteem diminishes and his choices are limited. The more he feels worthless, the more he feels powerless to change. The more he feels powerless, the fewer choices he feels he has. And the more he accepts the rules and introjects the parents' voices, *the more the child idealizes these rules so as not to separate himself from his parents.*

In other words, in order for a child to reflect on parental rules and find them wanting, *he would have to separate and stand on his own two feet in childhood*. A child cannot do this.

Once in adolescence, most of the child's energy is directed toward leaving the family, and it often appears as if adolescents are rejecting their parents' rules. In fact, the more fantasy-bonded an adolescent is, the more bonded he will become to his peer group, which serves as a "new parent." However, once this identity crisis is over, most adolescents return to the fantasy bond with their families. This is especially evident when a person settles down and starts his own family. What was famil(y)iar comes back and feels right, and this includes the rules for parenting. The poisonous pedagogy is transmitted multi-generationally as a sacred body of truth.

I stated earlier that these parenting rules are out of date. I contend that our consciousness and way of life have radically changed in the last 200 years. The poisonous pedagogy worked 200 years ago for several reasons.

First, life expectancy was much lower. Consequently, families were together a shorter period of time. Divorce was a rarity. The average marriage lasted 15 years and there was little adolescent family conflict as we know it. By age 13, most children had lost a parent. By 15, formal schooling was over. Puberty for women occurred in later adolescence.

Economically, families were bonded by work and survival. Father lived at home. Boys bonded to their fathers through work-apprentice systems. They watched and admired their fathers as they transformed the earth, built homes and barns, and created wonderful goods through manual labor. Today the majority of families have lost their fathers to the new world of work automation and cybernetics. Fathers have left home (someone estimated that the average executive father spends 37 seconds per day with his newborn).

Most children do not know what their fathers do at work. Mother-bonding and fathers' inability to break that bond due to absentee fathering have caused severe marital and intimacy problems.

Children, especially males, were once the greatest asset to a family. The old Chinese proverb underscores this: "Show me a rich man without any sons, and I'll show you a man who won't be rich very long. Show me a poor man with many sons, and I'll show you a man who won't be poor very long."

Today children are one of our greatest economic liabilities. Supporting children through the completion of college costs a pretty penny. It also necessitates close interaction between parents and children for 25 years.

The rules governing parenting and personality formation 200 years ago were also the result of scientific, philosophical and theological views of human nature that have changed drastically. Two hundred years ago, democracy, social equality and individual freedom were new concepts not yet tested by time.

The world was simpler then. Isaac Newton had mapped out the laws of nature. He conceived the world much like the machines that would emerge from the Industrial Revolution. Thinking and reasoning were what progress was all about. Man was a rational animal. Emotions and desires had great power to contaminate and therefore were very suspicious. Emotions needed to be subjected to the scrutiny and control of reason. Men were content to enjoy the security of a fixed order of things. God was in his heaven and all was right with the world . . . as long as men obeyed the laws of nature.

Those laws were also written into the hearts of men (and occasionally in women's hearts). This was the natural law. It was based on unchanging eternal truths.

Mothers and fathers carried God's authority. Their task was to teach their children the laws of God and nature and to be sure they obeyed these laws. Emotions and willfulness had to be repressed. Children were born with an unruly animal nature. Their souls, although made in God's image, were stained by original sin. Therefore, children needed discipline. Great energy was spent breaking their unruly passions and unbridled spirit. Spare the rod and you spoil the child. As Alice Miller reports, one 19th-century writer said:

> *"Blows provide forceful accompaniment to words and intensify their effect. The most direct and natural way of administering them is by that box on the ears, preceded by*

a strong pulling of the ear. . . . It obviously has symbolic sig-
nificance as does a slap on the mouth, which is a reminder
that there is an organ of speech and a warning to put it to
better use . . . the tried and true blow to the head and hair-
pulling still convey a certain symbolism, too." [4]

Any reaction to this punishment was deemed obstinate. Obstinate
meant having a mind of one's own. Those were the good old days!

The work of Einstein ended this world view. The quantum theory replaced Newton's clockwork deterministic universe and its
billiard-ball-like elements. Quantum theory challenged the basic
notions of space and time. Everything in the universe was relative
to everything else. Heisenberg's principle of uncertainty soon followed. He showed that while we can know that infinitesimal parts
of matter exist, we cannot measure them.

Quantum physics brought a revolution in our way of viewing
the universe. "Because of this," Dr. L. Dossey writes in *Space, Time
and Medicine,* "we can expect it to wreak astonishing transformations in our views of our psychophysical self."

The old world view was definitively shaken by World War I and
its 15 million dead.

Mankind had been basking in many illusions of inevitable
progress. Rationalism and technological advances assured everyone that progress was inevitable. After World War I, people asked,
"Where are reason and enlightenment?"

Stunned, the believers still espoused the faith. The League of
Nations and the Weimar Republic were safeguards that this could
not happen again.

Less than 20 years later, it did happen again. This time the modern world was shocked beyond any reason. Hitler and his followers were the agents of death for countless millions of people in the
space of six years. His regime programmatically exterminated several million Jews in gas chambers and death camps. The heinous-
ness of these crimes far exceeded anything known to human

---

[4] Miller, 44.

history. Their cruelty and inhumanity stretched beyond imagination. What would make a person want to gas millions of people? How could millions of others acclaim and assist him?

How Could Hitler Happen?

Germany had been a citadel of Christianity, the birthplace of the Protestant Reformation. Germany was a philosophical, theological and artistic giant among the nations of the world. How was it possible for all this to happen? *How was Hitler possible?*

Many answers to this question have been offered. None is satisfactory. Nevertheless, it is essential that we try to find such an answer. For at the end of the Nazi era came the new development of nuclear weapons, with their capacity for the annihilation of the human race.

How could Hitler happen? Certainly part of the answer lies in the harshness of the Treaty of Versailles, which robbed Germany of its lands. Another part of the answer lies in politics and economics. It has to do with self-interest, greed, the "haves" and "have nots." Part of the answer is sociological, having to do with special-interest groups and the laws that govern groups. This includes the shared focus and shared denials that group loyalty demands. And part of the puzzle of Hitler's Germany is psychological, having to do with the rules that govern the family structure.

The family is the place where persons are socialized. The rules governing the prototypical German family were almost a pure caricature of the patriarchal poisonous pedagogy. Indeed, obedience, rigidity, orderliness and denial of feelings taken to extreme led to the "black miracle of Nazism."

Erik Erikson voiced this powerfully in an article on Hitler. He writes:

> *It is our task to recognize that the black miracle of Nazism was only the German version, superbly planned and superbly bungled of a* universal contemporary potential. *The trend persists; Hitler's ghost is counting on it.* [Emphasis mine.] [5]

---

[5] Erik Erikson, *Childhood and Society* (New York: W.W. Norton & Co., 1963), 326.

The potential for this to happen again resides in the ever-present existence of the patriarchal poisonous pedagogy. Obedience and corporal punishment are still highly valued as the crown of parental discipline.

In the 1920s some did argue that the Weimar Republic would not succeed because of the totalitarian structure of the German family. The authoritarianism that gave the father such unequal rights over the mother and children did not provide a climate in which democracy could be learned.

Obedience Above All

Another factor in the black miracle was the patriarchal religious belief that all authority was from God and must be obeyed as a divine command. In its extreme form, this meant that one must obey authority, even if it is judged wrong.

Alice Miller has presented convincing evidence that Hitler was physically and emotionally abused as a child. His father was, in every sense, a totalitarian dictator. Some historians conjecture that Hitler's father was half-Jewish and illegitimate and acted out his rage on his children. Some believe that Hitler was reenacting his own childhood, using millions of innocent Jews as his scapegoats.

But Hitler could never have done this alone. What seems beyond all human logic is the fact that one madman could corrupt an entire elitist nation like Germany.

Erik Erikson has suggested that Hitler mobilized the dissociated rage of German adolescents. He was an adolescent gang leader who came as a brother and offered a matrix that institutionalized their rage. This rage was their unconscious response to their cruel upbringing and was neatly denied in the myth of the "master race." The scapegoated Jews represented the victimized part of themselves as they identified with their aggressive totalitarian parent. This national "acting out" was the logical result of an authoritarian family life in which one or two persons, the parents, have all the power and can whip, scold, punish, humiliate, manipulate, abuse or neglect their children—all under the banner of parenting and pedagogy.

In the autocratic German family, mother and children were totally subservient to the father's will, his moods and whims. The children had to accept humiliation and injustice unquestionably and gratefully. Obedience was the primary rule of conduct.

Hitler's family structure was the prototype of a totalitarian regime. His upbringing, although more severe, was not unlike that of the rest of the German nation. I believe that this similar family structure allowed Hitler to entice the German people.

Alice Miller has said that a single person can gain control over the masses if he learns to use to his own advantage the social system under which the people were raised.

At the Nuremberg war trials, murderer after murderer pleaded innocence on the basis of obedience to authority. People such as Adolf Eichmann and Rudolf Hess were trained to be obedient so successfully that this training never lost its effectiveness. To the end, they carried out orders *without questioning the content*. They carried them out just as the poisonous pedagogy recommended, not out of any sense of their inherent rightness, but simply because *they were orders*.

"This explains," writes Alice Miller, "why Eichmann was able to listen to the most moving testimony of the witnesses at his trial without the slightest display of emotion, yet when he forgot to stand up at the reading of the verdict, he blushed with embarrassment when this was brought to his attention."

Rudolf Hess' strict patriarchal Catholic upbringing is well-known. His very religious father wanted him to be a missionary. Hess writes:

> *"I . . . was as deeply religious as was possible for a boy of my age. . . . I had been brought up by my parents to be respectful and obedient toward all adults. . . . It was constantly impressed on me in forceful terms that I must obey promptly the wishes and commands of my parents, teachers, priests and indeed all adults, including servants, and that nothing must distract me from this duty.* Whatever they said was always right." [6]

---

[6] Quoted in Miller.

I believe that Nuremberg was a decisive turning point for the monarchial patriarchal poisonous pedagogy. Obedience, the star in the Christians' crown of glory, the meta-rule of all modern Western family systems, had reached its zenith of disclosure in terms of its potential for destruction. Suddenly the childhood idealism of the family structure was exposed as devastatingly destructive and with it, the whole substructure of life-denying rules.

Hitler and Nazism are a cruel caricature of what can happen in modern Western society if we do not stop promoting and proliferating family rules that destroy the self-esteem of human beings. Nazism marks the end of an epoch.

The Insidiousness of Total Obedience

Mine is an urgent, frantic plea for people to understand how insidious the rules that form the poisonous pedagogy can be. These rules are not insidious in themselves; they *become* insidious as absolutized and totalistic laws of human formation. Obedience and orderliness are essential to any family and social structure. Law as a guide to human safety through its protective structure is essential to human fulfillment. Learning to be agreeable, cooperative, unselfish and meek is useful and valuable.

However, *obedience without critical judgment and inner freedom* led to Nazism, Jonestown and My Lai. It was obedience absolutized and cut off from human sensitivity and natural law.

Similarly, cleanliness and orderliness without spontaneity lead to obsessive enslavement. Law and intellectualism without vitality and emotions lead to mechanical coldness and inhuman, heartless control. Considerateness, meekness, unselfishness without the essentials of inner freedom, inner-independence and critical judgment lead to a "doormat," people-pleasing type person, who can be ruled by almost any authority figure.

We programmatically deny children their feelings, especially anger and sexual feelings. Once a person loses contact with his own feelings, he loses contact with his body. We also monitor and control our children's desires and thoughts. To have one's feelings, body, desires and thoughts controlled is to lose one's self. To be de-selfed is to have one's self-esteem severely damaged.

"To live and never know who I really am" is the greatest tragedy of all. This tragic sense is a major cause of the rage that dominates our world. The rage is either directed against strangers in crimes of violence, or it is directed against ourselves as the shame that fuels our addictions.

My contention is that most families have dysfunctional elements because our rules for normalcy are dysfunctional. The important issue is to find out how specifically you were impacted by your family's use of these rules. Once you know what happened to you, you can do something about it.

SUMMARY

The key points covered in this chapter can be summed up using the letters from the word **CRISIS:**

Compulsive/Addictive Behavior Disorder

The range of compulsive/addictive behavior in modern society is awesome. The bubonic plague of today is compulsivity. It affects our everyday lifestyle; how and what we eat; how and what we drink; our work; our recreation; our activities; our sexuality; our religious worship. Such behavior is modeled and set up in families.

Rules for Child Rearing

The poisonous pedagogy promotes ownership of our children. It preaches non-democratic ways of relating. It especially espouses inequality of power. It promotes the denial of feelings and corporal punishment.

Idealization of Parents and Family

One of the rules of the poisonous pedagogy is that the rules cannot be challenged. This means that parents and family cannot be critically evaluated. Children naturally idealize their parents out of survival needs. They grow up to be adult children who carry out their parents' rules to the next generation. This creates more adult children.

Shame

Adult children are adults with a wounded child living inside of them. The true self is ruptured and a false self must be created. Shame is a being wound.

Ideological Totalism—Nazi Germany

The ultimate expression of the poisonous pedagogy was Nazi Germany. Hitler created the master/slave national state. He used the socialization structures of the German family to create the

Nazi regime. As long as the poisonous pedagogy goes unchallenged, the phenomenon of Hitler is still a potential in our society.

Social Systems

We now understand that social systems have laws, components and structural dynamics. Societies create "consensus realities" that ultimately become unconscious. Families are systems in which the whole is greater than the parts. Such systems have rules that, if left unchallenged, become closed systems, and such closed systems can go on for generations.

The Family as a
Rule-Bound Social System

The image of self and the image of family are reciprocally interdependent.

NATHAN ACKERMAN

In 1957, a researcher named Christian Midelfort, working at Lutheran Hospital in LaCrosse, Wisconsin, published his findings. He had been studying the relationships between his depressed, paranoid, schizophrenic and neurotic clients and their families. He concluded his study with the words:

> *This study substantiates the idea that all emotional illness develops in a family and is present in several members of the family.*[1]

Almost simultaneously in 1957, John Howells in Ipswich, England, after working extensively with families, concluded:

---

[1] Christian Midelfort, *The Family in Psychotherapy* (New York: McGraw Hill, 1957), 192.

In family psychiatry a family is not regarded as a back-ground to . . . help the present patient along. Family psychiatry accepts the family itself as the patient, the presenting member being viewed as a sign of family psychopathology.[2]

This type of research reached a zenith in the work of Margaret Singer and Lyman Wynne at the National Institute of Mental Health in Bethesda, Maryland. Wynne and Singer suggested that schizophrenia is not just an entity associated with certain clinical personalities, but is also caused by the manner in which a person is socialized. Wynne saw schizophrenia in terms of the family system. He boldly stated that it was a gross oversimplification to see the schizophrenic child as isolated in his sickness. Rather, he writes:

All family members, offspring and parents, are caught up in reciprocal victimizing and rescuing processes in which they are all tragically enmeshed.[3]

In 1951, Gregory Bateson began work that would engender an interpersonal notion of schizophrenia based on faulty and "crazy-making" communication. Commanding children to be spontaneous or telling them it is their duty to love their parents came to be known as "double binding." To command one to do something that by definition cannot be commanded is "crazy-making." Later research proved that schizophrenia is biochemically based. A sharp distinction must be made between mental and emotional illness. However, the work on whole family systems as the matrix of emotional illness was still relevant.

Virginia Satir aided Bateson in developing his theory of emotional illnesses based on a faulty and paradoxical pattern of interpersonal communication. Satir later elaborated her own theory of family system pathology. Others followed in research and thinking on the relationship between the individual who is considered emotionally dis-eased and the family from which he came. Murray

---

[2] John Howells, *Family Psychiatry* (Springfield, Ill.: Charles C. Thomas, Publisher, 1963), 4-5.

[3] Lyman Wynne, *Explaining the Base for Family Therapy* (New York: Family Service, 1961), 103.

Bowen and Warren Brodey added a multi-generational focus. Bowen established the role of the grandparents as significant in several cases. In one case he writes:

The grandparents' combined immaturities were acquired by one child who was most attached to the mother. When this child married a spouse with an equal degree of immaturity, it resulted in one child (the patient) with a high degree of immaturity.[4]

Basically Bowen saw the following scenario as the dominant pattern in producing emotional illness: Two people, carrying unresolved conflicts with their parents, get married. As the intimacy voltage rises in the marriage, these conflicts become more intense. The partners try to settle these issues with an emotional divorce, "a marked emotional distance." Very often both agree not to disagree and establish a pseudointimacy. The marriage looks good on the outside. There is a facade of happiness, but beneath the surface there are struggle, pain and loneliness.

When a child is born, he is "triangled" into the system. The child becomes the focus of the relationship. The child is locked into the system and finds it virtually impossible to leave the family. This child often becomes emotionally disturbed and is the identified patient who is sent to therapy. Actually the identified patient is only a symptom of the emotionally disturbed marriage. And the patient's so-called emotional illness can be seen and understood only in relation to the emotional system of which he is a part. There is emotional contagion in the whole family. The one who is labeled "sick" is the symptom-bearer of the whole sick emotional system itself.

Many brilliant and innovative therapists put these theories into practice with some extraordinary results. Salvador Minuchin, Carl A. Whittaker, Jay Haley and Virginia Satir are notable examples. Family systems thinking is grounded in the fact that we humans are inextricably social. My first beliefs about myself were formed from

---

[4] Murray Bowen, "A Family Concept of Schizophrenia," in Dr. Jackson, ed., *The Etiology of Schizophrenia* (New York: Basic Books, 1960), 348.

my mother's feelings and desires toward me. My self-definition and self-esteem literally began in the womb.

The Shaping of Our Lives

After birth, our self-image comes from our primary caregiver's eyes. How I see and feel about myself is exactly what I see in my caregiver's eyes. How my mothering person feels about me in these earliest years is how I will feel about myself. If my parents are shame-based, they will feel inadequate and needy. In such a state they cannot be there for me; they will need me to be there for them.

Our reality is shaped from the beginning by a relationship—we are we, before we are I. Our "I-ness" comes from our "we-ness." Our individuality comes from the social context of our lives. This is the basic foundation for the new thinking of the family.

Vincent Foley, in his *An Introduction to Family Therapy,* uses Tennessee Williams' play, *The Glass Menagerie,* to illustrate the family systems viewpoint. If one separates Laura from her family system (mother, brother), she appears to be a girl living in fantasy and unreality. She could be judged emotionally ill. She is sick and the labeled patient.

However, if we look at Laura from a systems viewpoint, we get a very different picture. We see her interaction with her mother and brother as crucial for keeping the family together. She is no longer the sick, frumpy sister waiting for a "gentleman caller," but a person necessary for the balance of the family system. The tensions between the son, Tom, and the mother, Amanda, are only tempered and kept in check by Laura. When the voltage of these tensions gets too high, Laura steps in and gets Tom and Amanda to focus on her. This distracts them and lowers the voltage. Thus, Laura performs a crucial and critical role. She keeps the family together.

The family system functions precisely because of Laura's intervention and not in spite of it. One could argue that it is blatantly false to label Laura sick. One could even call her the caretaker and unity preserver of the family. More precisely, one should say that the Winfield family system itself is sick and Laura is only a symptom of that system. *The shift from the person to the interpersonal is not just another way of viewing pathology; instead, it is a totally new and different concept of pathology.*

Families as Systems

The family as a system is a new reality that helps explain a bewildering array of behaviors. The very notion of emotional illness is no longer useful, since it implies some intrapsychic phenomena. The family systems model shows how each person in a family *plays a part in the whole system.* Family systems help us understand why children in the same family often seem so different. And seeing the family as a system helps us to see how the poisonous pedagogy is carried from generation to generation.

Emotional illness is never an insoluble, individualistic phenomenon. The theory of family systems accepts the family itself as the patient and views the presenting member as a sign of family psychopathology. The identified patient then becomes the symptom of the family system's dysfunctionality. The family itself is a symptom of society at large.

Over and over again, I have seen this family systems reality in my work. In our teenage drug-abuse program in Los Angeles, some 50 sets of parents (with drug-abusing teenagers) have completed a special eight-week parental enrichment series. This seminar helps these parents own the dysfunctionality of their marriages. They help me to see the drug behavior of their kids as an "acting out" to take the heat off their parents' marriages. In a certain sense, these kids have kept their families together by being drug addicts. They are the identified patients. But their systemic function is to get the family some help, and indeed, they have succeeded. Each of these families bears the scars of the poisonous pedagogy. Each operated their families on the basis of these rules. Each parent was also brought up in families using these rules.

Systems were first studied in biology. The German biologist Ludwig Von Bertalanffy defined systems as "complexes of elements in interaction." He went on to study systems and to deduce a set of principles that apply to all systems.

His position is called general systems theory. Independently of Bertalanffy, Dr. Murray Bowen, a psychiatrist at Georgetown University, developed a highly researched understanding of the family as an interrelated and holistic social system. Bowen's system is simply called "The Bowen Theory" in order to distinguish it from general systems theory. I will comment on parts of The Bowen Theory in the next chapter.

I shall spend the rest of this chapter summarizing in simple terms how Bertalanffy's general systems theory applies to families as systems.

Wholeness

Wholeness is the first principle of systems. The whole is greater than the sum of its parts. This means that the elements added together do not produce the system. The system results from the interaction of the elements. Without the interaction, there is no system.

The system of the family in *The Glass Menagerie* is not the sum of the individual personalities of Amanda, Laura and Tom Winfield, but is instead the vital outgoing interaction between them. Bertalanffy uses the term "wholeness" to characterize such interaction.

Relationship

The second characteristic of a system is *relationship*. Any family system is composed of connecting relationships. To study the family as a system, one must see the various connections and interactions between the individualized persons. Each person in the system relates to every other person in a similar fashion. Each is partly a whole and wholly a part. Each person within the system has his own unique systemic individuality, and at the same time he carries an imprint of the whole family system. I am my family as well as a person composed of whatever unique characteristics I have actualized as a person. I have both an individual and group identity.

A good way to grasp this property of relationship proportionality is by comparing it to holograms. A hologram is a three-dimensional picture made from interference patterns of a certain kind of light beam. If a hologram is divided, each half contains the whole picture. If cut in quarters, the whole picture is retained in each section, and so on. Many researchers believe that all organisms are holograms, that the human brain and the universe itself are holographic. The hologram is a good way to grasp the family system. If I am taken away from my family, all the realities of that family exist within me. My deep unconscious is totally related to all the persons in the system, and my reality has been formed by my relationship with each person in the system. The notion of wholeness is a way of expressing the deep organismic unconscious unity of any system, and the blood-connected family system especially.

An example from my own counseling practice may make this clearer. Several years ago a couple came to me because of their son. Both parents were high-achieving professionals. They were extremely intellectual and had almost a disdain for emotions. They would fit most models of work addiction. They were sexually dysfunctional in their marriage. They had not engaged in intercourse in five years. Each, however, had a fairly elaborate secret fantasy sex life. Their marriage was nonintimate and lonely. The only thing that they really enjoyed doing was eating out at good restaurants, which they did at least four times a week. The 13-year-old boy was their only child. He was the reason they came to see me. He was failing in school and at least 100 pounds overweight. He was unchildlike. He was somber, reclusive, had almost no affect and acted like an old man. Over several months I learned that he was compulsively masturbating. He revealed this with great shame. He had a secret ritual for masturbating, which was also a source of shame.

What was clear to me was that he was the symptom-bearer of his parents' marital dysfunction. He made their loneliness, their noncommunication and their secret sexual shame overt. He balanced their intense drive for achievement by underachievement. They liked to eat and he was grossly overweight.

Since he had started counseling, his parents' relationship had improved. He had been taken to several counselors before me.

Each had treated him differently. One therapist had put him on antidepressant drugs. None treated him as the symptom-bearer of his family system's dysfunction. My work was ultimately unsuccessful because the parents refused to see their marriage as the child's main problem.

Open and Closed Systems

Family systems can be either closed systems or flexible open systems. In closed systems the connections, structures and relationships are fixed and rigid and the process patterns remain essentially the same. This is useful knowledge when examining the family's problems. Whether the subject is money, sex, children or in-laws, the pattern will be the same.

Another aspect of family systems is that they, like all systems, relate through a process called feedback. It is the feedback loops that maintain the systems' functioning.

For example, in the White family, Dad is an alcoholic. He gets drunk and can't go to work the next day. Mom calls in sick for him. The children don't ask questions and pretend to believe that Dad is sick. While they purportedly do all this to save his job and the family's economic security, they in fact enable him to remain an alcoholic. He doesn't have to bear the consequences of his irresponsible behavior. He will go through a period of remorse and then begin drinking again. Soon the exact same sequence will take place.

In closed-system families, the feedback loops are negative and work to keep the system frozen and unchanging. This is called dynamic homeostasis. The more the Whites try to change Dad's behavior, the more it stays the same or gets worse. Feedback is also maintained in families by *rules* that govern the system. These rules can be overt, such as "children are to be seen and not heard," or covert, such as Father's loud and boisterous chauvinism with its covert message that women are to be feared and controlled. These covert rules are often a form of negative feedback. The poisonous pedagogy is carried both overtly and covertly. The poisonous pedagogy produces shame-based people who usually marry other shame-based people. Each has idealized their parents' rules. They raise their children the way their parents raised them. The children are shamed in the same way their parents were shamed. The cycle goes on for generations.

New Belief Systems

Positive feedback can break up the frozen status quo of a system. Positive feedback challenges destructive and unexamined rules, both overt and covert. Positive feedback comes in the form of new belief systems that precipitate new ways of acting by making old positions untenable. Challenging the assumptions of the poisonous pedagogy is a way to give positive feedback.

On my television series, I visually represented families with a six-foot stainless steel mobile created by a wonderful artist named Trudy Sween. To illustrate the dynamic homeostatic principle, I touched the mobile at the beginning of the program and pointed out later how it always came to rest in exactly the same position it had started.

I also illustrated the interconnecting interrelational principle by showing that when I touched one part of the mobile, every part moved.

An open family system could be illustrated by keeping the mobile in gentle motion all the time.

Family Rules

Family systems become chronically dysfunctional *not because of bad people,* but because of bad information loops, bad feedback in the form of bad rules of behavior. The same is true of society. Our parents are not bad people for transmitting the poisonous pedagogy. The rules once worked well. With our ever-evolving democratic consciousness, however, the patriarchal rules are no longer useful.

Families have a wide range of governing rules. There are financial, household, celebrational, social, educational, emotional, vocational, sexual, somal (sickness and health) and parenting rules. Each of these rules has attitudinal, behavioral and communicational aspects.

A household rule may be:

1. Attitudinal—The house should be neat and clean.
2. Behavioral—Dishes are cleaned after each use.
3. Communicational—Dad verbally reprimands if dishes are not washed.

Working out a compromise between the rules of each partner's family of origin is a major task in a marriage.

In addition to rules like the ones we have been discussing, all systems have components. In a family system, the chief components are the mother's relationship to herself and her relationship with the father, and the father's relationship to himself and his relationship with the mother. The status of these relationships dominates the system. If the marriage is functional, the children have a good chance of being fully functional. If the marriage component is dysfunctional, the family members are stressed and tend to adapt dysfunctionally.

Fulfilling the Family's Needs

Like all social systems, a family has basic needs. The family needs: a sense of worth, a sense of physical security or productivity, a sense of intimacy and relatedness, a sense of unified structure, a sense of responsibility, a sense of challenge and stimulation, a sense of joy and affirmation, and a spiritual grounding. A family also needs a mother and father who are committed in a basically healthy relationship and who are secure enough to parent their children without contamination.

Suppose Mother is a hypochondriac who obsesses on her every ailment, is often bedridden and uses illness to avoid responsibility. Because Mother is unavailable, the marriage has an intimacy vacuum. The family system needs a marriage. Someone in the system will need to be a partner with Dad in order to make a marriage.

Family Roles

In the example family above, one of the daughters will take on Mother's job. She becomes the Surrogate Spouse. Another child may take over the parenting function while Dad is busy working. This child will become super-responsible and a Little Parent. Another person in the system may be the one who adds joy to the family by being cute and funny. This person relieves a lot of the tension between Mother and Dad. He is the Mascot.

Another child will take the role of Saint and Hero, becoming a straight-A student, president of his class and winning honors. This person gives the family a sense of dignity.

Another child may take on Dad's unexpressed anger toward Mother by acting out antisocially. He may use drugs or get in trouble at school. This offers Mother and Dad a distraction. They may actually become more intimate through their mutual concern for this child. This child becomes the family Scapegoat.

In fact, like Laura in *The Glass Menagerie,* this child is the symptom-bearer of the family's dysfunction. The Scapegoat is often the service-bearer for the family. Because of the problems the Scapegoat causes, the whole family is often drawn into treatment.

I've capitalized these roles to show that they are *rigid.* They result from the needs of the system, not from anyone's individual choice. Nature abhors a vacuum. The children automatically work to provide for the system's overt and covert needs.

Everyone in the family is affected by Mother and Dad's relationship. As each person in the family adapts to the stress by taking on a particular role or roles, each loses his or her own true identity. As a role becomes more and more rigid, the family system closes more and more into a frozen trance-like state. Once this freezing occurs, the family is stuck. And the more each one tries to help by playing his or her role, the more the family stays the same.

In healthy family systems there are healthy roles. The parental role is mainly to model. Parents model:

- How to be a man or woman
- How to be a husband or wife
- How to be a father or mother
- How to be in an intimate relationship
- How to be functional human beings
- How to have good boundaries

Parents also play the role of nourishing teachers, giving their children time, attention and direction.

Children especially need direction in their role as learners. They are curious and filled with wonder. They need to learn how to use their powers to know, love, feel, choose and imagine. They need to learn to use these powers effectively and creatively so that their basic needs are met.

In healthy family systems the roles are flexible and rotating. The mobile is gently moving. Healthy role reversal and flexible interchange occur. Mother may be the scapegoat one month, Dad the next and one of the children the next.

Each family system is part of a larger system called a subculture. This involves nationality and religious preference. Each subculture has its principles, its rules and its components. Subcultures are part of cultures or actions. Each subculture and culture has an impact on the formation of rules and how the rules are enforced.

Birth Order Characteristics

One current model of family process work illustrates another aspect of family systems thinking. This model has to do with birth order. Birth order is predicated on the needs of any social system.[5]

In the Bach Model, every social system has four basic needs:

1. The need for productivity
2. The need for emotional maintenance
3. The need for relationship
4. The need for unity

As children are born into a family, these needs will be determined according to their birth order.

---

[5] What follows is a brief summary of the research done by Dr. Jerome Bach and his colleagues at the Bach Institute and the University of Minnesota. This material is taken from an unpublished paper. A full discussion of the Bach/Anderson birth order material has been published in the book *Birth Order and Sibling Patterns in Individual and Family Therapy* by Margaret M. Hoopes and James M. Harper (Gaithersburg, Md.: Aspen Publishers, Inc., 1987).

First Child

Usually the first child bears the family's conscious and explicit expectations. The first child carries more performance expectations than any other child due to the productivity needs of the system. The first child carries the family's dominant values and themes and will react to and identify most with the father (the productivity manager). A first child will make decisions and hold values consistent with or in exact opposition to the father.

The behavioral patterns of first children tend to be as follows:

1. They are other-oriented and socially aware. Firsts will be most conscious of social norms and images.
2. Firsts thrive on the explicit and obvious. They want detail and tend to go by the letter rather than the spirit.
3. Because of the expectation and pressure caused by parental youth and overcoercion ("first child jitters"), first children often have trouble developing high self-esteem.

Second Child

Second children naturally relate to the emotional maintenance needs of the system. Seconds respond to the covert and unconscious rules in the family system. A second child will normally bond with (react to or identify with) the mother. A second child will make decisions and hold values *vis-à-vis* the mother.

The behavioral patterns of second children are dominantly as follows:

1. They will act out the unconscious expectations and needs of others as well as their own. Seconds will often be an extension of a mother's unconscious needs or desires. A male second may become a man just like Mother wished she could have married. A female second may become promiscuous because the mother secretly wanted to be.
2. Second children carry the covert emotional issues in the family and so often have trouble putting their head and their

hearts together. What this means is that seconds will often be intuitively aware that something gamey is going on without knowing what or why. They will pick up "hidden agendas" immediately but may not be able to clearly express what they feel. Because of this, second children often seem naïve and puzzled. Subjectively, second children often feel crazy.

Third Child

The third child hooks into the relationship needs of the system. In the family system's process, thirds will identify with the marriage relationship. They will be the best symbol of what is going on in the marriage.

When thirds enter the family, relationships have already become established—the marital relationship, and the relationships between parents and the first and second children. Third children are assigned the task of keeping all the dyadic relationships in balance. They become especially responsible for the marital dyad, since it is the most important and explicit of the dyads. Because of their involvement in the existing dyads thirds have a hard time establishing a separate identity.

The behavior patterns of third children are generally as follows:

1. Relatedness is their main concern.
2. They appear very uninvolved, but are actually very involved.
3. They feel very ambivalent and have trouble making choices.

Fourth Child

The fourth child takes on the unification needs of the family system. The fourth child will catch and collect the unresolved family tensions. This might be any relational tension in the system. A fourth is like the family radar, picking up and identifying with every action and interaction in the family system.

From a behavioral pattern point of view, fourth children feel very responsible, yet powerless and helpless to really do anything about what is going on in the family. Fourths often resort to cutesy mascot-like behavior to distract pain and take care of the family. Fourths often appear infantile and indulged. They may be disruptive and scapegoats in the family in order to take care of it.

Only Children

Only children can take on all the birth order roles. When their parents' marriage is functioning well, only children fare the best.

In the example I previously gave of the high-achieving professional couple, the son is an only child. Only children will often carry all the family process functions. In a healthy functional marriage this can be excellent. And in healthy families only children fare well. In dysfunctional marriages, the only child carries the covert dysfunction.

My client in that earlier example, the 13-year-old boy, was an almost perfect readout for what was going on in the parents' marriage. He was overweight; their only "couple interest" was eating. He was sexually secretive; they had sexual secrets. He was lonely and showed little emotion; they were lonely and had almost no feelings in their relationship. He was noncommunicative; they had almost no communication in their marriage.

Any children beyond the fourth repeat the sequence. Fifth children operate like first children, sixth like second children, etc.

The Bach Model is a theory and can be useful in helping one identify certain personality tendencies that are more *systemically* included, rather than part of one's natural endowment.

The Family Trance

An interesting way to think of a family system is to think of a group of people in a hypnotic trance. Actually, a trance is a naturally occurring state. Most of us go in and out of trance many times during the course of a day. We daydream, we get absorbed in future fantasies, we relive old memories, we watch television, read novels or go to movies. All of these effect a state of trance.

In trance, a more holistic state of conscious absorption exists. Children are natural trance subjects because of their naïveté and trust, as well as their powerful interpersonal bonding with their parents. All that one learns in a trance state operates like a post-hypnotic suggestion. If Mom tells you that you will never be as smart as your sister, this message will operate until the trance is broken. It is broken by leaving home, growing up and breaking the bond with Mom.

The trance also functions in a circular feedback fashion. Each person is impacted by everyone else's behavior. Like a mobile, you touch one part and all the other parts are affected. Bowen referred to this as the family's undifferentiated ego mass.

The family trance is created by both parents' individual interactions with the children and by the marriage itself. Father's behavior impacts Mother, who responds or reacts with behavior that impacts Father.

For example, Mom may nag at Dad because he won't talk. When Dad is asked why he won't talk, he says it's because Mom bitches and nags. So Mom bitches and nags because Dad won't talk, and Dad won't talk because Mom bitches and nags. A circular loop is thus created. The children eat, breathe and are formed out of this dyadic trance action. The whole family is the trance that all the parts participate in.

The way that each person learns about his emotions is part of every family trance. The family dictates what feelings you can have and express. The parents model this. I call this the original family **SPELL.** SPELL stands for our **S**ource **P**eople's **E**motional **L**anguage **L**egacy. The fantasy bond is also part of our original SPELL. We all start our lives in our family SPELL. We are all in a post-hypnotic trance induced in early infancy.

The role of bonding is especially important in trance process. The children bond with one or both of their parents. This bonding is a powerful form of rapport. In rapport we enter the other's model of the world. We take on the other's map of reality. Bonding is the process by which the children are drawn into the trance created by their parents.

In dysfunctioning systems this bonding has severe and disastrous consequences. A child who is physically, sexually, emotionally, intellectually or morally abused will form a "traumatic bonding" to such abuse. He will experience the abuse as normal, since he doesn't know anything else or any other way to be in a family. Often he will identify with the persecuting parent. The child does this as a way to feel powerful. Once a child has identified with a parent, he carries the parent's feelings and beliefs.

For example, Jill, one of my clients in Los Angeles, had a violent and verbally abusive father. He shamed and humiliated her in front of boyfriends. He constantly accused her of being seductive and prophesied that she would be raped. Jill hated her father and had tremendous repressed anger for him.

When Jill married, she found a Caspar Milquetoast type of man whom she criticized, maligned and verbally abused. She copied her father's behavior and vented her rage at her father onto her husband. One of her daughters was raped four times!

Children who have been victimized by the poisonous pedagogy identify with their abusing parents and reenact the same abuse on their children by vehemently adhering to their parents' way of parenting.

Traumatic bonding and identification with the abuser explain the multi-generational carrying of dis-eased attitudes. Such identification is an ego defense and allows the child to survive.

The Family Trance Cycle

I. Family systems function through feedback loops that are cybernetic and circular, rather than casual. Therefore, in a family system, *everyone is involved in some way with everyone else.*

This organismic approach avoids labels, such as "sick" and "emotionally ill." It sees dysfunction as an organismic holistic imbalance caused by inadequate rules or belief systems that result in frozen feedback loops and circularity. This approach eliminates the need to *blame* the scapegoat with diagnostic labels. It eliminates the belief that illness is the breakdown of the person's intrapsychic machinery. It is the family that is diseased and not the individual person. The individual may, however, behave in a dysfunctional manner.

II. The whole is the behaviorally induced trance. In an open family system, the trance can change because of the flexible choices afforded by the healthy environment created by the marital dyad. In a closed family system, the trance is rigid and frozen. Any member can start the induction by his own particular role behavior. This is why a member can leave his family and still be in it. People from chronically dysfunctional families tend to stay in their rigid roles and carry the dysfunctionality into their later life.

III. The family is an incorporation of the subculture and culture of one's upbringing. Subcultures and cultures are created by individuals. They form the social construction of reality—culture's "consensus reality." This consensus reality is what all the culture's members agree to. Families are created according to the rules of the consensus reality. The current consensus reality rules for parenting are the poisonous pedagogy. Families also shape cultures in what Murray Bowen referred to as societal regression. For example, our penal systems often reproduce the same toxic shaming and abuse that put the inmates there in the first place.

IV. Systems theory explains how the poisonous pedagogy and other abuses can be passed on for generations. It is in understanding your own family system that you can rediscover how this poisonous pedagogy sets you up to play a role or act out a script and how your self-esteem was damaged. Connecting with your family history, you can discover what happened to your true self.

SUMMARY

The key points covered in this chapter can be summed up using the letters of the word **FAMILIES.**

Feedback Loops Versus Cause/Effect

The family systems notion sees the family as a dynamic social organism. Such an organism functions by means of interaction and interdependence. Dad won't talk because Mom bitches and nags, and Mom bitches and nags because Dad won't talk. Their behavior is cyclical rather than causal.

Autonomy or Wholeness

The family is a total organism—the whole is greater than the sum of its parts. Everyone in the family is affected by everyone else. Each individual is partly a whole and wholly a part. A whole new social concept of emotional dis-ease emerges from this realization. Individuals are not emotionally dis-eased—whole families are.

Marriage as the Chief Component

The marriage is the chief component in the family. The health of the marriage determines the health of the family.

Individual Roles

All families have roles. The role of parent is to model the following: how to be a man or woman; mothering and fathering; how to be a person; how to express feelings and desires. The role of child is to be curious and learn. In healthy families the roles are flexible; in dysfunctional families the roles are inflexible.

Laws or Rules

All families have laws or rules that govern the system. Laws include issues like household maintenance, body care, celebration, social life, financial issues, privacy and boundaries.

Individuation/Togetherness Tension

The tension in families results from the individuation/togetherness polarity. The need to be unique and self-actualized often clashes with the need to conform for the sake of the system.

Equilibrium

The members in a family tend to compliment each other. If Dad is frequently angry, Mom is mild and soft-spoken. Like a mobile, the system will always try to come to rest and balance. Families can be open (always in gentle motion) or closed (frozen or rigid).

Systems Needs

Like individuals, systems have needs. Families, like all social systems, have needs for productivity (food, clothing and shelter); emotional maintenance (touching, stroking, warmth); good relationships (love, intimacy); individuality and difference (self-actualization); stimulation (excitement, challenge, fun); and unity (a sense of belonging and togetherness).

Profile of a Functioning Family System

*If I am I
because I am I
And you are you
because you are you,
then I am and
you are.
But if I am
I because you
are you,
and you are you
because I am I,
then I am not and
you are not.*

RABBI MENDEL

Consider this the beginning of your quest for an enriched sense of self-esteem. Your major focus will be on your family of origin. Your original family was the unit from which you came. If it was a functional unit, that family was the source of your individuality and strength and gave you a permanent conviction of belonging. Your original family is where you lived out the most passionate and powerful of all your human experiences.

As you examine what a functioning healthy family is, you can also focus on the family you are now in or the one you are creating.

To say that something is functional is to say that it works. My car, for example, may have rust spots on the trunk, but if it drives well, then it is fully functional. It works.

43

A healthy family is one in which the members are functioning fully and the relationships between the members are fully functional. As human beings, all family members have available to them the use of all their human powers. They use these powers to cooperate, individuate and get their collective and individual needs met. A functional family is the healthy soil out of which individuals can become mature human beings. This involves the following:

1. The family is a survival and growth unit.
2. The family is the soil that provides for the emotional needs of the various members. These needs include a balance between autonomy and dependency and between social and sexual training.
3. A healthy family provides the growth and development of each member, including the parents.
4. The family is the place where the attainment of solid self-esteem takes place.
5. The family is a major unit in socialization and is crucial for a society if it is to endure.
6. The family is the matrix out of which the children's character and moral values are formed.

If the family is the soil for the creation of mature people, what does it mean to be a mature person? What are the essential components of maturity?

What Is Maturity?

The first component of The Bowen Theory is *self-differentiation*. A mature person is one who has differentiated himself from all others and established clearly marked ego boundaries. A mature person has a good identity. Such a person relates to his family system in meaningful ways, without being fused or joined to them. This means the mature person is emotionally free and can choose to move near without anger or absorption, and move away without guilt. Self-differentiation and self-esteem take time to develop. If a person accomplishes the various developmental tasks of childhood in a human (not perfect) manner, and if he negotiates his adolescent development without too many social setbacks, he should grow into adulthood with a solid sense of self-esteem. With a solid sense of self-esteem a person can separate from the family yet stay connected to it.

Self-differentiation also has to do with the ability to think about feelings and not be overwhelmed by them. This ability allows one to choose without reacting impulsively.

For example, one of the grown-up children in a family may decide to go on a Christmas holiday trip with his own family or network of friends. In a functional family, this would probably occasion some sadness in the other family members, but the parents and siblings would be glad that their fellow family member was happy and had a network of friends.

In a dysfunctional family, the other members would be angry. The parents would likely manipulate with guilt, and the person staying away for the holidays would surely feel guilty. Let's say the person felt so guilty that he canceled his plans and came home for the Christmas celebration. He would be resentful and angry while he was at home. This latter scenario is common in dysfunctional families.

The process of self-differentiation is essential to us all. Everyone is somewhere on the continuum in terms of degree of individuation and belonging. Our individuality is equivalent to our identity. Having a good identity means having a good sense of worth and a significant other or others who affirm that sense of worth. We cannot have an identity all alone. We need at least one significant other who verifies our sense of worth. Our identity is the difference about us that makes a difference. It must always be grounded in a social context—in a relationship.

Identity unites our self-actualizing needs with our need for belonging. Good identity is always rooted in belonging. In fact, the individuation drive and the need to conform and belong are always in polar tension. We cannot have one without the other.

Basic Human Needs

For individuation and differentiation to take place, the family must be stable and secure enough so that the members can get their needs met. A healthy family environment provides the opportunity for all members to get their needs met insofar as that is possible.

Each person needs:

- Self-worth, self-love, self-acceptance and the freedom to be the unique and unrepeatable one that he is
- Touching and mirroring
- Structure that is safe enough to risk growth and individuation; such a structure will change according to the stages of one's development
- Affection and recognition
- His feelings affirmed
- Challenge and stimulation to move through each stage of development
- Self-actualization and spiritualization

Spiritualization includes the need to love and care for others, the need to be needed, truth-seeking and the need for beauty and goodness. Spiritualization means living for something greater than oneself.

Each person is born with the powers to get these needs met. The power to know enables us to find out about ourselves and others, and to get enough knowledge mastery to survive and meet our basic security needs. The power to love enables each of us to love ourselves and others.

Basic Human Powers

Power to Feel

The word emotion is from the Latin *exmovere.* It literally means an energy that moves. Our emotions are one of our basic powers. Emotions give us signals from the body telling us of a need, a loss, a satiation. The energy is used to help us act effectively to take care of ourselves. Emotions are direct expressions of reality as opposed to thoughts, which translate or analyze our experience. Emotions give important information about what we need to do, what we want or how we want to change.

The power to feel allows each of us to know our own unique spontaneous reality. Emotions are tools that make us fully aware of where we are in fulfilling our needs. I sometimes hyphenate the word emotion as e-motion in order to indicate that an emotion is an energy that moves us. This energy (say, the beating of my heart and tensing of my muscles in anger) allows me to meet and resolve any threat to my basic needs. Without my energy (called anger), I am powerless to uphold my dignity and self-worth.

Fear is the energy of discernment. It raises awareness of danger zones in terms of satisfying our basic needs.

Sadness is the energy for saying good-bye and grieving loss. Life is a prolonged farewell, and therefore it is necessary to continuously say good-bye and complete cycles of growth. Grief and sadness give us the energy to complete the past. Saying good-bye to infancy and toddlerhood is essential in order to grow into the latency period of school age. Saying good-bye to school is essential in order for us to make our way and take our place in the world. Growth demands a continual dying and rebirth. Grief is the "healing feeling."

Guilt is the energy that forms our conscience. It is our moral shame. Without this energy, we would act shamelessly and become sociopathic and psychopathic. Guilt allows us to stand for something and to have an internal value system that leads to action and commitment.

Shame is the energy that lets us know we are limited and finite. Shame allows us to make mistakes and lets us know we need help. Shame is the source of our spirituality. This is very different from the neurotic shame induced by the poisonous pedagogy. That shame is no longer an e-motion; it has become the core of our identity.

Joy is the energy that signals all is well. All needs are being filled. We are becoming and growing. Joy creates new and boundless energy.

Power to Will

Each person has the power to choose, to want and to desire. This energy is usually called the volitional faculty, or will. Our will is the power of desire raised to the intensity of action. Our choices shape our reality and our life. Our will is the source of our love. Love is a choice. Love is the willingness to work on our relationships, even though it is hard work sometimes. Love also involves courage because when we love another person, we risk losing that person. He or she could reject us or die.

Power to Imagine

We have the power to imagine. This power allows us to look at new possibilities, and without it, we would be rigid conformists. Human imagination is the power that has forged new frontiers and given the world innovation, advancement and progress. Our national art galleries and museums are monuments to the power of imagination. Without this power we would gradually become hopeless, since hope involves seeing new possibilities.

Power to Know

A good family matrix provides a solid ground upon which we can exercise the powers to know, love, feel, decide and imagine. Such a ground needs to be developmentally proper. This means that we need to have the freedom to exercise our powers to get our needs met in a way proportional to the stages of our development.

The power to know, for example, develops gradually over the first 16 years, going through phases of symbolic, pre-logical, concrete logical, and finally abstract and symbolic thinking. We all need parenting sources who understand the specific way we think at each stage of development, so that parental expectations in the early stages are balanced by healthy challenge and awareness of a child's cognitive limitations. I outlined the magical pre-logical stage in the introductory chapter. A mature person updates the magical child within himself. He comes to see his parents as the real finite human beings they are. He updates their parenting rules with reason and logic and personal experience.

Sense of Worth

I believe that all of us are born with a deep and profound sense of worth. We are precious, rare, unique and innocent. We are born with all the powers and needs I've mentioned. We are, however, immature and totally dependent on our caretakers. Our early destiny is shaped to an awesome degree by those caretakers. To continue feeling precious and unique, we have to see our uniqueness and preciousness in the eyes of our caretakers. Our first beliefs about ourselves comes from their eyes.

The foundation for our self-image is grounded in the first three years of life. It comes from our major caretaker's mirroring. Our sense of our self needs to be mirrored by significant others who love and care and who are self-actualized enough not to be threatened by each new cognitive threshold we reach, with its expanding spontaneity and freedom. The more our major caretakers love themselves and accept all their own feelings, needs and wants, the more they can be there to accept all the parts of their children—their children's drives, feelings and needs.

Parents who have good self-worth and self-acceptance are getting their own needs met. They do not have to use their children to have a sense of power, adequacy and security. Such parent-partners are in the process of finishing their own business with their own family of origin. Each is becoming self-differentiated. Each has updated the destructive aspects of the poisonous pedagogy.

Emotional Intelligence

A healthy family exhibits a high level of what Yale psychologist Peter Salovey and New Hampshire University professor John Meyer call "Emotional Intelligence" (abbreviated as EQ). EQ, much more than IQ, determines a happy and enduring marriage. Parents who have EQ model it for their children. When children live with parents who have EQ, they develop EQ.

EQ is characterized by self-awareness or inner self-differentiation, empathy, persistence or self-motivation, and social deftness.

Self-awareness is the foundation for EQ because it allows us to have self-control and to differentiate between perceptions, think-ing, feelings and desires. The ability to think before reacting allows people to find a balanced response in interpersonal relationships. The ability to read our own internal cues helps us sort out the com-ponents of an experience and choose wisely. People who are self-aware have made their unconscious wounds conscious and therefore can take responsibility for them. This consciousness of wounds from the past allows each partner in a marriage to resist dumping old garbage on each other.

Empathy, another EQ characteristic, is an innate quality shaped by experience. Infants can be upset at the sound of another baby crying. Empathy is also a survival skill. Children from psychically damaged families frequently become hypervigilant because of their sensitive attunement to their parents' rage and anxious moods. Empathy is a buffer to cruelty and is conspicuously lacking in child beaters and child molesters.

Persistence is the ability to continually motivate oneself. It seems to be based on optimism. People who self-motivate have the abil-ity to be optimistic in the face of setbacks. They see some positive value in the mistakes they make. They are able to create new fan-tasies that offer real alternatives to the choices or inabilities that led to their setback.

Social deftness is the ability to manage interpersonal relation-ships well. Many studies of "derailed executives," the stars with promise who failed, show that they failed because of an interper-sonal flaw. They were too ambitious, too insensitive, too authori-tarian, too rebellious, rather than lacking in their technical competence. Social deftness allows one to get along well with oth-ers and to motivate other people.

For EQ to develop, children must identify and differentiate their feelings and their needs. They must also be able to contain their anger. If parents can name their own feelings and needs and con-tain their anger toward each other and their children in nonsham-ing ways, then the children will learn to do the same.

In his brilliant book *Emotional Intelligence,* Daniel Goleman has gathered an amazing amount of data pointing to the primacy of the emotional brain system over the thinking brain system.

We often *feel* without thinking, and the most damaging family transactions flow from emotional responses that bypass thinking. The more functional a family is, the more the members will be able to control their emotions and keep them from overrunning their reason. I will present data in this book suggesting that the more emotions are repressed, the more they contaminate thinking. The poisonous pedagogy tells us to repress emotion, thus damaging the possibilities of developing strong emotional intelligence.

What Is a Healthy Functional Marriage?

As I pointed out, *the chief component of the family as a system is the marital partnership.* If the marital relationship is healthy and functional, the children have the opportunity to grow.

A healthy functional couple commit to each other through the power of will. They *decide* and *choose* to stand by each other no matter what (for richer or poorer, in sickness and in health, until death do them part). A good relationship is based on committed love. It's not some maudlin feeling—*it's a decision.*

A healthy functioning relationship is based on equality, the equality of two self-actualizing spiritual beings who connect at the level of their beingness. Each is in the process of becoming a whole person. Each grows because of love for the other.

Both partners in a healthy functional marriage know that in the final analysis, they are responsible for their own wounds, actions and happiness. Happiness cannot be the fruition of a maturation process if it is dependent on something outside itself.

Maturity is a process of moving from environmental support to self-support. From puberty on, growing up and becoming mature means standing on one's own two feet and being independent and self-supporting. No relationship is healthy if it is based on incompleteness and neediness. Healthy relationships are mature, which means equal, self-responsible and mutually supportive.

The mature relationship image I like best is two people making music together. Both play their own instrument and use *their own unique skills,* but they play the same song. Each is whole and complete. Each is independent and committed.

Furthermore, in a healthy and committed relationship, each partner has a commitment to discipline. Each is self-disciplined and is willing to apply discipline to the relationship. Discipline utilizes four basic techniques that ease the suffering associated with life's inevitable problems. M. Scott Peck, in his book, *The Road Less Traveled,* outlines these techniques.

They are:

1. Delaying gratification.
2. Accepting responsibility for self.
3. Telling the truth and being dedicated to reality.
4. Bracketing ego needs for the sake of spiritual growth. [1]

Finally, discipline is both fueled by the commitment of love and is part of the commitment.

Healthy Functional Parents

When two people in a healthy relationship decide to be parents, they model their self-discipline and self-love for their children to emulate. They accept having children as the most responsible decision of their lives. They commit to being there for their children.

When such a relationship forms the foundation of a family, each child in the system has the safeguard of *needed age-specific dependency.* Age-specific dependency refers to the special needs a person has at each chronological age. Each child also needs the security to grow through experimenting with his unique individuality. In fact, the more stable and secure the parental relationship is, the more the children can be different. As long as Mom and Dad satisfy their own needs through their own powers and with each other, they will not use their children to solve these needs.

Functional parents will also model maturity and autonomy for their children. As they build a strong identity, they are in the

---

[1] M. Scott Peck, *The Road Less Traveled: A New Psychology of Love, Traditional Values & Spiritual Growth* (New York: Simon and Schuster, 1978).

process of resolving their unresolved childhood wounds. The children therefore do not have to take on their parents' unresolved unconscious conflicts.

Children of functional parents are then free to grow, using their powers of knowing, loving, feeling, deciding and imagining to reach their own individual self-actualization. The children are not constantly judged and measured by their parents' frustrated and anxiety-ridden projections. They are not the victims of their parents' "acting out" their own unresolved conflicts with their own parents.

What I'm saying here is the ideal. No human parent ever does this perfectly. If we are willing to replace the poisonous pedagogy with more deeply democratic methods, we can go a long way to stop toxic shaming and foster our children's self-esteem.

The Five Freedoms

Each person in a functioning family has access to his own natural endowment. Family therapist Virginia Satir calls this endowment the five freedoms.

These freedoms are:

1. *The freedom to see and hear (perceive) what is here and now, rather than what was, will be or should be.*
2. *The freedom to think what one thinks, rather than what one should think.*
3. *The freedom to feel what one feels, rather than what one should feel.*
4. *The freedom to ask for what one wants instead of waiting for permission.*
5. *The freedom to take risks in one's own behalf instead of choosing to be secure and always playing it safe.*[2]

These freedoms amount to full self-esteem and self-integration. Enormous personal power results from such freedoms. All of a person's energy flows freely outward, coping with the world while

---

[2] Viriginia Satir, *Making Contact* (Millbrae, California: Celestial Arts, 1976), 19.

getting personal needs met. This allows the individual to experience *full freedom* and *full functionality*.

The five freedoms oppose any kind of perfectionistic system that measures through critical judgment, since judgment implies measuring a person's worth. Fully functional families have conflicts and differences of opinion, but avoid judgment as a condition of another's worth. "I am uncomfortable" is an expression of a feeling. "You are stupid, selfish, crazy" is an evaluative judgment.

The poisonous pedagogy is based on inequality—a kind of master/slave relationship. The parental authority is vested by virtue of being a parent. Parents are deserving of respect simply because they are parents. Parents are always right and are to be obeyed.

In a family governed by the rules of poisonous pedagogy, critical judgment is not only okay, it is a duty and a requirement. Even the most mature parents will not be able to avoid the "I'm uncomfortable, therefore you are stupid, weird, crazy" distortion. Consequently, much emotional energy that belongs to the parent will be communicated as if it belonged to the child.

A client of mine felt terrible because she came home from work feeling frustrated, angry and hurt. Instead of saying to her children, "I need time alone. I'm angry, frustrated and hurt," she looked at the children's unkempt rooms and screamed at them, telling them how selfish they were and that "they never thought of anyone but themselves." She made them responsible for her frustration, anger and hurt. This is the judgment the Bible warns against. It is abusive because it attacks children's self-esteem.

The issue of judgment underscores what is perhaps the major issue differentiating functional families from dysfunctional families—the ability of each member to communicate effectively. Some theorists regard good communication in the family as the grounds for emotional health and bad communication as the mark of dysfunctionality.

Effective Communication

Good and effective communication centers around highly developed individual awareness and differentiation. Good communicators are aware of internal processes in themselves and external processes in others. Self-awareness involves my perceptions, my interpretations, my projections, my feelings and my desires. Other-awareness uses sensory observation skills, as well as the ability to translate words into sensory-based experiential data. Sensory observation involves real contact with others at a neurological level, seeing the other's accessing cues and hearing the other's words.

Accessing cues are things like breathing, facial expression and movement, voice tone and inflection. Every neurological cue is an indicator of an internal process occurring at the level of lived experience.

The ability to translate words into sensory-based experience requires listening both to the content and the process involved in speaking. This is called active listening. Active listening is listening for congruence. Congruence matches up content and process—i.e., does his body match his words? Saying "I'm not angry!" in a loud and aggressive voice tone is incongruent. If a person is not angry, he won't sound angry.

The mother who came home from work and yelled at her children failed to be aware of her own feelings. She disassociated from her feelings. She was emotionally abused as a child and learned to numb herself through her fantasy bond defense. Unaware of her feelings, and with no knowledge of self-responsible disclosure, she responded in angry judgment and criticism. Her egocentric and magical children can only translate her outburst as a judgment on themselves. Mother's anger and frustration translate into "I am bad."

The ability to translate words also has to do with challenging much of the shorthand we use in ordinary speech. Three examples of such shorthand are generalizations, deletions and distortions.

Generalizations are useful as shorthand, as when someone says, "Women are the physical child bearers." But generalizations are also dangerous, as in, "You can't trust a woman." In this case, the word "woman" needs to be translated into the concrete, specific woman or women the speaker can't trust.

Likewise, deletions are commonplace and useful. When we are making small talk at a cocktail party, it is useful to say, "My line of work is frustrating." It is not necessary to state how, specifically, our work is frustrating. However, if we want help for a frustrating problem at our job, we must translate that deletion into sensory information. This can be done when someone asks specifically how our work is frustrating.

Distortions include prejudices, mind-reading and cause-and-effect illusions. Statements like "Baptists are narrow-minded" or "Women are inferior" are *prejudicial distortions*. Statements like "You make me sick" or "You give me a headache" are *cause-and-effect distortions*. There is no real way to make another sick or to cause headaches simply by behaving in a certain fashion.

Examples of mind-reading are: "I know what you're thinking" or "I know you've never cared as much about me as I do about you." These are *mind-reading* distortions.

Each of these categories needs to be challenged in order to get below the surface to the experience the person is actually having or wants to have.

Good communication involves good self-awareness and self-differentiation. Good self-differentiation allows us to have very clear boundaries. We take responsibility for our own feelings, perceptions, interpretations and desires. We express these in self-responsible statements, using the word "I." Differentiation also means that I don't take responsibility for *your* feelings, perceptions, interpretations and desires.

When we have good boundaries, we know where we begin and end. We disclose in concrete, specific, behavioral detail. "I want you to take my suit to ABC Cleaners at nine o'clock tomorrow. Will that be possible?" rather than, "My clothes need cleaning." We check to see if the other person heard us clearly or if the other person understood clearly.

Thinking vs. Feeling

Another important aspect of healthy functionality is the internal self-differentiation that allows us to think about feelings. Being able to think about an event or a transaction allows us to contain our feelings and act upon them in an appropriate manner.

Separating thinking from feeling is a mark of solid selfhood and a part of emotional intelligence. Thinking about feeling allows us to have better choices. When we cannot differentiate thinking from feeling, we are reactive and impulsive.

Feedback

The last communication skill that makes for a healthy and fully functioning family is the courage and ability to give good feedback. Good feedback can take the form of confronting another with concrete sensory data on how the other looks, sounds and feels to the observer—for example, "You seem angry. Your jaw is tight and your fist is clenched. You haven't spoken in the last 20 minutes." Feedback also involves confronting another with our own internal response stated in sensory-based concrete data—for example, "I want to talk to you and I see you reading the paper. I feel rejected and frustrated." Confronting is important in good family relationships. It is an act of telling the truth. Caring enough to confront is an act of love.

Much more could be written on good communication. My purpose in outlining good effective communication is to show that it flows from good differentiation. Healthy partners communicate honestly with each other. They model this for their children.

To sum up, communication in a functional family will be concrete and experiential. It will be characterized by:

1. High levels of awareness about self and others.
2. Differentiation between thinking and feeling.
3. Concrete, specific, sensory-based behavioral data. A clear sense of "I"-centered self-responsibility.
4. Feedback apropos of the other's unaware behavior and apropos of our own responses.
5. A willingness to disclose what we feel, want and know.

Rules in a Functional Family

The rules in a functional family are overt and clear. Husband and wife are aware of their family differences in attitudinal, communicational and behavioral rules. These differences are understood and negotiated. Neither husband nor wife is right or wrong. Each acknowledges the other as simply different. Each partner works toward compromised solutions. This certainly does not mean they will never have any conflict. The capacity for conflict is a mark of intimacy and a mark of a healthy family. Good healthy conflict is a kind of contact. In dysfunctional families problems are denied. There is either fusion (agree not to disagree) or withdrawal.

Let's look at an example of healthy conflict. Because each person is unique and because each family system's rules are different, conflict is inevitable. For example, in my family of origin we opened our Christmas presents on Christmas Eve. We opened them fast and we didn't save the paper. In my wife's family they opened their presents on Christmas morning. They liked to spend time opening their presents. Others watched while each person opened his or her presents. They saved the ribbons and paper.

Now which way is the right way? Obviously, no one is right, and my wife and I recognized this. Our families represent two different sets of celebrational rules for Christmas. Celebrational rules have less voltage than parenting rules or financial rules. How to raise children, the right method of discipline, how to handle money, what should be spent and saved: these are rules with higher voltage. These rules lend themselves to conflict. Working out these differences is a process that may take many years.

Fair Fighting Rules

In a well-functioning marriage, the couple is committed to working out their differences. They do not stay in conflict, nor do they cop out with confluence (agreeing not to disagree). The couple strives for contact and compromise. Fighting is part of contact and compromise. Functional couples have problems and will fight, but they learn how to fight fair. While I don't profess to tell anyone an absolutely right way to deal with conflict, the following guidelines have proved useful:

1. Be assertive (self-valuing) rather than aggressive (get the other person no matter what the cost).
2. Stay in the now. Avoiding scorekeeping. "You are late for dinner. I feel angry. I wanted everything to be warm and tasty" is preferable to "You are late for dinner as usual. I remember two years ago on our vacation you . . ."
3. Avoid lecturing and stay with concrete, specific behavioral detail.
4. Avoid judgment. Stay with self-responsible "I" messages.
5. Honesty needs to be rigorous. Go for accuracy rather than agreement or perfection.
6. Don't argue about details—for example: "You were 20 minutes late." "No, I was only 13 minutes late."
7. Don't assign blame.
8. Use active listening. Repeat to the other person what you heard the person say. Get the person's agreement about what you heard before responding.
9. Fight about one thing at a time.
10. Unless you are being abused, hang in there. This is especially important. Go for a solution, rather than being right.

Covert Rules

When rules are covert, they present much greater conflict possibilities. For example, rules embodying the sex roles are often not present at a conscious verbal level. A highly successful husband who rants and raves about women's liberation may be hiding a nonverbal rule that says women should be feared and controlled. This rule may never have emerged during the "in love" courtship period. It may only come out after he is married, as he and his wife become homemakers. It may not emerge until after the first child. It is only then that his wife becomes Mother and he becomes Dad. As we take on mothering and fathering roles, our family of origin bonding comes back.

When we are "in love," our ego boundaries collapse. When we get married, they bounce back. In functional families, covert rules are brought into consciousness and dealt with. Very little is covert and unconscious. The children, therefore, do not have to act out a bunch of "secrets" or family system imbalances. Children in functional families will not be enmeshed in the covert rules of the family system. (In my book *Family Secrets,* I present a detailed examination of this phenomenon.)

Good functional rules allow each family member to express the five freedoms. Functional rules allow for flexibility and spontaneity. Mistakes are viewed as occasions for growth. Healthy shame is validated. Toxic shaming is strongly prohibited. Good functional rules promote fun and laughter. Each person is seen as precious, unique and unrepeatable.

Good Functional Rules

Functional family rules can be summed up as follows:

1. Problems are acknowledged and resolved.
2. The five freedoms are promoted. All members can freely and appropriately express their perception, feelings, thoughts, desires and fantasies.
3. All relationships are dialogical. Each person is of equal value as a person. Children's developmental limits are taken into account.
4. Communication is direct, congruent and sensory based—i.e., concrete, specific and behavioral.
5. Family members can get most of their needs met.
6. Family members can be different.
7. Parents do what they say. They are self-disciplined disciplinarians.
8. Family roles are chosen and flexible.
9. Atmosphere is fun and spontaneous.
10. The rules require accountability and consequences.
11. Violation of others' values leads to guilt.
12. Mistakes are forgiven and viewed as learning tools.
13. The family system exists for the individual's well-being.
14. Parents are in touch with their healthy shame.

One of the paradoxical aspects of functional and healthy families is that *as individuation increases, togetherness grows.* As people separate and move toward wholeness, real intimacy is possible. The poet says, "The mountain to the climber is clearer from the plain." We need separation in order to have togetherness. Needy and incomplete people seek others to make them complete. They say, "I love you because I need you." Individuated persons who have faced aloneness and separation know they can make it alone. They seek a partner because they *want to love,* not because they need completion. They say, "I need you because I love you." They offer love out of generosity, rather than need. They are no longer fantasy-bonded. It should be obvious that the rules of a healthy, functional family described here are quite different from the components of the poisonous pedagogy.

Figure 3.1. Functional Family System Chief Components

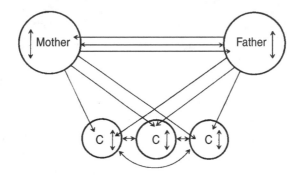

1. Whole greater than the sum of the parts.
2. System is dynamic—constantly seeks openness and growth, adjusting the feedback and stress.
3. Rules are overt and negotiable.
4. Mutual respect—balance—togetherness—individuation.
5. When anxiety is low interpersonally and intraphysically, the force toward individuation automatically emerges.
6. Five freedoms.

In figure 3.1, I have presented a visual picture of a functional family. Each person in the drawing has a complete and whole circle as his boundary. Each person has contact with every other person. The ($\updownarrow$) indicates that each person has good self-esteem. Mother and Father can share their inner lives with each other because their boundaries are semipermeable. However, the boundaries are strong enough to also keep each other out. They can say "no" to each other. They understand that while they are accountable to each other, they are not responsible for each other. If Mother responds angrily to Father, Father does not believe he *made* Mother angry. He knows that Mother's anger is about her own response (interpretation) and her own history (Father's voice may have sounded like her own father). Each takes responsibility for his or her own responses.

Because they are committed to each other, Mother and Father are accountable to each other. Father may be concerned about Mother's angry response and choose to do what he can to respond to her. He knows and she knows he is not to blame.

Family Accountability

In a healthy family, the mother and father have a disciplined love. They have the courage to do the work that love demands. Both loves themselves and are therefore self-disciplined. Because of this, they are *self-disciplined disciplinarians with their children.* They do what they ask their children to do. The children *are* disciplined.

In such a family, each person can pursue his own need fulfillment to a high degree. Of course, compromise and negotiation must take place from time to time. And *there will be conflict and boundary violation.* But all are accountable and committed to do the work of love, which means staying in there, fighting fairly and working it out.

This family will have their shame available as a wonderful and healing feeling. Mom and Dad will not act *shameless.* They will not play God by issuing "know-it-all" commands. They will not scream and curse. They will not criticize with over-responsible judgments or sarcastic and cutting remarks. They will exercise clear and firm boundaries as the mom and dad who are the architects and leaders of the family.

Does this sound like the family you enjoyed during your childhood? If it was, you are indeed graced and blessed.

For many of us, this type of family was not the context of our lives. For most of us, it would have been, had our parents known what to do differently. For most of us, our own parents had emerged from the poisonous pedagogy. They did the best they could within the limits of their awareness. Some parents are addicts and emotionally neurotic. They did *not* do the best they could.

Let us look next at how the poisonous pedagogy dysfunctions a family system. This will give you an idea of how dysfunctional your family of origin may have been. As you read the next five chapters, keep an open mind. Remember that the *idealization of family and parents is a natural and inescapable process, and that children who were severely abused or abandoned are set up to compulsively try to protect their parents. The issue here is not intentionality or blame.* Most parents would have done things differently if they had known that what they were doing was abusive. Most were probably abused themselves. Intention is not relevant. The issue is to discover our own actual history. What we want is accountability. By knowing your personal history, you will not have to repeat it. By knowing what actually happened to you, by making the abandonment real, you can change. You cannot change what you've denied or what is embedded in unconscious ego defenses and therefore isn't real. You cannot know what you don't know. Terry Kellogg states that,

> *By connecting with the past and making the abuse real, you can express the hurt and pain you had about the abuse. By expressing the anger or sadness, you can relieve the shame. You can then understand that* a lot of your behavior was about what happened to you and not about you. [3]

With that realization, a new self-acceptance and self-love can begin. Each of us has a real surprise in store for us, the surprise of rediscovering our own unique, valuable and precious self, and with that discovery will come new self-esteem.

---

[3] From an audiotape by Terry Kellogg.

S U M M A R Y

The key points covered in this chapter can be summed up using the letters of the word **FUNCTIONAL.**

Five Freedoms Expressed

In order to be fully functional, each human being needs to express freely the five basic powers that constitute human strength. These are: the power to perceive; to think and interpret; to emote; to choose, want (desire) and love; and to take risks through the use of imagination.

Unfolding Process of Intimacy

The marriage, as the chief component of the family, needs to be in the process of becoming intimate. This process goes through the stages of falling in love; working out differences; compromise and individualization; and high-level intimacy.

Negotiating Differences

Negotiating differences is the crucial task in the process of intimacy formation. To negotiate differences, a couple must have the desire to cooperate. This desire creates the willingness to fight fairly.

Clear and Consistent Communication

Clear and consistent communication are keys to establishing separateness and intimacy. Clear communication demands awareness of self and the other, as well as mutual respect for each other's dignity.

Trust

Trust is created by honesty. Accurate expression of emotions, thoughts and desires is more important than agreement. Honesty is self-responsible and avoids shaming.

Individuality

*In functional families, differences are encouraged. The unique-
ness and unrepeatability of each person is the number-one
priority in a functional family. When uniqueness is valued, a
strong sense of self-esteem can be developed. When differences
are acknowledged, a person can separate while staying connected. Strong individuality is based on self-awareness—the
ability to know the differences between one's thoughts, feelings,
needs and desires.*

Open and Flexible

*In a functional family, the roles are open and flexible. One can
be spontaneous without fear of shame and judgment.*

Needs Fulfilled

*Happy people are people who are getting their needs met. A func-
tional family allows all of its members to get their needs filled.*

Accountability

*Functional families are accountable. They are willing to
acknowledge individual problems as well as family problems.
They will work to resolve those problems.*

Laws Are Open and Flexible

*The laws in functional families will allow for mistakes. Laws can
be and are negotiable.*

Profile of a Chronically Dysfunctioning Family System

*They are
playing a game.
They are playing at
not playing a game.
If I show them I see
they are playing a
game, I shall break
the rules and they
will punish me. I
must play the game
of not seeing that
I play the
game.*

R. D. LAING

Dysfunctional families are primarily created by high levels of anxiety due to some form of stress. Our ability to deal with stress is a mark of our maturity level, which is partly measured by our ability to cope with the stressor effectively.

When two people with high levels of de-selfment and low self-esteem marry, the marriage is often characterized by the inability to cope with the stresses and strains of marriage and family life.

Think of the husband and wife as the architects of the family. When they cope in a dysfunctional way, the family starts dysfunctioning.

One of the tragic facts about dysfunctional individuals is that they almost always find other individuals who operate either at the same level of dysfunctionality or at a lower level.

Remember the family SPELL we discussed in chapter 2? Each person carries the whole family within himself. Individuals tend to exclusively seek relationships with which they have experience. The most impactive relationships a person has are those with his family of origin. We almost always choose a partner who bears many of the positive and negative traits of our parents. You may object that you have a relationship just the opposite of your parents' relationship. To choose the opposite is to still be dominated by the original trance. We are defined both by what we like or want and by what we don't like or don't want.

An observable fact about dysfunctional families is that they are part of a multi-generational process. Dysfunctional individuals who marry other dysfunctional individuals have come from dysfunctional families. So the circle remains unbroken. Dysfunctional families create dysfunctional individuals, who marry other dysfunctional individuals and create new dysfunctional families. Bowen called this the "multi-generational transmission process."

Five-Generation Genogram

Let me expand on this process by commenting on a family genogram. If you look at figure 4.1, you will see a five-generation genogram. A genogram is a family generational map. Genograms can be very useful for establishing multi-generational patterns. This genogram shows several striking patterns of dysfunctionality. First, there are five generations of alcoholism. Second, there are four generations of actual physical abandonment. Third, there was inappropriate and cross-generational bonding by both parents of the identified patient (IP). This is what I referred to as Surrogate Spousing. The IP carried on this generational pattern by marrying someone who was also a Surrogate Spouse. All the members in this genogram are co-dependent in the sense that they have a highly diminished sense of solid self-esteem. All members of this genogram need some form of treatment for emotional recovery. There are other subtleties in this multi-generational map, but they are of clinical concern. There are, however, many exceptions to the inevitability of the multi-generational process, and a great deal more work needs to be done to understand how and why certain individuals escape the consequences of the families' dysfunction.

In the last chapter we explored the components of a good marital relationship. Good functional marriages are dependent upon each partner's relationship to his/her self. If mother/wife loves herself and feels centered and growing in wholeness, she feels complete; likewise with the husband/father. I suggested that both partners feel complete and, therefore, don't look to the other for completion.

Without self-completion and self-esteem, we can hardly love another. When any natural organism is incomplete, its natural life drive is toward completion. So when two incomplete human beings come together, their drive will be toward self-completion rather than affirming each other. If we are in the process of self-completion, we can help the other to self-completion. In fact, a more realistic concept of marriage would be a state of union in which each partner is providing the other with the opportunity to self-actualize or self-complete. This is possibly what Rilke meant when he said:

> *Once the realization is accepted that even between the closest human beings infinite distances continue to exist, a wonderful living side by side can grow up, if they succeed in loving the distance between them which makes it possible for each to see the other whole against the sky. A good marriage is that in which each appoints the other guardian of his solitude.*[1]

This is also the sense of differentiation discussed in the previous chapter. Two people who have good differentiation are aware that:

1. Their feelings are distinct from their thoughts.
2. Their physical, emotional and intellectual selves are different from their partner's selves.
3. They are responsible for their individual personal happiness.

---

[1] Rainer Maria Rilke, *Letters of Rainer Maria Rilke,* trans. Jane Barnard Greene and M. D. Hester Norton (New York: W. W. Norton & Co., 1969).

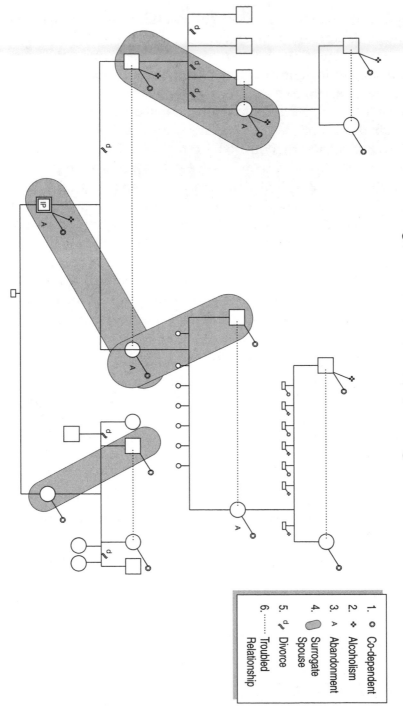

Figure 4.1. Five-Generation Genogram

1. ○   Co-dependent
2. ✧   Alcoholism
3. A   Abandonment
4. ⬭   Surrogate Spouse
5. ⌀ᵈ   Divorce
6. .... Troubled Relationship

People with such a solid sense of self-esteem are truly individuated and undependent. Being individuated and undependent does not mean that marital partners don't care for each other. It means that while they desire to love and care for each other and to be loved and cared for by each other, *they know they can survive alone.* They know that they are responsible for their own lives and happiness. They know that the other cannot make them happy. They know that the other is *not* their *better* half.

Arithmetic Lesson

The notion of husbands and wives being the other's "better half" actually exposes the common fallacy of our cultural patriarchal script on marriage. Our rigid sex roles promote two half-people joining together to make one whole person, as if one-half times one-half equaled a whole. One-half times one-half equals one-fourth, which is less than one-half. So two people who marry to be completed end up less complete than when they were incomplete.

Two half-people create an *entrapment* or *enmeshment,* rather than a relationship. In an entrapment, neither person has the freedom to get out. *Each is entrapped by needing the other for completion.* As the years roll on and the fear of going it alone increases, each becomes more and more trapped. I saw many entrapments in my marriage counseling. Such couples actually can't divorce. They are held together in an emotional symbiosis. They reenact the fantasy bond we described in the introduction. They are bonded by their neediness. The symbol I like for entrapment is the symbol of two people in a canoe. Whenever one moves, the other is forced to move.

In a healthy relationship, each person is bonded by desire and not out of neediness. Therefore, each is in the process of becoming whole. Two whole people who guard each other's wholeness come together and grow because of the guardianship of the other. Each, as Rilke suggests, provides the other the solid space (solitude) to grow. Each helps the other grow by giving up control, criticism, blame and judgment. In such a nonjudgmental space, each is free to exercise the five freedoms.

In a healthy relationship, such freedoms (which really amount to being loved unconditionally) let each partner accept himself or herself unconditionally. Unconditional self-acceptance is the royal road to wholeness. When you cannot feel, want, perceive, think or imagine what you are actually feeling, wanting, perceiving, thinking and imagining, you are split. The shoulds, oughts and musts of conditional love become internal measuring rods that cause you to split and alienate from self.

An inner warfare of self-talk ensures a constant enervating struggle. Existence itself is problematic rather than spontaneous. Everything is argued over. "Should I" or "shouldn't I" plays like a broken record. The self gets lost in the internal dialogue. You literally are beside your self. This is a good picture of dysfunction.

Dysfunctionality in a family sets up shoulds, oughts and musts by which each member is measured. The poisonous pedagogy measures all perceptions, thoughts, feelings, decisions and imaginings. "You shouldn't feel that way" or "Why do you want such and such?" or "How can you be so stupid?" or "You're just a dreamer," etc., etc., etc. In such an environment, natural powers are continuously discounted and judged as unacceptable. If you can't feel angry, your anger is split off and numbed by ego defenses. That anger is defended against and ultimately lost to consciousness. The same is true of your sexual feelings, your fearful feelings, your sad feelings, your thoughts, your desires and your visions. As pointed out in chapter 1, once you can't feel what you feel, your ego defenses take over and you become psychically numb.

When people marry out of deficiency and incompleteness, the relationship is headed for trouble. Each needs the other for completion. *In courtship, each is willing to give because of the long-range fantasy that by giving each will ultimately get the other to complete herself or himself.* This giving-to-get is one of the most troublesome and deceptive dynamics in relationships. Giving to get is a counterfeit form of love. However, each needy partner is connected by the illusion that the other is actually going to fulfill the incomplete self.

Courtship is a very deceptive and confused form of counterfeit love. Being "in love" is not love. It is probably a form of genetic bonding. Nature wants babies. So people "in love" have very powerful erotic drives for each other. When we are "in love," sex is "oceanic" in its feeling. Being "in love" is characterized by strong emotion. Actually, the emotion is undifferentiated from reason. You are literally "out of your mind" when you are in love. This out-of-mind state restores the primal symbiosis of the mother/child. If you are still in a state of undifferentiation apropos of this early state, you will feel that all of the deprived emotional needs of that earliest state can be fulfilled. This phenomenon is worth giving up parts of your self in the short term. There are no longer any boundaries. And so the dysfunctional cycle continues.

Power Struggles and The Need for Completion

Once marriage occurs, those evaporated boundaries return. Sally Hatfield is married to Bill McCoy. Now comes the power struggle between the two original families. The attitudinal, behavioral and emotional rules for each family swing into full consciousness. Both partners feel "at home" with their own *familiar* boundaries. Each family of origin system now vies for supremacy. "The way my family did it is what *feels right.*" It's what is *family-iar.* The power struggle begins and the differences must be negotiated. The "selected awareness" of being "in love" has given way to the new focus on actual differences.

The ability to accept others as different in whatever way they are different depends on your own level of differentiation. Two people with low-level differentiation cannot handle each other's differences. As the power struggle between these two people intensifies, both partners despair of ever getting the other to complete him or her. Either consciously or unconsciously, each begins to believe that by having a child or children, he or she can get completed. This belief is the beginning of the children's dysfunctionality. Born in the soil of their parents' alienated split selves, there is no way for the children to get what they absolutely need for healthy growth. More than anything else, they actually need models of good self-love and social interest. Since their parents are split and are not self-accepting, they cannot model good self-nurturing love. *There is no way for the children to learn self-love and social interest.* What they *will* learn are various forms of counterfeit love, resulting from contamination by their parents' weak, incomplete egos. They will be shamed through abandonment, and ultimately they will internalize the shame just as their parents did.

When children cannot get their dependency needs met, they become dysfunctional. And this is the best scenario we can paint. Add physical, sexual and emotional abuse to this picture, and we're talking about severe damage that can prevent a child from becoming fully functional.

Most parental mistreatment and abuse stems from the parents' own needs for completion. And the parents need completion because their own needs were never met because their needy parents were not there for them.

Parents who abuse their own children are struggling to regain the power they once lost to their own parents. Dysfunctional parents have usually been cheated out of their own feelings through abandonment. As children they were humiliated, laughed at, manipulated, intimidated, brushed aside, ignored, played with like a doll, treated like an object, sexually exploited or brutally beaten. What is worse, they were never allowed to express their rage, shame and hurt. Especially the hurt of wondering why their own parents were treating them so terribly. Beneath that hurt lies the magical egocentric belief that they must be very bad to be treated this way. This is what survives in the child who has now become parent—he is bad. As long as his own parents are idealized in the fantasy bond, the child continues to blame himself and to feel shame. *Parents who were abused as children were not even allowed to know what was happening to them.* Any mistreatment was held up as being necessary for their own good. When this mistreatment was most violent, they were told it hurt their parents as much as it hurt them. Or if that didn't work, they were taught to honor their parents no matter what. As children, their most fundamental need was their parents' protection; hence, abandonment was equivalent to death. So they obeyed and denied their own awareness (a) out of self-preservation, (b) because they possessed a magical and immature form of thinking and (c) *because they in fact did love their parents.* The fact that as children we cannot know what is happening to us is a crucial point to grasp.

The child-rearing rules that comprise poisonous pedagogy make it impossible for people to accurately remember the way they were actually treated by their parents.

The poisonous pedagogy demands that children give up their own wills and minds. The only emotion that is allowed is fear, as long as it is not so cowering as to make the parents feel guilty. Without their will, mind and emotions, children effectively lose any sense of self. They learn that they are most lovable when they are not being themselves. It is because of this radical deselfment that these children become adults who cannot understand that they were treated abusively by their parents.

Another reason abused children who are now adults do not grasp the poisonous pedagogy as abusive is because it was the normal way children were treated. They believe that because everyone for generations raised their children with the poisonous pedagogy, then it must be right. The philosopher Alfred North Whitehead called this the "naturalist fallacy." When we believe that some form of behavior is "right" simply because everyone else believes as we do, we risk the naturalist fallacy.

As adults, people act the same way their parents acted *in an attempt to prove that their parents behaved correctly toward them— i.e., really loved them and really did it for their own good.*

Alice Miller suggests that only when we have children of our own do we see for the first time the vulnerability of our earliest years (which has been dissociated or denied with the ego defenses that created the fantasy bond). In controlling our own children and putting them through what we went through, we struggle to regain the power and dignity we lost to our own parents.

All recovery from dysfunction depends on our leaving the family trance. This amounts to self-differentiation. As long as we remain in the trance, we remain in delusion and denial. I'll return to this point in chapter 9 when we discuss recovering your disabled will.

Narcissistic Deprivation

Children need to have their healthy narcissistic needs met. Narcissus was the Greek god who was condemned to fall in love with his own reflection in the lake. The story is almost always interpreted in a way that makes narcissism, or self-love, seem bad. The story needs to be seen as a symbolic statement about emerging self-image and self-consciousness.

We humans would never know who we were without a mirror to look at in the beginning. That mirror needs to reflect ourselves as the person we really are at any given time. The original mirror is almost always the mothering person who raises us, especially in the first three years of life. The mothering person needs to mirror, admire and take us seriously. Each child needs to see his instinctual drives (orality, defecation, sexuality) and aggressive feelings mirrored in the mothering person's face. Obviously, this requires a high degree of security, self-confidence and completeness in the mothering person. When this is the case, Alice Miller writes, the child can:

1. *Have his aggressive impulses so they don't upset parents' confidence.*
2. *Strive toward autonomy and be spontaneous because such strivings are not experienced as a threat to the parents.*
3. *Experience his true self—his actual feelings, wants, perceptions, thoughts and imaginings because his parents do not impose moralistic shoulds, oughts and musts at a time when the child is pre-moral.*
4. *Learn to please himself and doesn't have to please his parents, since they are self-confident and complete.*
5. *Separate successfully from his parents, i.e., achieve differentiation.*
6. *Use his parents to meet his dependency needs, since his parents are mostly complete and unneedy. These dependency needs are insatiable in the early years. The child needs his parents' time, attention and direction all the time during the early years.*[2]

---

[2] Alice Miller, *The Drama of the Gifted Child* (New York: Basic Books, 1981), 33-34.

Obviously, this is a large order. Parents who never had these needs met are themselves needy. They therefore cannot give to their children what they do not have themselves. When the mothering persons have been deprived of their own healthy narcissism, they will try to get it for the rest of their lives through substitute means.

The most available object of gratification for narcissistically deprived parents is their own child or children. The children are in their control; will obey them because not to obey is equivalent to death; will never abandon them; will possibly try to extend their parents' lives through the fruits of their achievements and performances. The child becomes the sole possession of the parents' lost narcissistic gratification.

The child thus becomes an instrument of the parents' will. Once this occurs, the child's true self is abandoned and a false self must be created. The false self is a cover-up for the *being wound* suffered by one's true self. If I can't have my feelings, my needs, my thoughts, my wants, then something must be wrong with me. I must be flawed as a person. I am worthless of my parents' time and attention. I am worth-less. This is internalized shame. The tragedy of all this is that individuals or generations get caught up in a repetition compulsion, a vicious cycle of repeating over and over again the quest for the lost paradise, only to find that each substitute is an illusion. Compulsively seeking fame, status, new sex partners, a certainty of salvation, security in a political party and so on cannot give you that deep inner unity that was lost with your child-self. The lost self is an inner problem, not an outer one. *Nothing* on the outside can bring back what was lost. Your lost child is lost forever.

The poet Omar Khayyám writes:

The Moving Finger writes; and, having writ,
Moves on; nor all your Piety nor Wit
Shall lure it back to cancel half a Line,
Nor all your Tears wash out a Word of it.[3]

---

[3] Omar Khayyám, *The Rubáiyat of Omar Khayyám,* trans. Edward Fitzgerald (New York: Doubleday, 1879), st. 71.

However, your tears are the beginning of your healing. And it is only through *mourning* that we can be completed and comforted. It is what many will have to do in order to leave home and break out of the fantasy-bonded poisonous pedagogy.

What is crucial here is to see that dysfunctional parents reenact their own original pain on their children. It is very difficult for us to understand that most persecutors were once victims. But understand it we must, or the sins of the fathers go on and on. The abused child in the persecutor is angry and hurt. Directing that anger toward our parents is forbidden. Since the anger is strictly forbidden, we project it onto others, turn it against self, or "act it out."

Boundaries

Dysfunctional families have either enmeshed or walled boundaries within the system. Enmeshment is the term used to describe the violation of ego boundaries. Figure 4.2 is a drawing of enmeshment. As you can see, all the boundaries are overrun. There is *no real possibility* of intimacy in such a family because there are no whole people to relate to. Each one plays at being intimate. What exists is pseudo-mutuality. The rules in enmeshed families are confused and covert. They are never direct and concrete. No one has a solid sense of self. Murray Bowen described the enmeshed family with the phrase "undifferentiated ego mass."

The other extreme of a boundary problem is "walled" boundaries. As you can see in figure 4.3, the boundaries are so thick, no interaction or intimacy can occur. This family can look good on the outside, but on the inside each family member has lost contact with his true self. Each is playing his respective role. Each is in an "act" and even though the boundaries are walled, each person is still ruled by the family system. Members of families with walled boundaries are usually lacking in spontaneity. There is little real contact between members, a situation described clinically as non-mutuality. Members of walled families experience loneliness. There are high levels of anxiety in both types of families.

Roles

In enmeshed families, the members play rigid roles. Their roles may be those of loving family members or good Christians. However, the role is an act. No one is really in touch with his own feelings, needs or wants. Since all are pretending, no one really knows anyone else. As we look at these families, we see a collage of images who are eternal strangers to each other. Each false self covers a core of secret inadequacy and shame. Each false self is rigid and creates a narrow range of concealing behaviors, which keep family members from revealing what they really think, feel or want.

Shame governs the entire family. The rigid roles are cover-up defenses against the shame core. Each person is in hiding and each is afraid to be his true self. This shame is inherited generationally and is perpetrated through the rigid roles and ego defenses. Shame begets shame. The self-contempt experienced in shame is maintained through the idealization of the parents and their rules for parenting. Shame is the organizing principle in most dysfunctional families.

Ego Boundaries

Figures 4.2 and 4.3 describe the intrafamily boundaries. Feeling incomplete inside is an individual *ego boundary* problem. Not having the ability to differentiate thoughts, desires and feelings is an individual ego boundary problem. Boundary problems contribute to the intimacy vacuum in dysfunctional families. I refer to this overall condition as the yin/yang disorder. People with ego boundary problems poison their thinking with unresolved feelings. These unresolved feelings block freedom of choice through the contamination of the mind.

Loss of Freedom

The blocking of choice is what I call the "disabled will." Once our will is disabled, we lose our freedom. Since toxic shame binds all one's emotions in a chronically dysfunctioning family, all its members have greatly impaired freedom. This is perhaps the greatest casualty of dysfunctional families.

Figure 4.2. Dysfunctional Family System with Enmeshed Boundaries

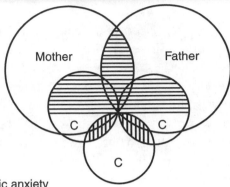

1. High-level chronic anxiety
2. Fusion of boundaries
3. Confused and covert rules
4. System is rigid and static with rigid roles
5. Undifferentiated ego mass
6. Pseudo-mutuality

Figure 4.3. Walled Boundaries

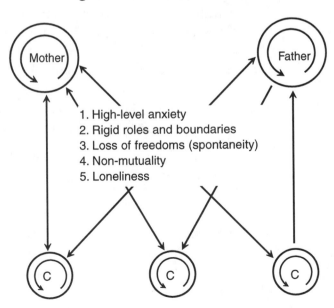

1. High-level anxiety
2. Rigid roles and boundaries
3. Loss of freedoms (spontaneity)
4. Non-mutuality
5. Loneliness

In the following diagrams (figures 4.4, 4.5 and 4.6), I try to give you a visual picture of what happens to the power of choice when our feelings are repressed. In these diagrams I borrow freely from Harvey Jackins' presentation of blocked emotion in his book, *The Human Side of Human Beings*. Jackins developed a method of working through the blocked emotions from the past called Reevaluation Counseling. I have borrowed his basic diagrams, but I've changed these drawings for my own purposes. While Jackins' focus is on the blocked emotion, my concern is on how the *human will becomes disabled by the emotionally contaminated mind*. I also believe that there is a higher level of consciousness beyond what Jackins describes in his drawings.

The drawings are quite rough and are not intended to be scientific specimens. They will give the reader a visual glimpse of what happens to our will when the mind is blocked by emotion.

The will needs the eyes of perception, judgment, imagination and reasoning. Without this source, the will is blinded. The mind cannot use its perception, judgment, reasoning and imagination when it is under the impact of repressed emotion.

One part of the brain, the amygdala, is especially impacted by repressed emotion. The amygdala is part of the limbic brain (the seat of emotion), which bypasses reason. We have the ability to react without thinking for the purpose of survival. When our brain signals us that something is dangerous, we respond immediately with either fight or flight.

Childhood abandonments, especially in the form of traumatic abuse, dramatically imprint the amygdala. Thereafter, when something seems to resemble that original moment of distress, the amygdala recognizes the similarity and guides our response in a split second, before the thinking brain has time to ponder what is happening or what the consequences of our reaction will be.

Trauma needs to be grieved through expressing the emotions appropriate to grief. When we repress the appropriate emotions (because our source figures prohibit their expression), they come out in inappropriate hysterical outbursts of anger, fear or sadness. We may also act them out in irrational behaviors, like choosing one abusive partner (resembling our source figure) after another.

The repressed energy has to be discharged before the mind can function effectively. When the emotion is repressed, it forms a frozen block that chronically mars the effective use of reasoning. Anyone who has had an outbreak of temper or been depressed has experienced how difficult it is to think under the power of these emotions. In figure 4.4 we see a model of what our raw intelligence looks like in an uncontaminated state. Our 3 trillion-circuited, 13 billion-celled computer brain is capable of a new and creative response to any new experience that occurs in our life.

Figure 4.4. Uncontaminated Raw Intelligence

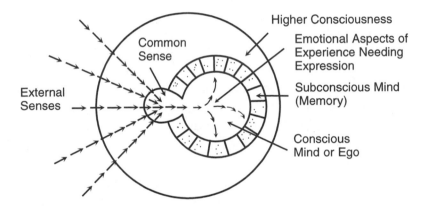

Our external senses take in new data that is given meaning and stored in our memory banks. When new information comes in, it is compared against what is already known and either stored accordingly or becomes a new bit of stored memory. The information cannot be computed if it has emotional content that is unresolved. When an experience is not resolved, it cannot be stored appropriately. Unresolved experience results from the lack of emotional discharge and meaning. The mind cannot function when biased by emotion.

When a child is abandoned through neglect, abuse or enmeshment, one of three transactions usually occurs:

1. Mythologies are created to explain the abandonment.
2. The child is given reasons for the abandonment that make no real sense and shame the child.
3. The child is told he cannot express the feelings he has about the abandonment—usually fear, hurt (sadness) and anger.

All three transactions are aimed at repressing the child's true feelings, which are the core of his inner self.

Mythologies are meanings given to events or actions in order to distract from what is actually happening. For example, in a family dysfunctioned by work addiction, the work-addict father, *who is actually emotionally abandoning his children,* is explained away by the enabling wife/mother by saying, "Your father works so much because he loves you and wants you to have nice things."

In the second transaction, the poisonous pedagogy has all kinds of reasons for the abuse. For example, "I'm doing this because I love you" or "This hurts me more than you."

In the third transaction, the emotionally blocked parents cannot handle their child's emotions. Mother's own sadness is stimulated by the child's crying. This is distressful. So Mom forbids the child to cry.

In every case, the distress experience cannot be stored *because the emotions cannot be discharged.* What occurs is a frozen pattern of blocked energy, pictured in figure 4.5.

This frozen pattern dogs your creative intelligence. It forms a trigger that functions like the "on" button of a tape recorder. Whenever any new or similar experience happens, the old recording starts to play. Here we see the force and power of behavioral conditioning. Like Pavlov's dog, whenever stimulation occurs, the response automatically takes place. This is the basis of reactions or reenactments. The past so contaminates the intelligence that new and creative responses are not possible. Blocked emotions take over the reasoning and judgment of intelligence, and the effect is cumulative.

Whenever we are confronted with a new experience that is in any way similar to the original unresolved stress, *we feel compulsively forced to reenact the old experience. We act compulsively; we do the exact same things that never worked before; we say things that are not pertinent and we have intense feelings that are totally inappropriate to what is actually happening.*

Figure 4.5. Frozen Pattern of Blocked Energy

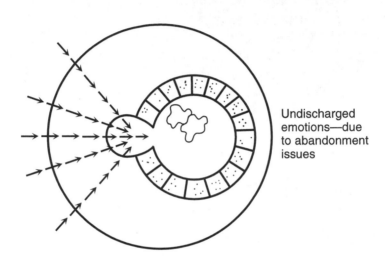

Undischarged
emotions—due
to abandonment
issues

Undischarged Emotions

Like a snowball rolling downhill, getting larger and larger, once shamed, we act out of shame and create more shame. Once a false self is created to cover the secret private self, each new shaming event solidifies the false self even more. With each new abuse that precipitates anger and sadness, the old triggers are turned on and the old frozen record starts playing. This is the basis of what we refer to as reactive behavior or overreactions. When a person represses over the course of a number of years, intelligence is greatly contaminated and diminished. The frozen patterns become chronic patterns. It is as if the "on" button is stuck and plays all the time. Figure 4.6 shows how little intelligence is left uncontaminated.

Figure 4.6. Chronic Frozen Emotions

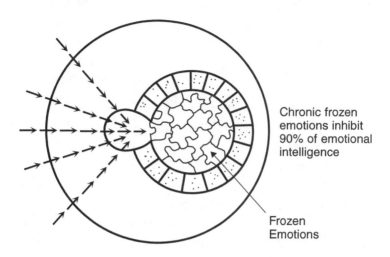

Chronic frozen
emotions inhibit
90% of emotional
intelligence

Frozen
Emotions

The Disabled Will

Contaminated intelligence seriously lessens one's decision-making process, since the will needs perception, intelligence and imagination in order to make decisions. The human will becomes "disabled."

Since the will is blinded by contaminated intelligence, it has no resource for its choice-making. The only object left for the will to use is itself. When we will ourselves to will, we become willful (literally full of will). As Leslie Farber points out in *The Ways of the Will*, the will becomes the self. With each act of willing for the sake of willing, we feel whole and complete. This is the basis of impulsiveness. To act on impulse is to will just because you can. In every "act of will," we feel complete. Just by willing we can get a feeling of oneness with self.

When we can only will to will, we become grandiose. We play God. Self-will has run riot. As Farber so brilliantly points out, we become addicted to our own will.

As children we are naturally willful, grandiose and absolutist. By not getting our developmental emotional needs met (especially the need to identify and express emotions), we are set up to become grandiose as adults.

Most children from chronically dysfunctional families have the disabled will problem. The forms this disability takes in actual life experience are:

1. We are impulsive; doing things for no reason.
2. We are gullible.
3. We have trouble with decisions and make faulty decisions, especially in matters of trust.
4. We attempt to control what cannot be controlled—e.g., an addict believes he can control his addiction, the spouse believes she can cure the addict, parents believe they can control their children. We believe that we can control our emotions.
5. We always look for the grand experience—the perfect spouse, lover, child, parent, orgasm, etc.
6. We are driven and compulsive.
7. We see everything in extremes—black and white, good or bad, for me or against me, love everything about me or you don't love me at all.

Family Roles

In chronically dysfunctioning families, the family members are selectively cut off from many of their feelings and are in rigid role performances. There are many kinds of roles, such as The Hero, Scapegoat, Lost Child, etc.

In themselves, roles are not bad, and as Shakespeare wisely pointed out, we all play many roles in our lives. The roles in chronically dysfunctional family systems are different. They are not chosen or flexible. *They are necessitated by the covert or overt needs of the family as a system.* They function to keep the family system in balance. If Dad is a workaholic and never home, one of the children will become Mom's Emotional Spouse since the system needs a marriage for balance.

In an alcoholic family, one child will be a Hero or Heroine because the family system needs some dignity. If the family system has no warmth, one child will become the Emotional Caretaker and be warm and loving to everyone. If the system is ravaged with unexpressed anger and pain, one child will become the Scapegoat and act out all the anger and pain. In each case, the person playing the role gives up his own unique selfhood in order to keep the system in balance. *In chronically dysfunctional families, the individual exists to keep the system in balance.* The whole family is dis-eased. The roles are capitalized to signify their rigidity. Because the chronic stress is not relieved, each person lives in reaction to the distress coming from chemical abuse, incest, violence, work addiction, eating disorder, parental rage or sickness, or whatever the compulsivity is.

Rigid Roles and Control

In addition to balancing the chronically dysfunctioning family, rigid roles are the false selves that shame-based family members use in order to have a sense of control over the distress the family is experiencing.

Control results from the disabled will and is one of the major defenses for shame. Shame-based people will attempt to control all the relationships they are in. Shame is the feeling of being flawed and worth-less. It demands that we hide and live in secret. Shame-based people guard against unguarded moments. In an instant of unguardedness, you could be exposed, and that would be too painful to bear. Shame-based parents control their children. Children in shame-based families play their rigid roles as a way of controlling their parents. Always being Helpful, always being a Hero, a Rebel, a Perfect Child, a Scapegoat, etc., is a way to control the family that controls you. This control madness is another way dysfunctional families set their members up for addiction. Addictions are ways to be out of control. Addictions provide relief.

Co-dependency

Co-dependency is the core outcome of dysfunctional family systems. I will expand the discussion of co-dependency in chapter 8. Co-dependency is a dis-ease of self-esteem. People who are co-dependent no longer have their own feelings, needs and wants. They react to the family distress and play out a rigid role. They learn what feelings their role demands and what feelings they may not have. For example, I was my family system's Hero. As a Hero, I had to be brave and strong. I learned to play a role of always being "up" and competent. In playing this role, I had to give up my fear and vulnerability. Since my fear and vulnerability were real parts of me, I gave up parts of myself. My role became my false self. It was an act whereby I played my enmeshed role in my alcoholic family's script.

These rigid roles are ways to survive the intolerable situation in a dysfunctional family. They function like ego defenses. They become part of the total family's fantasy bond. We are a happy family. We love each other. Each member plays his part to keep the system closed and rigid. Each member shares the mythology of the family trance. Each unconsciously agrees to share a certain focus and to share a certain denial. The denial constitutes the family system's "vital lies." Each member believes that exposing the lie would be unbearably painful and would break up the family.

Denial

We will see the trait of denial most vividly when we look at incest families. The *shared secret* and the *shared denial* are the most horrible aspects of incest. Perhaps nothing so accurately characterizes dysfunctional families as *denial.* The denial forces members to keep believing the myths and vital lies in spite of the facts, or to keep expecting that the same behaviors will have different outcomes. Dad's not an alcoholic because he never drinks in the morning, in spite of the fact that he's drunk every night. Chronically dysfunctioning families are also delusional. Delusion is *sincere* denial.

A client of mine sincerely believed that her brutally violent father was not an alcoholic because he quit drinking every Lent.

This delusion and this denial also apply to our false self roles. We become so identified with each role that we could pass a lie detector test. Our true self has been buried so long in the unconscious family trance, we think the role is who we really are. In my book *Creating Love,* I refer to this as *mystification.*

Cultural and Subcultural Boundaries

In addition to the intrafamily and ego boundaries, the family system has a third boundary. This one exists as an invisible line around the whole family. I call it the cultural or subcultural boundary. Nationalities and religious affiliations are the strongest factors in this type of boundary. Italians, Greeks, the Irish, etc. have their own special rules and "vital lies." Likewise with Pentecostalists, Catholics, Baptists, Mormons, Jews, etc. These subculture boundaries control the flow of information coming into and going out of the family. These boundaries also govern behaviors with the "other": the strangers, the ones outside of our clan. These boundaries can contribute greatly to the family's level of dysfunctionality.

For example, a client of mine who was a rigid Christian fundamentalist engaged in incest with her father because she had no right to disobey him. Her interpretation of her religion supported the poisonous pedagogy belief in parental ownership.

These subculture boundaries can also contribute greatly to keeping the system closed. They control knowledge and information. A major factor in getting out of a dysfunctional family is awareness about abuse and dysfunctionality. If your religion prohibits reading psychological works as part of secular humanism, you may not be able to understand many kinds of abuse and family dysfunction.

Thus, a characteristic of chronically dysfunctional family systems is that the more they try to change, the more they stay the same. They have no new information to break the old beliefs that form the circular feedback loops in the system. If parents are sacred and must be honored at any cost, one cannot even look at the possibility that they were abusing you.

Rules

The overt rules that create dysfunctionality are the rules of the poisonous pedagogy. The parents are dysfunctioned as a result of these erroneous rules, which they carry within their own psyches. The parents parent themselves with these rules. Without critically questioning and updating them, they pass them on to their children. Thus, parents become unintentional carriers of a virus. Add to this parents who are in advanced stages of addiction and the voltage is intensified.

The commonalities of dysfunctional families we have been describing can be summarized as a body of covert rules that operate unconsciously to create the distress in families. These rules are:

1. RULE OF CONTROL

You must be in control of all interactions, feelings and personal behavior at all times. This is a cardinal rule in all dysfunctional, shame-based family systems. Once you control feelings, all spontaneity is lost. Control gives each member a sense of power, predictability and security. Control madness is a form of severe disability of the will. Someone suffering from control madness will try to will away what cannot be willed away, such as the fundamental insecurity and unpredictability of life.

2. RULE OF PERFECTIONISM

Always be "right" in everything you do. This tyranny of being right can be about any norms the multi-generational family system has preserved. The norm may be about intellectual achievement or moral self-righteousness or being upper class and rich. The perfectionistic rule always involves an imposed measurement. There is a competitive aspect to this rule. There is a one-up, better-than-others aspect to this rule that covers up the family members' sense of shame.

The fear and avoidance of making a mistake is the organizing principle of life in a perfectionistic family. The members live according to an externalized image. They become self-image actualized. If you suffer from this rule, you will be busy observing your own actions in a situation while internally self-monitoring:

"Am I coming across okay?" "Am I getting it right?" You are committed to impression management and you constantly compare yourself with an external norm in an attempt to measure up.

No rule leads to hopelessness more powerfully than this one. Since the ideal is a mental creation, it is fantasy rather than reality. The perfectionistic ideal is shameless since it disallows mistakes. Shame as a healthy human feeling lets us know we are finite and incomplete. Shame lets us laugh at our mistakes. Shame tells us we are always in need of feedback and human community. Shame lets us know we are not God. Shame lets us know we are human. Following the perfectionism rule leads to hopelessness because to be perfectly human is to be imperfect. Perfectionism is inhuman.

3. RULE OF BLAME

Blame is another defensive cover-up for shame. Blaming behavior covers our shame or projects it onto others. Since a shame-based person cannot feel vulnerable or needy without being ashamed, blame becomes an automatic way to avoid our deepest feelings and true self.

Life's spontaneity and unpredictability inevitably break down the control rule. Blame is habitually used to regain the illusion of control. Blame is how the shaming process continues to function. As we feel the danger of vulnerability and exposure, we shame the others with blame.

4. RULE OF DENYING THE FIVE FREEDOMS

This rule follows the perfectionist rule. "You shouldn't think, feel, desire, imagine, see things or hear things the *way you do.* You should see, hear, feel, think, imagine, desire the way the perfectionistic ideal demands."

5. THE NO-TALK RULE

Don't talk openly about any feelings, thoughts or experiences that focus on the family's constant state of distress. This rule is a corollary of Rule 4. The denial of expression is a fundamental wound to humanness. Human beings are symbolic animals who speak and express themselves in symbols. We create new life and new frontiers through the symbolic function of the imagination. Certain family secrets can be maintained for generations because of this rule. I explored this idea in my book, *Family Secrets.*

6. THE NO-LISTEN RULE

Family members live so defensively that we are not present when others speak. The need to engage in "impression management" necessitates thinking about our next response rather than listening to what is being said.

7. INCOMPLETION RULE

Don't complete transactions. Keep the same fights and disagreements going for years. This rule may be manifested in two ways. One is through chronic fighting and conflict without any real resolution. The second is through enmeshment and confluence; agreeing never to disagree. The family has either conflict or confluence, but never contact. Members stay upset and confused all the time.

8. UNRELIABILITY RULE

Don't expect reliability in relationships. *Don't trust anyone* and you will never be disappointed. Since our parents never got their dependency needs met as children, they cover up this insatiability with fantasy-bonded illusions of self-sufficiency. By acting either aloof and independent (walled boundaries) or needy and dependent (enmeshed boundaries), everyone feels emotionally cut off and incomplete. No one gets his needs met in a functional manner.

Figure 4.7 sums up the profile of a dysfunctional family. This chart is a composite of the actual types of dysfunctional families I will discuss in the next three chapters. The Rigid Roles are not listed accurately; they are simply listed. I encourage the reader to use this chart and the next three chapters as a checklist for your own personal self-discovery. Most of our present human dysfunctions can be described by the term compulsivity. Violence, sexual disorders, eating disorders, emotional and religious addictions are the ills that destroy people's lives. Let us look at these now.

Figure 4.7. Profile of a Dysfunctional Family System

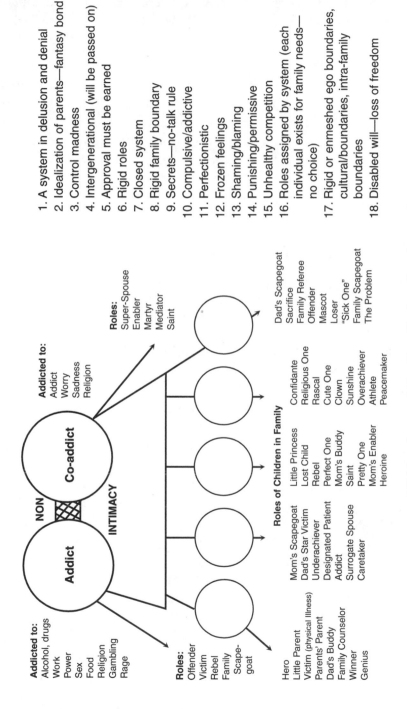

Addicted to:
Alcohol, drugs
Work
Power
Sex
Food
Religion
Gambling
Rage

Roles:
Offender
Victim
Rebel
Family Scapegoat

Addicted to:
Addict
Worry
Sadness
Religion

Roles:
Super-Spouse
Enabler
Martyr
Mediator
Saint

Roles of Children in Family

Hero — Little Princess — Confidante — Dad's Scapegoat
Little Parent — Lost Child — Religious One — Sacrifice
Victim (physical Illness) — Rebel — Rascal — Family Referee
Parents' Parent — Perfect One — Cute One — Offender
Designated Patient — Mom's Buddy — Clown — Mascot
Addict — Saint — Sunshine — Loser
Surrogate Spouse — Pretty One — Overachiever — "Sick One"
Caretaker — Mom's Enabler — Athlete — Family Scapegoat
Genius — Heroine — Peacemaker — The Problem
Family Counselor
Winner

1. A system in delusion and denial
2. Idealization of parents—fantasy bond
3. Control madness
4. Intergenerational (will be passed on)
5. Approval must be earned
6. Rigid roles
7. Closed system
8. Rigid family boundary
9. Secrets—no-talk rule
10. Compulsive/addictive
11. Perfectionistic
12. Frozen feelings
13. Shaming/blaming
14. Punishing/permissive
15. Unhealthy competition
16. Roles assigned by system (each individual exists for family needs—no choice)
17. Rigid or enmeshed ego boundaries, cultural/boundaries, intra-family boundaries
18. Disabled will—loss of freedom

All Members of the Family Are Co-dependent

SUMMARY

The key points covered in this chapter can be summed up using the letters of the word **DYSFUNCTIONAL.**

Denial and Delusion

Dysfunctional families deny their problems; hence, the problems never get solved. Such families also deny members the Five Freedoms.

Yin/Yang Disorder

There is an intimacy vacuum in a dysfunctional family. The intimacy vacuum contributes to the dysfunction.

Shame-based

Nonfunctional families are shame-based. The parents have internalized their shame and act shameless toward their children. The children often feel ashamed of the family.

Fixed, Frozen and Rigid Roles

Roles are created by the needs of the family as a system. Children give up their reality to take care of the needs of the system.

Undifferentiated Ego Mass

Members of dysfunctional families are enmeshed in each other's boundaries. If Mom is scared, all feel scared. Members feel for other members.

Needs Sacrificed to the System

Members of a dysfunctional family cannot get their individual needs met. Individual needs are put aside for the needs of the system. There is almost always low-grade anger and depression in a dysfunctional family.

Confluence or Conflicted Communication

The communication style in dysfunctional families is either open conflict or the agreement never to disagree (confluence). There is rarely any real contact.

Togetherness Polarity Dominates

Individual differences are sacrificed for the needs of the family system. In dysfunctional families, the individual exists for the family. It is difficult to leave dysfunctional families.

Irrevocable Rules

In nonfunctional families, the rules are rigid and unchanging. The poisonous pedagogy helps to set up these rules. The dominant rules are control, perfectionism, blame, denying the Five Freedoms, no-talk, no-listen, incompletion and unreliability.

Open Secrets

The open secrets are part of the vital lies keeping the family frozen. Apropos of open secrets, everyone knows what everyone pretends not to know.

Nonchanging Closed System

Everyone plays his role to control the controlling distress. But the more each plays his role, the more the system stays the same. The French proverb, Plus ça change, plus c'est la même chose *(the more something changes, the more it remains the same), sums up the dilemma of the closed family system.*

Absolute and Grandiose Will

The major catastrophe of the dysfunctional family is that members have their wills disabled. Each person's birthright of freedom is impaired. Control itself is a product of the disabled will. The no-talk rule results in frozen feelings that contaminate one's emotional intelligence. The will to will or self-will taken to the extreme creates chaotic and unpredictable behavior in chronically dysfunctioning families.

Lack of Boundaries

Members of dysfunctional families give up their ego boundaries as a way to maintain the family system. Giving up ego boundaries is equivalent to giving up your identity.

Compulsive Families: Checklist for How Your Self-Esteem Was Damaged in an Addicted Family

The open secrets. Everybody knows about them and nobody is supposed to know that everybody knows.

R. D. LAING

After 17 bitter years of painful alcoholism, I put the cork in the bottle 30 years ago. In many ways the last thing I would have believed as a child was that I would become an alcoholic. I cried myself to sleep many a night because of my father's drinking and his abandonment. Frozen with fear in my bed at night, I waited for him to come home, never knowing exactly what was going to happen. I hated alcoholism and all it stood for. I obsessed about his drinking day in and day out. At 30 years old, I wound up in Austin State Hospital on a voluntary commitment for the treatment of alcoholism.

As paradoxical as it seems, *many* children of alcoholics become alcoholics. And if they don't become alcoholics, they often marry alcoholics or

97

people with some other compulsive, addictive personality disorder.

This paradoxical pattern focuses on the truth of "families as systems" more than any other single factor. Some 20 years ago, persons from alcoholic families started realizing that there were commonalities in their lives that seemed to have less to do with them and more to do with their families of origin. Led by Robert J. Ackerman, Claudia Black, Sharon Wegscheider-Cruse, Janet G. Woititz and Wayne Kritsberg, the Adult Children of Alcoholics (ACoA) movement formed. With the Adult Children's movement, the family systems concept took a giant step forward.

During the first decade of my recovery from alcoholism, I knew nothing of the Adult Children's phenomenon. I had dabbled intellectually with family systems. I had incorporated the work of Virginia Satir, Jay Haley and R. D. Laing into my adult theology classes at Palmer Episcopal Church in Houston. But I never got the connection with my own alcoholic family of origin. I thought that my addiction to excitement, my people-pleasing and approval-seeking, my overly developed sense of responsibility, my intimacy problems, my frantic compulsive lifestyle, my severe self-criticalness, my frozen feelings, my incessant good-guy act and my intense need to control were just personality quirks. I never dreamed that they were characteristics common to adults who as children lived in alcoholic families.

Even though I was recovering from alcoholism, I was still acutely compulsive. My compulsivity was causing life-damaging consequences. I was working, buying, smoking and eating compulsively. This realization led me to seek further treatment for my still-addicted personality.

The work in chemical dependency and especially the ACoA movement has helped me understand the nature of compulsivity and how it is set up in families who use ineffective coping skills to deal with anxiety and distress.

Adult Children of Alcoholics

The fact that there are common characteristics of children who grew up in alcoholic families betrays an underlying structure of disorder. I've outlined some traits of ACoA using the first letters of the phrase *Adult Children of Alcoholics.*

A Addictive/compulsive behavior or marry addicts
D Delusional thinking and denial about family of origin
U Unmercifully judgmental of self or others
L Lack good boundaries
T Tolerate inappropriate behavior

C Constantly seek approval
H Have difficulty with intimate relationships
I Incur guilt when standing up for self
L Lie when it would be just as easy to tell the truth
D Disabled will
R Reactive rather than creative
E Extremely loyal to a fault
N Numbed out

O Overreact to changes over which they have no control
F Feel different from other people

A Anxious and hypervigilant
L Low self-worth and internalized shame
C Confuse love and pity
O Overly rigid and serious, or just the opposite
H Have difficulty finishing projects
O Overly dependent and terrified of abandonment
L Live life as a victim or offender
I Intimidated by anger and personal criticism, or overly independent
C Control madness—have an excessive need to control
S Super-responsible or super-irresponsible

From this checklist it's clear that as children of alcoholics, we are not just reacting to the alcoholic's drinking. We are reacting to the relational issues: the anger, the control, the emotional unavailability of the alcoholic parent. These traits are a response to the trauma of the abandonment and ensuing shame that occur in alcoholic families.

For the children of alcoholics, this shame is primarily rooted in the broken relationship with their parents. Our index of traits shows that most of the problems ACoAs have are relationship problems. These traits also give us a clue to understanding the roots of compulsivity. The World Health Organization's definition of compulsive/addictive behavior is "a pathological relationship to any mood-altering experience that has life-damaging consequences."

The propensity for *pathological relationships* is rooted in and set up by the shame of the parental abandonment. Let us look at our index of traits in more detail.

A. **Addictive/compulsive behavior or marry addicts.** You are or have been in an active compulsive/addictive pattern of behavior. You are or have been in a relationship with a compulsive/addicted person.

D. **Delusional thinking and denial about family of origin.** You either consciously or sincerely deny your partner's or parent's drinking problem. You are in a fantasy-bonded idealization of your parents. You idealize your nonaddicted parent. You minimize and deny your feelings and the impact on your life and/or your children's lives of the relationship you are in with an alcoholic partner or parent.

U. **Unmercifully judgmental of self and others.** You constantly criticize yourself. What you do is not good enough. You project your own self-critical judgment onto others.

L. **Lack good boundaries.** *You* take an aspirin when your spouse has a headache. You don't know where your feelings end and others' feelings begin. You let everyone touch you or let no one touch you. Your opinion is the same as the opinion of the person you are with.

T. **Tolerate inappropriate behavior.** You guess at what normal is. In your relationships, you are now tolerating what you said you would never tolerate. You believe that your abusive childhood was more or less normal.

C. Constantly seek approval. You are a people-pleaser and will go to almost any lengths to have people like you. In your primary relationships, you drive others crazy with your need to know where you stand.

H. Have difficulty with intimate relationships. You confuse *intimacy with enmeshment* and *contact with conformity*. You believe that if you love someone, you will both like the same things. You are attracted to destructive relationships and are turned off by healthy, stable, caring people. You sabotage any relationship that starts getting too close.

I. Incur guilt standing up for self. You feel guilty whenever you stand up for yourself, act assertive and ask for what you want. You feel guilty that you are in recovery and the rest of your family is not.

L. Lie when it would be just as easy to tell the truth. You find yourself lying for no good reason when it would be just as easy to tell the truth. Or you are just the opposite—you adhere to the letter of the truth.

D. Disabled will. You are compulsive, impulsive, stubborn, grandiose, overly dramatic and controlling, and have difficulty making decisions. You try to control what cannot be controlled.

R. Reactive rather than creative. Your life is one reaction after another. You overreact. You say things that are not relevant, feel things that are disproportionate to what is going on. You spend so much time worrying and reminiscing over others' behavior that you have no time for your own.

E. Extremely loyal to a fault. You stay loyal even in the face of evidence to the contrary, or you are loyal to no one.

N. Numbed out. You are psychically numb. You deny your feelings. You don't know what you feel and wouldn't know how to express your feelings even if you did know.

O. Overreact to changes over which you have no control. You ruminate over things you cannot change, like mistakes you've made in the past.

F. Feel different from other people. You never feel like you really belong. You always feel self-conscious. You are secretly jealous and envious of others' seeming normalcy.

A. Anxious and hypervigilant. You are always on guard. You have an intense level of nameless fear and catastrophic expectation. You have a feeling of impending doom. You are jumpy and easily startled. You enjoy your vacations most after they are over and you are showing the slides.

L. Low self-worth and internalized shame. You feel defective as a human being. You cover up with roles like Caretaker, Super-Responsible One, Hero, Star, Heroine, the Perfect One. You are perfectionistic, controlling, power-seeking, critical and judgmental, rageful, secretly or openly contemptuous, gossipy and backbiting.

C. Confuse love and pity. You are attracted to weak people. You go to great lengths to help pitiful-looking people. You enter relationships with people you can fix. You mistake pity for love.

O. Overly rigid and serious, or just the opposite. You are somber and rarely play and have fun. Life is problematic rather than spontaneous. You are perfectionistic and super-responsible. Or you are irresponsible and never take things seriously enough.

H. Have difficulty finishing projects. You have trouble initiating action. You have trouble stopping once you've started. You never quite finish important things, like getting degrees.

O. Overly dependent and terrified of abandonment. You stay in relationships that are life-damaging and severely dysfunctional. You have trouble ending anything. You stay in a job that has no future. You are possessive and suspicious, and cling to the relationships you are in with spouse, lover, child, friend.

L. Live life as a victim or offender. You have been physically, sexually, emotionally abused. You live in a Victim role, finding yourself victimized wherever you are. You are attracted to either offenders or victims. You expend much energy dramatically describing your victimizations. Your identity comes from being a victim.

I. Intimidated by anger and personal criticism, or very independent. You are manipulated by anger and criticism. You will go to great lengths to stop someone from being angry at you or critical of you. You will give up your needs to stop their anger or criticalness, or you are a rageaholic.

C. Control madness. You have an excessive need to control. You control by being "helpful." You feel frightened when you feel out of control. You avoid anyone or any situation where you can't be in control.

S. Super-responsible or super-irresponsible. You take responsibility for everything and everyone. You try to solve others' problems even when they don't ask for help. Or you take no responsibility and expect others to be responsible for you.

This kind of index helps researchers see just how dysfunctional you can become simply by living in an alcoholic family. This index also helps to focus on the causes for compulsive behavior.

The alcoholic family is a compulsive family. Everyone in the system is affected by the distress caused by the anxiety over the alcoholic's drinking. Someone compared living in an alcoholic family to living in a concentration camp. And like survivors of a concentration camp, ACoAs carry what has been compared to post-traumatic stress symptoms. In fact, if one takes a list of the disorders experienced by war veterans or any other severe trauma victims, one will find that a large number of the post-trauma symptoms match a large number of ACoA characteristics. Children who live in alcoholic families, if untreated as children, carry these characteristics of post-trauma stress into later life.

Abandonment

Because of the chronic distress caused by the alcoholic's drinking, each person in the family must find a way to adapt. To some degree, each person in the alcoholic family becomes hypervigilant, anxious and chronically afraid. In such an environment, it's difficult for anyone to get his basic human needs met. Each person loses self-esteem.

The major consequence of this chronic stress is a feeling of abandonment. There may be several characteristics of abandonment experienced by the members in an alcoholic family. First, since alcoholism is an all-pervasive addiction, the addict's time is consumed with alcohol. Such involvement leaves little time for the care of children. Alcoholic parents, no matter how good their intentions, physically abandon their children. They also neglect their children's basic dependency needs, which is a second form of abandonment. There is no one there for the child. There is no mirroring face to affirm the child's preciousness and no one the child can depend on. If Dad's the alcoholic and Mom is addicted to Dad, Mom is co-dependent. She can't be there for her children's needs because she is also an addict.

As addicts, both parents are needy and to some degree shame-based. A second form of abandonment occurs because it is extremely difficult for two needy, shame-based people to give love and model self-love. A normal child has healthy narcissistic needs, but there is no way these needs can be met in an alcoholic family. So each child turns inward to a fantasy bond of connection with their parents, and often to self-indulging habits and pain-killing ways to alter mood.

A third form of abandonment comes from abuse. Alcoholic families foster every kind of abuse. Because alcohol lowers inhibitions and knocks out the rheostat that regulates impulse control, physical, sexual and emotional battering are commonplace in alcoholic families. Some estimates say that two-thirds of ACoAs were physically violated as children. Studies have shown that 50 percent of incest fathers are alcoholic.

Alcoholic families are severely enmeshed. Enmeshment is another way the children are abandoned. As the alcoholic marriage becomes more entangled and entrapped, the children get caught up in the needs of both their parents, as well as the needs of the family system for wholeness and balance. Nature abhors a vacuum.

When the family system is unbalanced, the children attempt to create a balance.

In my family, my dad was never there. By the time I was 11 years old, he was, for all practical purposes, gone. I was the oldest male. The system needed a husband. I became my mother's emotional husband (Surrogate Spouse). My mom did not decide this, the system demanded it. I also became my brother's Little Parent, since the system needed fathering. When I was 13, I was giving *him* an allowance.

In one family I worked with, as the drinking husband's alcoholism intensified, the oldest daughter became Mom's Scapegoat. Mom had been pregnant with her at the time of her marriage. In fact, she was the reason Mom and Dad got married. As Mom realized Dad was an irresponsible alcoholic, she turned her anger onto the girl child.

In this same family, the third child came at the height of the parents' marital conflict. He was an accidental pregnancy. He felt the emotional abandonment in the womb. His role was Lost Child in the family. Literally the parental message he got was, "Get lost, child, we can't handle another child."

In alcoholic families the discipline is modeled by *unself-*disciplined disciplinarians. The rules of the poisonous pedagogy offer justification for a lot of so-called discipline. Very little of it is really discipline. It is often contaminated by the parents' irritation and rage about their own lives. Most of the time this discipline has nothing to do with the child—i.e., it doesn't stem from the child's behavior or help the child improve. Punishment occurs frequently and is usually inconsistent. The parents model this inconsistency.

What all this adds up to is that the children who need their parents' time, attention and direction for at least the first 15 years of their lives do not get it. They are abandoned. Abandonment sets up compulsivity. Since the children need their parents all the time, and since they do not get their needs met, they grow up looking and talking like adults, but having within them an insatiable little child who never got his or her needs met. They have an inner emptiness, and this drives their compulsivity. They look for *more and more love,* attention, praise, booze, money, etc. And since none of us can be a child again, and we cannot go back and have a mom or a dad take care of us, these needs cannot be filled *as a child*. They *can* be dealt with as they are recycled in adult life. But they can only be dealt with as an *adult*.

The Compulsive Family in General

I've used the alcoholic family as a prototype of the compulsive family. Historically, the studies in chemically dependent families revealed the dysfunctional structure of other types of families. Through studying alcoholism and the alcoholic family, a new model emerged that explained how other forms of compulsivity cause similar patterns of dysfunctionality in families.

The pattern was clear. Shame-based compulsive people create needy marriages and engender families in which children are shamed through abandonment. The victimized children from these marriages often become equally compulsive and continue the cycle.

The poisonous pedagogy, with its master/slave inequality, is intensified in families parented by addicts. However, *these addicts were often set up for addiction by being discounted and having their needs denied by the poisonous pedagogy in their families of origin.*

Power, control, perfectionism, criticism, contempt, blame and rage are ways that shame is interpersonally transferred. Parents who are covering up their shame with their own fantasy-bonded ego defenses, their own rigid roles and their own addictions become shameless. Acting as if they know it all, criticizing, controlling, condemning, blaming and punishing themselves, each other and their children, these parents play God. Such shameless behavior necessitates that the children carry their parents' shame.

Let's take rage, for example. Rage is common in alcoholic families. It is also a common addiction in itself. A rageaholic parent can cause a family to be every bit as dysfunctional as an alcoholic parent can. Rage serves a self-protective function by insulating the self against exposure and by actively keeping others away. For example, suppose a father goes on a drunken spree. He misses several days of work. When he goes to work, his boss chews him out.

As he comes home, he feels the piercing shame of his behavior. He sees his son's bicycle lying in the front yard. Using his poisonous pedagogical rights, he seeks out his son and begins raging at him. This spontaneous behavior enables the father to feel good about himself (doing his fatherly duty) and lose all contact with the pain of his own shame. By being shamed, the son takes on the father's shame. Rage is a strategy of defense aimed at making the son feel shame in order to reduce the father's shame.

Since there is so much shame present in an alcoholic family, the interpersonal transfer of shame goes on continuously. The poisonous pedagogy actually supports the parents in their strategies of interpersonal transference of shame. Power, control, blame, criticism and perfectionism are encouraged and justified by the poisonous pedagogy.

Children idealize parents through the fantasy bond. Because they are idealized, parents can easily pass their rage, hurt, loneliness and shame onto their own children.

Compulsivity as Addictiveness

I've been using the words compulsivity and addiction more or less synonymously. This needs to be clarified.

Compulsivity is a more comprehensive term than addiction. Compulsivity comes closer to meaning "addictiveness." Addictiveness is the inner emptiness we try to fill up with any mood-altering behavior. The word addiction has often been limited to chemical substances like alcohol, nicotine and other drugs that have their own inherent addictive properties.

This understanding narrows down the meaning of addiction. There are many types of nonchemical addiction. Activities such as gambling, sexing, working, eating and starving can also be full-fledged addictions. The common root of every addiction is compulsivity understood as addictiveness.

When I stopped my alcohol addiction, I did not stop being compulsive. My compulsivity turned into other addictions, like working and eating. This distinction is important because if we do not understand it we cannot really get at the root of the problem. Until I dealt with my compulsivity, I didn't stop my addictions.

Compulsivity is set up by the kinds of abandonment I've been describing. Healing the unresolved grief resulting from abandonment is the way to heal compulsivity. I discuss this fully in chapter 10.

Compulsive/Addictive Behavior

I believe that our most pressing human problems focus on compulsive/addictive behavior. Addictions narrow our minds and disable our wills. Our life is no longer a conscious choice.

It is false thinking to believe that addiction is only about dope fiends in dark alleys or belligerent and stumbling drunks. *Addiction touches the lives of many people in our culture.*

In my own work as president of the Palmer Drug Abuse Program, I found a very stereotyped conception of addiction. While we treated teenagers abusing chemicals, we also dealt with their parents and families. All around me I found work addiction, religious addiction, eating disorders, co-dependent people addicts, parents addicted to their children, cigarette addicts and rageaholics.

It is important to expand the definition of addiction. If people can identify their own compulsivities—their own life-damaging relationships with mood-altering experiences—we can create a community of concern about a very *common modern crisis*.

An addiction is a pathological relationship with any mood-altering experience that has life-damaging consequences. The inability to relate in a healthy manner is the result of shame, since shame is the result of broken relationships. Once the interpersonal bridge with caretakers or survival figures is broken, children believe that they do not have the right to depend on anyone. They quit trusting themselves and others and start depending on their fantasy bond and self-indulging patterns of behavior. They are set up for pathological relationships.

Pathological implies a delusional quality to the relationship. Delusion and denial are the essence of compulsive/addictive behavior. In denial, you deny that what you are doing is really harmful, either to yourself or to others. In delusion, you keep sincerely believing that what is happening is not happening, in spite of the facts. Robert Firestone's "fantasy bond" is a form of delusion and denial. In my opinion, all addictions are fantasy bond reenactments.

The fantasy bond is reenacted in several ways. It can come with the grandiosity of being in love; the ecstasy of feeling good and righteous; sexual conquest and orgasm; the *ful-filled* feeling of eating; the altered state of consciousness induced by starving; the magical possession of money and things; the high of drugs. In all compulsive/addictive behavior, *the illusion of connection* is restored. In the ecstatic moments of the addiction, you feel that you are not alone. You believe that you have overcome separation and aloneness. Delusion and denial keep away the "legitimate suffering" that comes with feeling the pain of emptiness and aloneness. Addicts minimize the effects of their compulsivity in their life. They rationalize the life-denying consequences of their behavior.

Compulsive/addictive behaviors are not about being hungry, thirsty, "horny" or needing to work. They are about mood-alteration. They help us manage our own feelings. They distract us or alter the way we are feeling so that we don't have to feel the loneliness and emptiness of our abandonment and shame.

The mood alteration that comes from distractive activities is mostly unrecognized in our culture. We promote hard work and competitive achievement. We are a God-fearing, God-worshiping nation. We are sports-minded, with an array of entertainment the whole world seeks and envies. All of these activities can become addictions. They are all ways that we can revel in an adrenaline rush and excitement and distract ourselves from whatever we are feeling.

Gambling is perhaps the most dramatic example. For gamblers, "the action is the distraction." But any activity can distract and therefore mood-alter. Work addiction and religious addiction are major addictions in our country.

Emotional Addictions

Emotions themselves can be addictive. We can substitute one emotion for a less painful emotion. Men are frequently taught to substitute anger for fear. Almost everyone has met an angry man.

Such men have internalized their anger. Men are supposed to be warriors. Warriors have to be super-strong and totally adequate. Any hint of inadequacy makes one less a man. Consequently, men are afraid of feeling inadequate and often cover that feeling up with anger. Anger feels powerful. Inadequacy feels weak.

I came home from work one summer evening and my wife greeted me at the door with the news that our air conditioner had stopped working. It was in the middle of summer, humid and unbearably hot. A voice in my head told me, "Real men know how to fix mechanical things." Since I can't fix anything mechanical, I felt inadequate. I didn't even know where our air conditioner was located. So instead of saying, "Gee honey, that's awful. Let's go to a hotel and call someone to get it fixed," I said angrily, "What did you do to it now? Can't I count on you for anything?" Anger feels potent; fear feels wimpy. This example shows you how anger works as a mood alterer. Of course, an occasional episode of mood alteration does not make one an addict. But I counseled folks who were chronically angry. Their anger created life-damaging consequences.

Any feeling can be used to mood-alter other feelings, and *when it has life-damaging consequences,* I call it an addiction. One person may be a full-fledged sad addict. I'm sure you've met a "sad sack"—a person who is always sad. That's probably an addiction.

Chemicals, activity and emotions are powerful ways not to feel what you are feeling. Remembering that abandonment is a major setup for compulsivity helps us to see why we want to mood-alter. When abandoned, we feel rejected, lonely, sad and angry. And, of course, we feel shame. Deep internalized shame is excruciatingly painful. Therefore, we want to mood-alter it.

Compulsive Thinking

There are also other ways to be compulsive. Certain obsessive thought patterns are excellent ways to distract and cut off emotions. Obsessive worrying, ruminating, engrossment in minute details, generalizing and abstract thinking are all ways to cut off our feelings.

Obsessive thought patterns play a major role in all compulsivities. The thought pattern in sexual addiction is called lusting. A sex addict may be lusting in his head for hours before he begins his ritualized behavior—cruising, obtaining pornography or looking for a child to victimize. The lust itself is an addictive part of the addiction process.

The most crucial aspect of any compulsivity is the *life-damaging aspect of it*. Life-damaging means that the compulsive/addictive behavior causes personal dysfunction. Compulsivity of any sort blocks us from getting our needs met through our own basic human powers. The compulsivity takes up all our energy. Our choices are narrowed. Our freedom is lost. Our will is disabled. Compulsivity is a state of inner barrenness. We are totally externalized, without any self-reflection and interior life. How can we have an inner life when we feel flawed and defective as a human being? This shame core keeps the addict from going inward. The true self hides behind a masked false self.

Compulsivity is also about bad habits that become vicious over a period of time. Philosophers speak of habits as second natures. Good habits are virtues, which are strengths added to our personhood. Bad habits are vices and have the power to control our lives and take it over. Bad habits are a very dominant part of the euphoric type of mood alterers such as drugs, sugar and sex. Drugs and food also have the added factor of having their own intrinsic chemical power. These chemicals are in themselves addicting.

In 15 years of working with teenage drug abusers, I've never found a single one who was what I'd call *only a chemical addict*. As powerful as many of the current market drugs are, especially cocaine and crack, I've never yet worked with an addict who didn't have the inner emptiness. I've been in my personal recovery for 30 years and I've never met a person in recovery from chemical abuse who didn't have abandonment issues in the sense I have defined them.

Perhaps nothing is more important for adult children of dysfunctional families than to connect their abandonment violation with the behavioral dysfunctions and problems that abandonment causes. For example, in the checklist I've given for ACoAs, each of the behavioral characteristics is a response to being violated.

Abandonment violates our rights, our boundaries and our needs.

Our violated true self stays in hiding because we have lost the connection between what happened and the response to what happened. Since the fantasy bond idealizes our persecutors, we can only conclude that our neurotic, dysfunctional behavior is about us and not them.

But once we become aware that our responses to violence are about what happened to us and not about who we really are, we can begin our recovery process. We can demythologize our idealized parents and can see that *we are not bad, flawed or defective.*

I'd like to sum up this chapter by presenting a profile of four types of compulsive families. Each family is a composite profile of people I've actually counseled, people who have shared in my workshops and people from my own experiences. All key members will be disguised in such a way as to protect their personal ego boundaries. At the same time, these profiles will reflect what is happening in real flesh-and-blood family systems. The four types of compulsive families are: chemically addicted, eating disordered, religion addicted and work addicted. I will be talking about sexual addiction, physical violence, emotional battering and co-dependence in the chapters that follow.

Chemical Addiction: The Blue Family

Jesse is the father of this family. He is an alcoholic. He was inappropriately bonded with his mother and was abandoned by his own father. He had two stepfathers. They were both alcoholics. One was physically abusive to Jesse and his mother. His mother carried the poisonous pedagogy in denying her son his sexual feelings as well as his anger. Jesse is very passive-aggressive. He was taught that real men don't cry and are not afraid. At 16 Jesse met Jessica and impregnated her, and they married.

Jessica was inappropriately bonded with her father since her mother was the adult child of an alcoholic, an incest victim and addicted to sickness (her mother was bedridden most of her life). Jessica's father was sanctified by Jessica and her seven sisters. Actually, Jessica's father was an enabler, allowing his wife to stay addicted by walking on eggshells and living in reaction to her feelings, needs and wants. Jessica's family looked very respectable. They were staunch churchgoers. Only appropriate feelings were ever shown.

Jessica and Jesse had three children. Their first child (the reason they married), Gweneviere, was born to her 16-year-old mother. She was not wanted and felt this from birth. She became the Lost Child, as well as Superachiever and Super-Responsible first child. She was Mom's Scapegoat and felt this conflict all her life. She went to work early. She twice divorced addicts and lived in chronic depression and isolation until she found a recovery group.

Jack was born 13 months after Gweneviere. He was the first male in two generations and bore the unconscious sexualized rage of two generations of man-haters. He became the family Caretaker. Jesse abandoned all the children with his active alcoholism. Jack bonded inappropriately with Jessica and played the role of Surrogate Spouse.

Jack was also Super-Responsible and a Superachiever. He also took the role of Caretaker by being grandmother's, aunts' and Mom's helper. He later acted out his alienated rage for having to be Jessica's emotional spouse and the family caretaker by becoming alcoholic himself. He started drinking in secret at age 13, and by age 15 was seriously addicted, having had several alcoholic blackouts. In spite of this, Jack developed a Hero role by being the class president and salutatorian in high school.

After one year of college, Jack decided to be a celibate minister. This ensured both his inappropriate bond role and Hero role. His active addiction destroyed his ministry. He got help in AA and sobered up. He married a pregnant girlfriend, reenacting Jesse and Jessica's marriage. He had two children and lived in nonintimacy for seven years. Jack later found ACoA and continues in it to this day.

The third child, Jacob, was also a Lost Child—another accidental pregnancy. He came at the apex of Jesse and Jessica's ever-accelerating dysfunctionality. He carries the loneliness and sadness of the marital relationship. Jacob was also the Protected One. Gweneviere and Jack became his Little Parents, hoping that Jacob would not experience the pain of the family's trauma. In fact, Jacob felt so totally abandoned that he still reenacts the abandonment by running away and totally disappearing. He married at 17, also to a pregnant girlfriend, reenacting Jesse and Jessica's marriage. He also married an Adult Child and had three children, as his parents did, later abandoning them, as his father had done to him. His oldest daughter became the Super-Responsible One and Little Parent to her sisters, and later Parent to her own parents. The other two daughters both became serious drug addicts.

The foregoing is a classic example of how alcoholism controls the lives of all the people in the family. Each child was doubly addicted—both to Jesse's alcohol and Jessica's co-dependency (her addiction) to Jesse. All of these people are enmeshed, having to give up their own uniqueness and individuality. The whole family needs to be treated.

Someone estimated that each drinking alcoholic affects the lives of four other people. When you look at the alcoholic family multi-generationally, you see what a devastating effect alcoholism has on the family.

Eating Addiction: The Orange Family

Jake Orange is the perfect product of the poisonous pedagogy. He is authoritarian and rigid, and controls his emotions. He also attempts to control the emotions of all those around him. Jake is an overachiever and has made millions of dollars.

Jake married Jonelle, who had a rigid and authoritarian mother. Jonelle is a perfect lady. She graduated from Southern College and was elected Miss Southern Belle. She would be physically striking were it not for a weight problem. Although not obese, she struggles with a fat/thin obsessive eating disorder. She stays so preoccupied with fat/thin thinking that she can avoid her low-grade depression, which is really anger at herself. She is angry at herself for never standing up to her mother and for staying in a marriage she wanted to leave after two months.

Jonelle is also addicted to Jake. She constantly obsesses about how awful he is. She spends hours talking to lady friends about him. She has no time to be in touch with her own feelings.

Jake and Jonelle have four children, two girls and two boys. The girls are 14 and 12, the boys are 8 and 2 years old.

The 14-year-old, Priscilla, is anorexic. Her weight fluctuates between 60 and 85 pounds. She is very much in denial and minimizes that the family has any problems. Her anorexia "coincidentally" emerged when her mother had an affair and was caught by the father. The anorexic condition has lasted for two years. The younger sister is beginning to act out by getting in trouble in school. The eight-year-old is isolated, nonathletic and obese. Jake is very depressed about his children. He coerced Jonelle into having their two-year-old because he wanted another chance at parenting. Jonelle is extremely depressed over having the child.

Priscilla is the Caretaker for the family. She serves to unify her parents' marriage. She carries her mother's unexpressed rage, equating that rage with food. Priscilla fears this rage. Therefore, if she eats, she believes she will have to feel the rage. The starvation and vomiting keep her mood altered. She acts out the rigidity and severe authoritarianism of her childhood by her severe and austere self-management. Priscilla controls her father, as well as the entire family. She has made certain that her mother and father will not divorce.

The father still attempts to control Priscilla but is shaken and deeply frustrated by her. This is a classic picture of an eating-disordered family. The mom's weight problem is about unexpressed anger, which covers her hurt and sadness about her own childhood. She has reenacted that childhood by marrying someone controlling like her mother.

The third child is a Lost Child. He was an accidental pregnancy. He carries the loneliness and isolation of the marriage. He is 90 pounds overweight and eats to fill the emptiness he feels. This family needs help.

Let me turn the discussion now to a type of compulsive family that looks good on the outside but carries its pathology at a very covert level. In alcoholic and eating-disordered families, the pathology is more overt and obvious. The families look bad and are clearly in trouble. The children play obvious roles to balance the system.

In the next two examples, the parents look good and are not obviously in trouble. Their behavior is acceptable according to societal standards. The family pathology is more covert, more hidden, and the members of the family feel more confused and crazy.

In one of our sample profiles, Mom is a religion addict. It is very difficult to be in a conflict with someone who is on a pedestal, who looks and acts holy. In our second example, Dad is a highly successful public figure. He looks like a "perfect 10" in the American way of making it. Yet both families are extremely dysfunctional.

The children are caught up in the covert family system. Since one of the functions of children in a system is to make the covert explicit, the children act out the pathology.

Religion Addiction: The Purple Family

Pevilia Purple is married to Biff. Biff is a traveling salesman. He has had several affairs and is a sex addict. He is the classic "good old boy." He gets by on his job. But he is really lazy, a jock at heart, who would rather pitch softball than be intimate.

Biff was raised by a domineering and controlling mother who divorced his father at an early age and bad-mouthed him until he died. Any time Biff wanted money or anything that cost money, his mother would blame his father because she couldn't give it to him. She sexually abused Biff by continuously demeaning his father to him. She categorized his father with all men "who think with their penises." Biff became an irresponsible kind of person—always messing around and always looking for fun.

Pevilia is emotionally Biff's mother. She provides for him beautifully by keeping an immaculate house and by being a consummate cook. She continually nags, lectures, quotes Scripture, gripes, and on occasion goes hysterical because of Biff's lack of responsibility. Biff gets out of the house every chance he can, even though he's only home for three weekends a month. Pevilia tries to control everyone and everything within her reach. She is avidly religious. She has changed churches several times. The reason is always that the church is not true enough to the Bible. She has finally found a spiritual guru who she thinks is a true messenger of God. She studies the Bible daily with this self-appointed biblical authority. He is attached to no denomination, as he believes denominations are the devil's creation. His followers claim that he has affected several miraculous cures.

Pevilia takes two of her daughters, Mary and Sue Ellen, to Bible class daily. They are 9 and 12. The 12-year-old, Sue Ellen, was sexually abused by her 16-year-old, drug-addicted brother, Raldo. Raldo was in therapy for homosexuality for six years and has been in drug programs for the last three years. He seems incorrigible and has now dropped out of school. There is another boy, Billy, who is 4 years old, and another older daughter, Maggie, who is 19 years old.

Maggie is a perfect daughter. She is in her first year of college. While she is not a born-again Christian like her mom, she is rigid. She has dated one boy from Sunday school for five years. She has literally never been kissed. She was a straight-A student, the valedictorian of her high school class. She tries to be perfect.

The young son, Billy, is prone to violent outbursts of temper. This is usually blamed on 16-year-old Raldo, who is also rageful. Biff, who also rages, has had actual fist fights with Raldo over the years. Biff has never liked him and makes no bones about it.

Pevilia herself was in therapy for nine years until she realized that therapy was a form of secular humanism. She entered counseling because of her marriage, spending three years basically talking about Biff. She has been trying to control Raldo's therapy for years. She has been advised to put him into an in-house treatment center, but she can't bear to do this to him. She enables him by giving him money and defending him. When he sexually abused his sister, the family completely hushed it up and it remained a family secret until Sue Ellen started acting out with obsessive-compulsive behavior concerning venereal disease. When she passes a bar or strip joint, she becomes hysterical over the possibility that venereal germs have soiled her.

In spite of all of this, Pevilia smiles incessantly. She thanks God for sending her such misfortune and has been told over and over again how much God must love her because of her problems. Pevilia always seems to know what is right. When the children are hurting, she consoles them with scriptural quotations and moral exhortations.

This family is a compulsive family. Mom is addicted to the ecstasy she feels when she experiences her sense of righteousness in prayer or moralizing with biblical readings or in religious services. She uses this feeling of goodness to distract herself from how lonely, disappointed, sad and angry she feels. She plays the role of being good and righteous—Saint Mom. The children call her a saint. Mom is also severely co-dependent, staying in her head worrying so much of the time that she doesn't have to feel her own loneliness and emptiness.

The oldest daughter, Maggie, takes some of the heat off the parents' marriage by being the Perfect One. She's like a robot, always saying the right thing. Her achievements are a source of pride to her parents.

The drug-abusing son, Raldo, is the family Scapegoat. He acts out the covert rage of his parents. He takes the heat off the non-intimacy and utter loneliness of his parents' marriage. He carries his father's secret sexual addiction, as well as his father's unresolved sexual abuse, and acted it out with his sister. His purported homosexuality has to do with his father's unconscious abandonment issues with his own father, as well as Raldo's actual abandonment by his father, Biff. Raldo seeks the nurturing of a man. He also distracts the family with the homosexual issue.

Sue Ellen is the family Victim. She's the third child and is totally confused. Her role is to take care of her parents' marriage. She does this by being a victim. The times of greatest closeness between Pevilia and Biff are when they deal with Sue Ellen's issues. The fourth child, Mary, is a Lost Child. She was an accidental pregnancy. Pevilia refuses to use any birth control methods. She says they are non-biblical. Mary tries to be perfect and not bother anyone. She plays alone a lot and is referred to by Biff as his "good child." Pevilia calls her a gift from God.

Little Billy already carries the system's rage and acts it out. He is athletic and gets special attention from Dad when Dad is home. Pevilia sometimes wonders in the secret, most honest recesses of her heart whether she really is specially loved by God. In fact, she feels completely confused by the disproportionate grace that life seems to offer. She would never talk about her doubts.

This family often looks good to the outside world. Pevilia sees to it that they all go to church on Sunday. This family needs outside help.

Work Addiction: The White Family

Mickey and Matilda White live in the most luxurious section of their city. They are millionaires. Each has been married before. They have two children of their own and each has a child by a previous marriage.

Mickey is the president of a large manufacturing company founded by his grandfather, who died at age 89 "after a hard day's work." "He worked every day of his life" is a frequently heard family quotation.

While Mickey is sick of hearing this, he still likes to quote it in public when talking about White Enterprises. Mickey's dad is still alive and also comes to work daily. Both Granddad and Dad were womanizers and modeled this to their sons.

Mickey has five brothers; three are partners in the company. The youngest is totally screwed up with alcoholism, and the second son is a religious fanatic. Mickey started out with a lot of pressure to do as well as his father and grandfather. At first, he worked in a totally acceptable manner, working from nine to five and occasionally on Saturday. Slowly over the years, he's worked longer and longer hours. Nine to five became five to nine. Saturdays are entertainment days with clients. And even though Mickey says he loves his family, Sunday is a dreaded day.

Mickey's daughter by a previous marriage has been diagnosed as having a borderline personality. She's been in several of the most lavish psychiatric treatment centers. Currently she's on psychoactive drug treatment.

Mickey's first wife was "a raving bitch" who constantly accused him of sleeping around. She overprotected their child and has used the child to take sides against Mickey. Their child witnessed the most violent emotional fights between her mom and dad. Mickey's work intensified during his divorce and during his joint therapy sessions with his daughter.

Matilda is altogether different. She was raised as a perfect lady. She graduated cum laude from a fine Eastern school. She does volunteer work at several hospitals and is past president of the Junior League. She constantly defends her husband to their teenage sons and to her daughter. The children, ages 13, 12 and 10, love their dad and love to be with him, except he's never there. He breaks promises about going fishing and playing golf. The boys are set up not to feel their anger by being told that Dad works so hard for them. Mom constantly points to all the toys and luxuries they have as a result of Dad's working so hard. They feel guilty when she tells them this.

The oldest son is a star athlete. Dad makes some of his games. The youngest son is awkward, noncompetitive and nonathletic. Both sons are failing in school.

Mickey believes in strong discipline. He often states how the "teenage drug crisis" could be solved with hard work and strong physical discipline.

Mickey appears self-assured, even arrogant at times. But underneath he is shame-based. He was not a good athlete, nor was he academically bright. He punched out a friend who ridiculed him for not having the capacity to make it without his father's money. He has always been afraid he couldn't make it on his own. His father was physically abusive. Mickey was verbally shamed as a child.

Mickey and Matilda have been sexually dysfunctional for most of their 15-year marriage. Neither has any real desire for the other. They never talk about it. Matilda is the perfect wife in every other respect. She is a wonderful hostess and charms her guests with generous hospitality.

Her child, Suzette, who is 13 years old, admitted to her therapist that she's been compulsively masturbating for nine years. She also has some obsessive/compulsive cleaning disorders, going through ritual washings before and after school.

Mickey is the most celebrated layman in his religious denomination. He and the whole family have gone to church every Sunday for years. They look like a perfect family. Recently the oldest son has refused to go to church. Sundays are becoming a battlefield.

At home, Mickey stays busy all the time. He's always doing something. Basically, his belief is that he is what he does. His wife is severely co-dependent. She never refers to herself. She stays busy all the time—worrying, driving the children places, instructing the maids, doing volunteer work, planning parties. She stops her children from having any emotions other than two positive ones—joy and go-getter determination.

The children are all underachievers, the oldest son being the exception in sports. He is the family Star and, like his dad, he only feels okay when he is performing.

The younger son is a Lost Child as well as Dad's Scapegoat. Mickey vows he will not lose his temper at him but does so over and over again. Mickey's daughter is the Scapegoat for the entire blended system. Mickey is idolized by all the children. Each, however, is shamed by not being *worth* Dad's time.

Mickey is a severe work addict and Matilda enables him by continually defending him. The whole family is compulsive and needs some form of therapy.

The no-talk and no-feeling expression rules govern all of these families. Since the problems are denied and minimized, they cannot be solved. As the children are forced to repress their emotions, they lose touch with their vital self-esteem. They lose touch with their own reality. To be in denial about your feelings is to be in a state of numbness and withholding. Functionality calls for vitalization and spontaneity. These families are emotionally dead. They no longer even feel their shame. They have internalized it.

When we are abandoned by our parental figure, we continue to look for that parent's love. Freud called this ongoing search the "repetition compulsion." The repetition compulsion, more than anything else, underscores the hopelessness of addiction. The repetition compulsion is the continual acting out of the original pain in a vain attempt to find connection and overcome alienation and aloneness. Each new cycle promises the intimacy and original connection of love that we needed with our source figure(s) as a foundation of growth and self-acceptance. And each new cycle ends in a deeper sense of loneliness and depression, coming from the pain and sadness of loss. As each new layer of shame is accrued, a more grandiose and delusional false self is strengthened. As each cycle of repetition compulsion is enacted, the hopelessness and powerlessness engender despair.

READER/CUSTOMER CARE SURVEY

We care about your opinions! Please take a moment to fill out our online Reader Survey at **http://survey.hcibooks.com.**
As a **"THANK YOU"** you will receive a **VALUABLE INSTANT COUPON** towards future book purchases as well as a **SPECIAL GIFT** available only online! Or, you may mail this card back to us and we will send you a copy of our exciting catalog with your valuable coupon inside.

(PLEASE PRINT IN ALL CAPS)

First Name   M.I.   Last Name

Address   City

State   Zip   Email

1. Gender
❏ Female   ❏ Male

2. Age
❏ 8 or younger
❏ 9-12   ❏ 13-16
❏ 17-20   ❏ 21-30
❏ 31+

3. Did you receive this book as a gift?
❏ Yes   ❏ No

4. Annual Household Income
❏ under $25,000
❏ $25,000 - $34,999
❏ $35,000 - $49,999
❏ $50,000 - $74,999
❏ over $75,000

5. What are the ages of the children living in your house?
❏ 0 - 14   ❏ 15+

6. Marital Status
❏ Single
❏ Married
❏ Divorced
❏ Widowed

7. How did you find out about the book?
(please choose one)
❏ Recommendation
❏ Store Display
❏ Online
❏ Catalog/Mailing
❏ Interview/Review

8. Where do you usually buy books?
(please choose one)
❏ Bookstore
❏ Online
❏ Book Club/Mail Order
❏ Price Club (Sam's Club, Costco's, etc.)
❏ Retail Store (Target, Wal-Mart, etc.)

9. What subject do you enjoy reading about the most?
(please choose one)
❏ Parenting/Family
❏ Relationships
❏ Recovery/Addictions
❏ Health/Nutrition
❏ Christianity
❏ Spirituality/Inspiration
❏ Business Self-help
❏ Women's Issues
❏ Sports

10. What attracts you most to a book?
(please choose one)
❏ Title
❏ Cover Design
❏ Author
❏ Content

Comments

S U M M A R Y

The key points covered in this chapter can be summed up using the letters of the word **COMPULSIVE.**

Children of Alcoholics Are Guideposts for Understanding the Compulsive Family

The common traits possessed by Adult Children of Alcoholics have provided the greatest proof for the family systems approach. ACoAs have also offered immense insight into the structure of compulsive families. ACoAs are helping us to grasp how compulsivity is set up in dysfunctional families.

Out of Control and Controlling

One of the strange paradoxes of compulsive families is that while the members are out of control with their compulsivity, the family system is dominated by control. The control domination can result from one member (Dad's drinking) or from a strict rule of control.

Major Responses to Alcoholism

The checklist in this chapter offers the most common traits exhibited by adults who have grown up in alcoholic families. These traits are natural responses to the violation imposed by the alcoholic and co-alcoholic's behavior.

Pathological Relationships

Compulsive/addictive behavior is a pathological relationship to any mood-altering experience that has life-damaging consequences. The pathological relationship is rooted in the original relationship of abandonment. Compulsivity is set up in families by abandonment.

Unmet Dependency Needs

The abandonment creates an environment where there is no one there to depend on for the fulfillment of our basic dependency needs. We thus grow up with an insatiable child living inside us. As children, we need our parents for the first 15 years of life. Since we cannot go back and actually be children again, these needs are insatiable.

Loss of Vitality and Spontaneity

When we have to give up our own feelings, needs and wants, we develop a false self. This false self is a mask and is unreal. When we live life as someone else, we lose our vitality and spontaneity. The only way we can feel alive is when we engage in compulsive/addictive behaviors.

Shame-Based and Shameless Caretakers

Compulsive families are created by shame-based people. Shame is the fuel of the compulsive/addictive behavior. Shame-based people defend against shame by acting shameless. They act shameless by using cover-ups for shame like control, superior power, perfectionism, criticism, contempt and rage.

Idealization of Caretakers and the Fantasy Bond

Shameless caretakers transfer their shame to those they take care of. Their superior power and control, coupled with children's cognitive egocentrism, result in the child carrying the caretaker's shame. Children naturally idealize parents (create a fantasy bond) and are vulnerable prey to their shame-based caretakers' "shameless" cover-ups.

Violation of Self

Once children take on their caretaker's shame, they feel flawed and defective within themselves. A flawed, defective person must develop a defensive false self.

Expanded Notion of Compulsive/Addictive Behavior
with Examples

In this chapter, I have expanded the common notion of compulsive/addictive behavior. Addiction is usually limited to ingestive addictions. I include activity addictions (working, gambling, entertainment, spending), as well as emotional, thought and sexual addictions in the total definition of compulsive/addictive disorders. We examined four examples of compulsive families illustrating chemical, eating, religious and work compulsivity.

The Persecuted: Checklist for How Your Self-Esteem Was Damaged in a Sexually or Physically Abusing Family

The abused children are alone with their suffering, not only within the family, but also within themselves. They cannot share their pain with anyone. They cannot create a place in their own soul where they could cry their heart out.

ALICE MILLER

It was my older brother. He would expose himself to me and make me touch him. I worried about him all the time. I stayed outside as long as I could. It was like being hunted. I felt like an animal. I finally gave up. I would let him do whatever he wanted to. I felt soiled and contaminated. I thought of suicide every day of my life. I couldn't be with people. I wondered why people were interested in things—why they laughed or wanted to go to school. I would wander in fields in order not to be. I just wanted "not to be."

These statements were uttered by Cathy, a 46-year-old woman. This was the first time she had told anyone her

story of abuse. I had counseled with her 10 years earlier concerning the death of her 13-year-old son. He had been killed in a
car wreck. I had also counseled with her after her second husband
had verbally terrorized her. Cathy has been depressed all her life.
She was physically abused in her first marriage and has been the
victim of psychological battering in her second marriage. She
bears the wounds and manifests the patterns of an incest victim.

Incest is defined by Webster as "sexual intercourse or inbreeding
between closely related individuals . . . when they are related . . .
within degrees wherein marriage is prohibited by law or custom."

I agree with Susan Forward that we should expand the definition to include people who

> *perceive themselves to be closely related including steppar-
> ents, stepsiblings, half-siblings and even live-in lovers if they
> have assumed a parental role.*[1]

I understand incest to include overt, covert and emotional types
of sexual abuse. I differentiate molestation from incest. Molestation
is a sexually abusive act performed by a stranger. The effects can
be equally as damaging.

Incest is usually more shaming than any other form of abuse.
But incest has the added element of betrayal by someone who is
supposed to be your protector. When children are incested, they
frequently believe it was their fault. Children generally don't think
that their parents are bad. If Daddy *can't* be bad and the child feels
icky and bad, then it must be the child who is bad.

Children also internalize their parents at their worst. What this
means is that when the parent is acting in the way that is most
threatening to the child's survival, the child records this most
vividly. A raging drunk and out-of-control violent father is much
more dangerous to a child's survival than a verbally scolding
mother. The child adapts to the threat and internalizes it for the
sake of survival. The child needs the parent for survival.

---

[1] Susan Forward, *Betrayal of Innocence: Incest and Its Devastation* (New York: Penguin Books,
1979), 3-4.

Incest dramatizes in the most powerful way the tragedy of the abandoned child. Incest is a form of violence—the violation of a child's sexuality. This amounts to the violation of one's very being, since sexuality is something we are, rather than something we have.

The incest drama is played out on the stage of an innocent child's naïve trust. It is fueled by a natural sense of respect and desire to please. It reaches its denouement in the idealization of the parent at the expense of a ruptured and soul-wounded self that will never be the same again. It is no wonder the incest taboo is found in all human societies.

Dissociation

Incest is a dramatic form of abandonment and has dramatic consequences. One major consequence is the disconnection between the act of victimization and the response to being victimized. Because the violation is so profound, the defense is equally profound. "Instant numbing" is my phrase for it. The technical word is dissociation. In dissociation the violence is so intolerable that the victim leaves his or her body. When incest abuse is chronic, the victim often loses the connection with the memories of what happened. This is why incest is difficult to deal with. The survivor may have no conscious memories of what happened. It is also why the prosecution of offenders is difficult. A terrified child being harassed by an adult lawyer on a witness stand is at a profound disadvantage.

Fortunately the victim's body does retain the *feelings* of what happened, because sometimes these "body memories" allow healing work to take place. Through a process called debriefing, the memories and the feelings are reconnected. Because the memories are dissociated from the feelings and because the feelings are so intense, the victim experiences life as unreal. The victim feels crazy. The victim thinks there is something wrong with him or her. The victims often lose the connection with what was done to them.

When anyone is violated, the first feeling response is raw fear and terror. The victim wants to run away from the threat and fear. But he or she is helpless and out of control. The more intolerable the situation, the greater the need to dissociate. The body records and imprints the terror. Later the feelings of hurt, anger, abandonment and shame are recorded. When victims dissociate from the memories, they often depersonalize the offender, especially if the offender is their parent or relative. Later they may have recurring nightmares or other sleep disorders. They may experience blip memories that come like a momentary flashback. Or they may just feel crazy without any true psychosis.

The increased intensity of traumatization may cause a personality split or even multiple personalities. Since victims are dissociated from the memories, they feel as though these symptoms are about them. Their defenses have severed the relationship of their feelings with the traumatizing event. In reality, these defenses are *natural responses* to the violence.[2]

In order to heal, sexual abuse victims must do debriefing work in which they go back into the memories. The emphasis is on the survivor getting in touch with the concrete sensory-based details of the abuse as much as possible. This allows victims to connect with what actually happened. In this way, they connect the feeling responses to the sexual violation itself. They become aware that what they feel and the way they behave are about *what happened to them and not about them.*

The poisonous pedagogy plays a role in the tragedy of incest and sexual abuse in general. I believe it implicitly gives permission for any kind of abuse by promoting a kind of ownership of children. It is the ownership principle that justifies the inequality. If children must obey and honor their parents at any cost, then the parents implicitly have rights over their children's bodies.

I have two clients who were abused exactly on these grounds. One was taken in the bathroom by her father at age 14 and told to spread her legs so that he could see if she was still a virgin. She claimed he was very religious and said he was doing his parental duty. Another, at age 11, was spread-eagled and tied to the bed while her mother examined her for a vaginal rash with the father watching. Since he was her parent, he had a right to be there.

---

[2] Much of the information in this section has been taken from lectures by Renee Frederickson, an expert on sexual violation. See her book *Repressed Memories* (New York: Simon & Schuster, 1992).

I certainly believe that many patriarchal parents are appalled by sexual abuse and would not allow it to happen. But the implicit belief that parents own their children creates an environment of greater risk.

Cheryl McCall's *Life* magazine article of December 1984 begins with the words: "There are perhaps 34 million of us in America—adult women who were victims of sexual abuse."

These figures shock most people because the common conception of sexual abuse is limited to a kind of "horror story abuse." Horror story almost always means sexual intercourse (physical penetration). Most people have the idea that if there is no physical penetration, then there is no sexual abuse. There is a growing consensus that this is not true. Many people bear the scars of sexual abuse without having engaged in sexual intercourse with their offender.

There is almost no good data on male sexual abuse. The figure often quoted is that 1 out of 12 males is abused by the time he has finished adolescence. My own opinion is that the figures may be higher if we look at the whole range of sexual abuse.

What follows is a checklist of traits that are common psychological and behavioral responses to sexual violence. *No single trait indicates sexual violation, and several are necessary before one would begin to make a case for being sexually violated*—so be very careful in your own self-analysis. Incest is traumatic and carries the same symptomatic consequences as any other traumatic violation. There is real danger in hastily concluding that one has been incested.

A Age-inappropriate behavior, knowledge inappropriate to age
D Denial, delusion, dissociation, displaced feelings,
      depersonalization, psychic numbness
U Unreality
L Loneliness, isolation and withdrawal
T Terrors, excessive fears, phobias, anxiety, hypervigilance

C Compulsive disorders, addictions
H Hostility, sexualized rage, passive/aggressive behavior
I Internalized shame
L Lives life as a victim
D Delinquency, criminal behavior, prostitution

R Reenacts the abuse
E Employment and work problems
N No-talk rule—keeping the secret

O Offender status
F Feelings are somatized (psychosomatic disorders)

S Split personality (multiple personality)
E Eating disorders
X "X'd out," confused identity
U Underlying depression
A Aggressive and seductive behavior
L Loss of sexual identity and functionality

V Violated sexual boundaries
I Intimacy problems
O Objectification of self and others sexually
L Love confused with sex
E Excessive dependency and clinging to sexual partners
N Nightmares and sleeping disorders
C Cross-generational bonding and role reversal
E Early childhood symptoms

A. **Age-inappropriate behavior or knowledge inappropriate to age.** In children, this behavior may appear as the child making coital movements or trying to insert a penis-like object into someone or something, frequently touching or trying to touch grown-up genitals, imitating intercourse with animals or toys, and a girl child putting objects in her vagina. Later on the behavior may involve early promiscuity, early masturbation, early prostitution or frequenting of prostitutes, becoming the high-school lover boy or slut. In adulthood it may appear as sexual dysfunction either in or out of marriage. "Disorder of desire" in marriage is sometimes a symptom of emotional incest.

D. **Denial, delusion, dissociation, displaced feelings, depersonalization, psychic numbness.** These are all ego defenses.

Dissociation is an out-of-body kind of defense. The victim goes somewhere else mentally and imaginatively. This is the major cause of memory loss. The feelings are often displaced, or the experience can be displaced when a child may, for example, start seeing monsters in the hall or having hallucinations. The child often depersonalizes the incest offender when a parent or relative is involved. Denial and delusion are the result of the child believing he is bad and idealizing the family or parents. Even if idealization does not occur, the child still feels he is bad.

U. Unreality. The victim feels that his "now" experience is not real. He has no understanding of so-called normal reality, finding it hard to understand why people are interested in the things they are interested in. Victims may lose interest in life.

L. Loneliness, isolation and withdrawal. The person withdraws physically, wants to be invisible and often is not noticed unless acting out seductively. He tends to run away from things and may run away from home, school, any conflict or problems. He wants to run away from life and often thinks of suicide.

T. Terrors, excessive fears, phobias, anxiety, hypervigilance. The major consequence of being violated is raw terror. The person who once felt helpless and victimized is traumatically and chronically stressed. This nameless terror may manifest itself as a phobia or many phobias.

C. Compulsive disorders, addictions. The major addictive range includes: co-dependency, drug (alcohol) addiction, eating disorders, sex addiction.

H. Hostility, sexualized rage, passive/aggressive behavior. Anger patterns depend on whether one becomes a victim or offender. Offenders will be aggressive and rageful. Victims will be more passive/aggressive. The victim usually experiences the rage at the end of a relationship.

I. Internalized shame. The victim internalizes the shame and feels soiled, flawed and defective as a human being. He will act in a self-destructive manner, e.g., drug addiction, smoking, overeating—all of which are forms of chronic suicide.

L. Lives life as a victim. The victim trusts untrustworthy people and ends up being victimized. He is attracted to other victims and confuses love and pity. He makes an identity out of being a victim.

D. Delinquency, criminal behavior, prostitution. Behaviors may appear in childhood as aggressive and destructive, such as setting fires, destroying property, hitting and stealing. Later it appears as delinquency, breaking the law. In some studies, 85 percent of prostitutes were sexually abused as children. A high percentage of female drug addicts claim they were sexually abused.

R. Reenacts the abuse. The victim may reenact the abuse on others or experience his own victimization in adult relationships. Multiple relationships, marriages and affairs that end with offender/victim polarity are often outcomes of sexual abuse.

E. Employment and work problems. Often sexual abuse victims go from job to job and have inconsistent work habits. They seem to have lost their effectiveness and competency. This frequently begins in school with underachievement.

N. No-talk rule—keeping the secret. Keeping the secret is a major factor in the rupture between the violence and the sexual abuse victim's responses to that violence. Many have *never told anyone* about what happened. Often if they tell, they are told to keep the secret for the sake of keeping the family together. Or they may be told that they imagined what happened. The no-talk rule keeps the victim from expressing the feelings about what happened and, therefore, working through the violence. (I discuss this further in my book, *Family Secrets*.)

O. Offender status. Victims often identify with their offender as a way of feeling less helpless. They bond with them and almost literally become them. They then reenact the offense onto others.

F. Feelings are somatized (psychosomatic disorders). Since the feelings cannot be expressed, they are often somatized. The victim gets sick and is then "allowed" to feel as bad as he really feels. Sickness may come out in the same areas of the body that the original abuse occurred, such as vaginal rashes or pain, sore throat, anal or bowel dysfunction, upper respiratory asthma, chronic chest congestion and a sore back.

S. Split personality (multiple personality). When a victim is in his normal social role, he acts very differently from when he is at home in private. The private, at-home self reenacts what happened in childhood—but now with safety, since it is not the feared parent or relative, but the victim's spouse, lover or children. When the distress has been of the "horror story kind," a person can develop several personalities.

E. Eating disorders. I mentioned this earlier under the general topic of compulsivities. Nongenetic obesity is a common way that sexual victims protect themselves. Fat is considered a sexual turn-off, so it protects the victim. Fat is insulation. It is as if the fat person builds a fence around himself. Often the victim puts the weight on in the area the abuse was done—a sagging stomach can hide one's genitals.

X. "X'ed out," confused identity. Victims feel different from others. They feel as though they are defective merchandise. Victims also often feel crazy without any concomitant psychosis.

U. Underlying depression. The victim may suffer from post-traumatic stress disorder. The act of violence is shocking. The betrayal makes it more shocking. A chronic sense of sadness and grief ensues.

A. Aggressive and seductive behavior. Often sexual abuse victims feel that the only way they are desirable is sexually. They therefore use sex as a way of gaining control. The seduction behavior also has the symbolic sense of getting control of the offender and getting it over with. Sexual victims and offenders find each other with unbelievable regularity.

L. Loss of sexual identity and functionality. This is the opposite of the victim only having an identity by being sexual. Since sex is at the very core of our being, sexual violation strikes at the very core of our identity. A common consequence of this violation is sexual dysfunction. The victim may later experience impotence, frigidity, disorder of desire and/or flashbacks while in the act of sex. The victim may need sadomasochistic fantasies in order to function sexually.

V. Violated sexual boundaries. Sexual abuse violates the core of the victim's being—his physical, emotional and spiritual boundaries. Victims have a doorknob on the outside with little control over who comes in. Violated boundaries are like a country without borders or laws. The response to such violations is to have sex either with everyone or with no one (walls).

I. Intimacy problems. The betrayal and chronic shock set up a kind of emotional numbness. The fear of closeness is the fear of betrayal and pain. For sexual abuse survivors, this may come up over and over again in marriage and relationships. Victims often move away from real love, affection and closeness and are attracted to an abusive, rejecting person. Victims have an impaired ability to evaluate the trustworthiness of others. Victims are enmeshed in the family violence and often seek enmeshed relationships. They may set up old fantasy-bond dilemmas. If only I give more, try harder, give more sex, then maybe he'll really love me. They often reenact this dilemma with an offender-type spouse or relationships.

O. Objectification of self and others sexually. Once violated, a person withdraws into self. The withdrawal into self and self-indulging habits and painkillers is the opposite of having friendships and mutuality. Once a victim is used, that victim becomes an object. Since there is no nurturing parent there for the child, the child objectifies himself. Thumb-sucking and early masturbation are self-indulging and objectifying habits. Once a person objectifies himself, he tends to project that outward onto others. Sexual objectification is an outcome of sexual abuse. Our whole society wholeheartedly supports sexual objectification. A good woman is a "10." Pornography is extreme objectification and glorifies genitals at the expense of personhood.

L. Love confused with sex. Victims of sexual abuse often confuse love with sex. They believe they are only lovable if they are sexually desirable. They believe they must be the best possible sex partner or else they will be abandoned and rejected.

E. Excessive dependency and clinging to sexual partners. Because the abandonment and shame destroy the interpersonal parent/child bridge, sexually abused children have no one to depend on. Their natural developmental dependency needs are neglected. They therefore grow up with an excessively needy child within them. Clinging is a defensive strategy to avoid abandonment.

N. Nightmares and sleeping disorders. The victim has often been violated in his own bed at night. Night terrors, recurring nightmares, sleeping excessively and fearing to go to sleep may all be the result of sexual violence.

C. Cross-generational bonding and role reversal. Children are victimized by being drawn into the family system's needs for balance. If Mom and Dad's marriage is sexually and emotionally barren, Dad may make his daughter his Little Princess. He may later have sexual fantasies about her. Even though they are never acted on, the child carries the impact of the covert fantasies. The daughter may become Dad's emotional spouse and take care of his emotional needs or his affectionalized sexuality. Mom may do the same with one or all of her sons. Either parent may also surrogate spouse children of their same sex.

E. Early childhood symptoms. Along with age-inappropriate knowledge of behavior, several other phenomena may be the result of early sexual abuse. These phenomena are: unexplained bruises; age regression, such as starting to wet or soil himself after potty training is over; public display of age regression; playing with or smearing feces at an inappropriate age; bowel disorders; vaginal disorders (pain, rashes); traumatic response (for example, shrieking or screaming in response to a vaginal exam); prolonged bed-wetting; prolonged thumb-sucking; dramatic mood changes; aggressiveness; sudden and unprovoked behavior; self-mutilation and suicidal thoughts or talk; picking at skin or scabs until they bleed; hitting self; cutting self; slapping self; wearing two or more pairs of underpants and refusing to change; chronic somatic complaints like sore throats, stomachaches, gagging, asthma and upper respiratory disorders.

The checklist is by no means exhaustive. If you think you were sexually abused but have no memories of it, this list may help you discover whether you are an adult child of a sexually abusing family. Be *very* careful in your assessment of sexual abuse. Trust your own experience if it feels as if you are being persuaded to find memories of sexual abuse.

In recent years, a number of people have come forward who claim their therapists have convinced them that they were sexual abuse victims. They claim that their therapists' suggestions led them to retrieve false memories. Some believe that there is a "false memory syndrome." I am not competent to judge these claims. I do believe that the induction of false memories is possible. People who have suffered abandonment in the form of traumatic abuse often take others' suggestions as if they were orders to be obeyed.

If you have no memories of being sexually abused, consider all the following guidelines before you conclude that you were:

1. Identify with several (five or six) symptoms on the checklist presented here.
2. Find an expert (proper license and reputation) and get his or her expert opinion on whether or not you were incested.
3. If at all possible, find at least one collaborating witness or some facts clearly supporting your belief that you were abused.

4. Live for six months with the belief that you are a survivor of sexual abuse and see how this belief gives you answers to family issues and makes sense out of your life and past behavior. If it doesn't fit, let the belief go.

Above all, do not confront your offender until you have worked out the post-traumatic stress disorders stemming from the abuse. Do not consider any kind of confrontation without your therapist's or friends' support. Confronting someone for sexual abuse is a legal matter as well and should not be done impulsively.

Our common understanding of sexual abuse is extremely limited. One out of 100 people have been through the kind of horror story abuse that hits the newspapers, the crisis hot lines and the child protection agencies. This is bad enough! If one out of a hundred people had a serious disease, we would be vaccinating everyone against it.

Sexual abuse involves whole families. Pia Mellody, who is a pioneer in treating co-dependency and survivors of childhood abuse at The Meadows Treatment Facility in Wickenberg, Arizona, divides sexual abuse into the following categories:[3]

1. Physical Sexual Abuse

This involves hands-on touching in a sexual way. The range of abusive behaviors that are sexual includes sexualized hugging or kissing; any kind of sexual touching or fondling; oral and anal sex; masturbation of the victim or forcing the victim to masturbate the offender; sexual intercourse.

2. Overt Sexual Abuse

This involves voyeurism and/or exhibitionism. This can be outside or inside the home. Parents often sexually abuse children through voyeurism and exhibitionism. The criterion for in-home voyeurism or exhibitionism is whether the parent is being sexually stimulated. Sometimes the parent may be so out

---

[3] I have taken this classification from the audiotape lectures of Pia Mellody. She is a pioneer in our ever-expanding understanding of the range and consequences of sexual abuse.

of touch with his own sexuality that he is not aware of how sexual he is being. The child almost always has a kind of "icky" feeling about it.

One client told me how her father would leer at her in her panties coming out of the bathroom. Others speak of having no privacy in the house, much less the bathroom. I've had a dozen male clients whose mothers bathed their genital parts up through eight or nine years old.

Children can feel sexual around parents. This is not sexual abuse unless the parent originated it. It all depends on the parents. Here I'm not talking about a parent having a passing sexual thought or feeling. It's about a parent using a child for his own conscious or unconscious sexual stimulation.

3. Covert Sexual Abuse

(a) Verbal. This involves inappropriate sexual talking—for instance, Dad or any significant male calling women "whores" or "cunts" or objectified sexual names; or Mom or any significant female deprecating men in a sexual way. It also involves parents or caretakers having to know about every detail of their children's private sexual life, asking questions about a child's sexual physiology, or questioning for minute details about dates.

Covert sexual abuse involves not receiving adequate sexual information. I've had several female clients who didn't know what was happening when they began menstruating. I've had three female clients who did not know that their vagina had an opening in it until they were 20 years old.

An overt kind of sexual abuse also occurs when Dad or Mom talks about sex in front of their children when the children's age level is inappropriate. It also occurs when Mom or Dad makes sexual remarks about the sexual parts of their children's bodies. I've worked with two male clients who were traumatized by their mother's jokes about the size of their penis and with female clients whose fathers and stepfathers teased them about the size of their breasts or buttocks.

(b) Boundary Violation. This involves children witnessing parents in sexual behavior. The children may walk in on it frequently because parents don't provide closed and locked doors.

Boundary violation also encompasses the children being allowed no privacy. They are walked in on in the bathroom. They are not taught to lock their doors or given permission to lock their doors. Parents need to model appropriate nudity—i.e., they need to be clothed appropriately after the children reach a certain age.

Children are sexually curious. Beginning at around age three or between ages three to six, children start noticing parents' bodies. Children are often obsessed with nudity. Mom and Dad need to be careful walking around nude with young children. If Mom is not being stimulated sexually, the nudity is not sexual abuse. She simply is acting in a dysfunctional way. She is not setting good sexual boundaries.

The use of enemas at an early age can also be abusive in a way that leads to sexual dysfunction. The enemas can be a body boundary violation.

4. Emotional Sexual Abuse

Emotional sexual abuse results from cross-generational bonding. I've spoken of enmeshment as a way that children take on the covert needs of a family system. It is very common for one or both parents in a dysfunctional marriage to bond inappropriately with one of their children. *The parents in effect use the child to meet their emotional needs.* This relationship can easily become sexualized and romanticized. The daughter may become Daddy's Little Princess, or the son may become Mom's Little Man. In both cases the child is being abandoned. The parent is getting his needs met at the expense of the child's needs. The child needs a parent, not a spouse.

Pia Mellody gives the following definition of emotional sexual abuse. She says that when "one parent has a relationship with the child that is more important than the relationship he has with his spouse," there is emotional sexual abuse.

Sometimes both parents emotionally bond with a child. The child tries to take care of both parents' feelings. I once worked with a female client whose father would come and get her in the middle of the night and put her in bed with him in the guest bedroom. He would do this mainly to punish his wife for sexually refusing him. The daughter has suffered greatly with confused sexual identity.

Cross-generational bonding can occur with a parent and a child of the same sex. A most common form of this in our culture is mother and daughter. Mother often has sexualized rage. She may fear and hate men. Mother then uses her daughter for her emotional needs and also contaminates her daughter's feelings about men. I know of several cases where mothers' sexual abuse of their daughters was physical.

This issue is whether the parent is there for the child's needs, rather than the child being there for the parent's needs. And while children have the capacity to be sexual in a way appropriate to their developmental level, *whenever an adult is being sexual with a child, sexual abuse is occurring.*

Some sexual abuse also comes from older siblings. Generally, sexual behavior by same-age children is not sexually abusive unless one of the children has been sexually abused and is acting the abuse out on the other child. The rule of thumb is that when a child is experiencing sexual "acting out" at the hands of a child three or four years older, it is sexually abusive.

Sexual Offenders

Let us look at the profile of sexual offenders. Incest offenders are sexually excited by children and ostensibly see nothing wrong with gratifying themselves at the expense of children. This is not true in every case. But more often than not, *the offender sees the child as having no rights.* Most offenders have been victimized themselves. Half have been sexually abused, the other half abused in some other way. Most often the other abuse is physical. Almost all offenders are sex addicts, although all sex addicts are not pedophiles. Most are emotionally retarded and feel inadequate in an adult world. They turn to children to get respect, affection and sex. The offenders are often alcoholic or chemically addicted. They have poor impulse control—especially over sexual matters. Most had poor relationships with the parent of the same sex and have a very shaky image of what it is to be a male or female.

Child sexual abusers live a secret life, hiding their behavior from spouses, colleagues and closest friends. Lucy Berliner, a Seattle therapist quoted in Cheryl McCall's article, says, "Most of us think of child molesters as hideous, until we find out we know one." They are members of our club or elders in the church. In fact, a disproportionate number of sex offenders are outwardly religious.

Incest Family Systems

Male sex offenders are by far the most dominant. Of 4 million known offenders, only five percent are women. Males are the most dominant part of the sexual addiction population. Women are more often co-dependents of sex addicts. This is true of the incest family. The mother is co-dependent and may be in a collusive role when the father is victimizing the children. *Just as in the other compulsive families, there is the addict and the co-addict spouse or co-dependent.* The spouse may tolerate the abuse actively or passively.

Active collusion means that the spouse participates in the abuse either actually or by knowingly allowing it to happen.

Passive collusion occurs when the spouse is so bonded to the offender, either by addictions or by being abused, that she is out of touch with what's going on.

In an incest family, the members are seriously dis-eased and need some form of help. Even if you were not the one sexually abused in your family, you still carry the covert secrets of the family system. Children function to make the covert overt in the family system. The children act out the unconscious of the family and the family secrets. This acting out can even occur in a future generation. Two clients of mine are carrying unspoken sexual secrets from past generations.

One of these clients, Rothgahr, comes from a rigidly religious family. His father was authoritarian and controlling. He is the sixth of nine children. Second and sixth children often bond with the mother. Bonding means taking on Mother's emotional issues—both conscious and unconscious. Rothgahr's mother is an incest victim who never resolved her victimization. She's never done the debriefing work. Therefore, Rothgahr carries her unresolved sexual secret through bonding. He came to me because he was frightened of dreams and actual fantasies he was having about molesting children.

Rothgahr is what the psychologist Patrick Carnes, in his book *Out of the Shadows: Understanding Sexual Addiction,* calls a Level I sex addict. Level I involves womanizing, manizing, compulsive masturbation, pornography with or without compulsive masturbation, cruising and prostitution. Carnes sees voyeurism, exhibitionism, indecent liberties and phone calls as Level II sexual addiction, with rape, incest and molestation as Level III sexual addiction.

The levels signify increasing risks of sexual behavior apropos of culturally sanctioned behavior. Levels II and III always involve a victim and are punished by law. Level III is the most victimizing and incurs the greatest legal punishment.

My client was a womanizer. He was terribly disturbed by his molestation fantasies. He wasn't even aware that he was a sex addict, confusing Level I with just being a "good ol' boy." My belief was that he carried his mother's unresolved incest issues. This was the basis for his molestation fantasies. He was also acting out the "internalized shame" produced by his religiously addicted family. This was the core of his sexual addiction.

Another client, Ophelia, has the same bonding issues. She carries her mother's unconscious unresolved incest. She has dealt with her sexual terrors by totally shutting down sexually. She is a rigid and devout Catholic. She has abstained from sex for 40 years, refusing to date or remarry out of commitment to her faith. She inappropriately bonded with her three sons. Each son is a sex addict and carries her sexualized rage. Each has been affected adversely by her repressed sexuality. She was often exhibitionistic with her sons. She behaved this way unconsciously—in other words, without being conscious of what she was doing and how this would impact her son's sexual lives.

Incest families are common in our culture. The sexual victimization is carried on through the offender/collusive victims' incest family system. Offenders were once victims who bonded with their offenders out of helplessness. They continue to reenact the abuse on their offspring. They do to their children what they wish they could have done to parents who abused them. The fantasy bond keeps the child in the adult idealizing the parent and feeling bad and shamed. And the cycle goes on.

Adult Children of Physical Violence

I'll never forget Hub. He was one of the most striking men I've ever met, physically handsome and incredibly bright. He had been close to making a fortune on several occasions. He knew how to do everything except complete the deal. He would always "almost make it." He had been married several times. I met two of his wives. They were not what I'd ever have suspected. Both were markedly unattractive and both hated men, myself included, as I learned in the counseling sessions.

Hub was an ACoA, and like a lot of ACoAs, he was physically abused as a child. An estimated two-thirds of ACoAs are victims of physical violence. When I first asked Hub about his childhood, he told me that his dad had knocked him and his brother around a lot. "But," he quickly added, "we deserved it."

It took me several sessions to get the gory details. The knocking around often consisted of his father dunking Hub's head in the toilet and slapping him across the face several times. And as if this wasn't horrible enough, his father would urinate before sticking Hub's head in the toilet. The usual offenses that *deserved* such punishments were things like spending his lunch money on candy, not making his bed and talking back to the maid.

Many researchers believe that physical abuse is the most common form of abuse. *The poisonous pedagogy teaches that corporal punishment is a useful way to teach children to respect their parents and be obedient.* Violence against children (and women) and the condoning of that violence is part of an ancient and pervasive tradition.

No form of abuse is more binding than physical violence. The victim bonds to the abuser out of terror—terror for his or her life. The offenders are usually more developmentally retarded than any other abuser. Impulse control is learned from about two years old on. So the spouses and children in violent families are living under the reign of an adult person whose behavior is quite immature.

The profile of a physically abusing parent includes the following: isolated; poor self-image; lacks sensitivity to others' feelings; usually physically abused himself; deprived of basic mothering; unmet needs for love and comfort; in denial of problems and the impact of the problems; feels there is no one to turn to for advice; totally unrealistic expectations of children; expects the children to meet his needs for comfort and nurturing; when children fail to meet his needs, interprets this as rejection and responds with anger and frustration; deals with children as if they were much older than they are. Interestingly, in the category of biological parents, biological mothers are offenders about 5 percent more than fathers.

There is no good data on the extent of physical abuse. The usual data covers only those cases that are actually reported. It excludes those cases not treated by a physician, those treated by a physician but not identified as abuse, and those identified as abuse but not reported. It's estimated that there are 200 unreported cases for every case reported.

Physical violence against children has a long history. R. I. Light, in an article in *The Harvard Educational Review* dated November 1973, claims that in colonial America, a father had absolute rights over his children. It was common to flog children without provocation to break them of their willfulness.

Our commonly quoted nursery rhyme about the "old woman who lived in a shoe" attests to the common acceptance of physical spankings. I remember as a child wondering what was the point of this nursery rhyme. What a splendid way to end the day— porridge without bread and a sound whipping.

The ownership of children by parents and the belief that children are willful and need their wills broken form the basis of the rationale for spanking children.

The Bible is also often quoted to support this practice. The rod spoken of in the Bible was originally the shepherd's rod. It was an oak stick about three feet long, tipped with flint or metal to beat away the wolves and to guide the timid sheep over difficult *wadis* (stream beds). The shepherd's rod was later expanded into the rod of authority by Moses. The rod symbolized God's presence and was mostly used to gently guide the people along right paths. Almost nowhere in Scripture is there any widespread permission to spank children. A few isolated texts have been made into an entire pedagogical edifice. Society was also totally non-democratic in biblical times.

Physical violence is the norm in many dysfunctional families. This includes actual physical spankings; having to go get your own weapons of torture such as belts, switches, etc.; punching, slapping and/or slapping in the face; pulling on or yanking on a child; choking, shaking, kicking, pinching; torturing with tickling; threatening with violence or abandonment; threatening with being put in jail or having the police come; witnessing violence done to a parent or sibling.

This last category is a major issue in homes where wives are battered. A child witnessing his mother's battering is equivalent to battering the child. A witness to violence is a victim of violence.

In 1988 I spoke at the mayor's conference on battered women in Houston, the city in which I live. In my hometown at that time, one woman out of four was a battered woman. Professionals continue to document the cases of battered women, and these cases continue to increase at an alarming rate.

Bonding to Violence

Bonding to physical violence is perplexing and paradoxical. You would think that the trauma of physical violence was so great that the victim would never get near it again. Actually, the exact opposite is closer to the truth. Being beaten and humiliated are so shaming that the victims' sense of self-worth diminishes. The more the victims are beaten, the more their self-worth diminishes. The more victims think they are lowly and flawed as human beings, the more *their choices diminish*. They become bonded to violence.

Learned Helplessness

The theory of learned helplessness attempts to explain the paradoxical bonding to violence. This theory was developed by Martin Seligman. He hypothesized that dogs subjected to non-contingent negative reinforcement could learn that their voluntary behavior had no effect on controlling what happened to them. If the original kind of stimulus was repeated, the dogs' motivation to respond lessened.

Various types of experiments have been conducted to support this hypothesis. These have included testing dogs, cats, birds, rats, mice, fish, primates and humans. Some animals learned to be helpless at a faster rate and became more helpless across a greater number of situations. For some the learning only occurred in one situation; others generalized it and were helpless in all areas of stressful behavior.

Seligman's study is the most illustrative. His research team placed dogs in cages and administered electrical shocks at random and varied intervals. The dogs quickly learned that no matter what response they made, they could not control the shock. In the beginning, the dogs tried various movements in an attempt to escape. When nothing they did stopped the shocks, they ceased any voluntary action and became submissive. Later the researchers changed the procedure and attempted to teach the dogs that they could escape by crossing to the other side of the cage. The dogs still remained passive and helpless. Even when the door was left open and the dogs were shown the way out, they refused to leave and did not avoid the shock.

The earlier in life the dogs received such treatment, the longer it took to overcome the effects of this so-called learned helplessness.

A graphic illustration of learned helplessness was reported in a Florida paper I once read. It seems that 100 nice hotel beds and rooms were made available for some of the street people in a Florida city. Only four people took the offer.

When applied to the physical battering of women and children, this theory helps demonstrate why battered children and battered wives believe that they are helpless. The children tend to set up the exact kind of relationships later on, and the wives do not attempt to free themselves from the battering relationship.

The battered person's belief in helplessness is the most important aspect of this phenomenon. The battered child or wife is determined by a negative cognitive set, a negative belief system. They really believe that the situation is hopeless. This is the reason victims of violence do not attempt to free themselves from the battering relationships.

Children are actually as helpless as they believe themselves to be; women believe they are helpless, but they are not. Children victimized by physical violence tend to generalize the feeling of helplessness. They feel helpless in other adverse situations. Such children become "externalizers." They believe that most of the events that occur in their lives are caused by factors outside their control.

Often the physically abused child is in a family where the mother is being battered. A little girl victimized by witnessing her mother's violation grows up to believe that she cannot escape being battered. She believes with her mother that women cannot escape men's overall coercion.

A little boy may become the victim of the mother's repressed rage and be battered by her. If he witnesses his father's violence, he may grow up believing in male supremacy and in the stereotyped picture of male supremacy in the family. Boys identify with the violent offenders and become offenders more often than girls. Bonding with the offender is a way to overcome the feeling of helplessness and powerlessness. The person bonding with an offender literally loses his own reality and becomes the offender. In that way he feels he can survive. Most offenders were once victims who bonded with their offenders. Battering husbands and parents were probably once helpless victims.

I was fascinated at my own intense response to the movie *First Blood*. Obviously massive numbers of others were fascinated with it, too. In this movie, Rambo is hunted by abusing and unjust authority figures, represented by the sheriff and his deputies. Rambo subsequently kills them all and totally annihilates the town where he encountered them. The abusive treatment of Rambo touches the abused and revenge-seeking child in all of us. While my law-abiding adult is horrified by Rambo's mass killings, my child cheers him on.

Boundaries and Abuse

Both sexually and physically abusive families tend to be dominated by the rules of the poisonous pedagogy. The family profiles show strong and rigid boundaries around the family. The boundaries are often established by strong religious beliefs as well as the belief in following perfectionistic and rigid rules. Thus the whole family is oriented toward an externalizer-type boundary dynamic. The hurt and pain are carried as the family secret. The child is forbidden to talk because of the rule of obedience to the adults. No new information can come into the family because of the rigidity of the system and the hierarchical control. The religious rules often call anything outside the family religion (usually fundamentalistic or highly authoritarian) "secular humanism." Anything psychological is looked upon with suspicion. Hence, the very material that could give new permissions and offer guidance is rejected.

Physical violence affects a level of shame second only to sexual abuse. Slapping, jostling, pinching, shoving, etc. are often done in public. It may be in public places or in front of brothers and sisters or older children. Shame is the feeling of being exposed before you are ready to be exposed. Shame is often associated with being looked at—having eyes on you before you're ready to be seen. Shame is associated with being caught naked, with your pants down, as it were.

Children are frequently made to take their pants down to get spanked. Many other debilitating consequences flow from the shame. Feeling flawed lessens a person's motivation to initiate action. Believing that there is nothing you can do to control your life greatly reduces your ability to learn and to solve problems. Thus the range of responses a person can choose from is greatly narrowed by shame. The will becomes disabled; the person becomes blind to options. A deep, profound, chronic depression sets in.

Look at the following checklist. Many of the symptoms of adult children of physically and sexually violent families are identical to the symptoms of people who have been chronically stressed, such as war victims or victims of concentration camps. Using the letters of the phrase *Adult Children of Physical Violence,* check out whether you may have damaged your true self-esteem through physical violence.

A Abuse feels normal
D Delusion and denial
U Unreality
L Loss of the ability to initiate projects or solve problems
T Trust issues

C Criminal behavior
H Hostility and internalized rage
I Intensely jealous and possessive
L Loneliness, alienation, isolation
D Dissociated and depersonalized
R Rigidity
E Eating disorders
N Numbed out and apathetic

O Objectification of self and others
F Fixated personality development

P Prostitution and sexualized rage
H Hypervigilant and fear of losing control
Y Yearning for parental approval
S Shame-based
I Illness—real or imagined
C Co-dependent
A Acting-out behaviors
L Loss of boundaries

V Victim role
I Incensed at parents
O Offender status
L Low-grade chronic depression
E Externalizer
N Nightmares or dream repression
C Compulsive/addictive behavior
E Extremely split

A. **Abuse feels normal.** You continue to live in abusive situations. You feel that there are no other choices. This is your lot. I had a woman client who married three abusive alcoholics. She told me she thought it was normal for men to drink and be violent.

D. **Delusion and denial.** You idealize your parents. You minimize their physical punishments. You never think you can leave the physically abusive relationship you are in. You still think you can control the physical abuse by being more perfect or by pleasing your offender.

U. **Unreality.** You often feel like things and events around you are unreal. You can't understand why people are so interested in certain aspects of life. You have little real interest in anything.

L. **Loss of the ability to initiate projects or solve problems.** You can't get started, have trouble completing thought processes, and can't seem to see any alternatives. You feel confused a lot.

T. **Trust issues.** You trust no one. When you have risked trusting, your judgment was bad. You don't trust your own perceptions, feelings or thoughts. You're not attracted to those who seem to be truly trustworthy.

C. **Criminal behavior.** You are or have been in trouble with the law. You were a delinquent. You secretly steal or have stolen in the past. You feel that nothing is wrong with cheating or stealing if you can get away with it. You are a criminal.

H. **Hostility and internalized rage.** You are angry a lot and inflict your nasty moods onto others, or you are terrified of anger and manipulated by it. You are passive/aggressive. You feel like lashing out at everyone.

I. **Intensely jealous and possessive.** You control your spouse and children. You are possessive and jealous. You are offended at the slightest withdrawal of their attention.

L. Loneliness, alienation and isolation. You feel lost. You feel different from other people. You feel as though you don't really belong. You feel crazy without any attendant psychosis.

D. Dissociated and depersonalized. You don't have control over your physical self. You are disconnected from your body. You don't know when you are tired, hungry or having sexual desires. You are cold and distant. You do not have warmth or intimacy with anyone. You have no memories from childhood. You have catastrophic fantasies. You are paranoid. You have lots of accidents.

R. Rigidity. You operate with fixed and rigid rules. Your body is rigid and without much feeling. You are inflexible.

E. Eating disorders. You don't know when you feel empty or hungry. You eat to fill up. You eat to feel full. You repress anger and eat to cover it up.

N. Numbed out and apathetic. You are numb. You deny your feelings. You feel apathetic and listless. You have low energy.

O. Objectification of self and others. You do not experience others as persons but as objects to be used. You treat yourself as an object. You indulge yourself. You indulged in early and chronic masturbation. You objectify sex partners.

F. Fixated personality development. You are emotionally a child. You are extremely needy. You have impulse control problems. You are insatiable in your need for affection and love. You are fixated at the age you were when the physical abuse occurred.

P. Prostitution and sexualized rage. You are now or have been a prostitute. You were manipulated and used physically by your parents. You have open or secret contempt for the opposite sex.

H. Hypervigilant and fear of losing control. You live in a state of readiness for attack. You feel jumpy and are easily startled. You have attacks of sudden fear or panic. You fear losing control.

Y. Yearning for parental approval. You still seek your parents' approval and love. You do things you think will please them, only to be disappointed over and over again.

S. Shame-based. You feel inadequate and flawed as a human being. You feel you deserved what happened to you in childhood. You think you are bad and deserve all the bad things that have happened to you. You are self-destructive and have tried to mutilate yourself on occasion. You feel you are almost always wrong.

I. Illness—real or imagined. You have been sick a great deal in your life. You go to doctors often. You have been told that there is no organic cause for many of your physical illnesses. You have many headaches, stomachaches, backaches. You are accident-prone.

C. Co-dependent. You have no sense of your own reality. You do not know what you feel, need or want. You have great trouble making decisions. You have a great need to control others' behavior.

A. Acting-out behaviors. You commit violent behaviors. You do to your children what was done to you. You do to other people what was done to you. You reenact either as an offender or victim what was done to you in childhood.

L. Loss of boundaries. You have very poor physical boundaries. You let everyone touch you, or put up walls so that no one touches you. You have sex when you don't want to. You have sex with people you don't want to have sex with. Or you won't have sex with anyone. You allow your partner to physically abuse you.

V. Victim role. You continually end up being a victim. You feel you can't control being victimized.

I. Incensed at parents. You hate your parents. You resent them and obsess on the wrong they did to you. You haven't seen them in years. You are abusive to them.

O. Offender status. You have been called an offender. You beat your spouse. You beat your children. You violate others' rights. You break the law and feel no compunction. You rage at those around you. You seem to have little capacity for empathy or sympathy.

L. Low-grade chronic depression. You have been depressed as far back as you can remember. You have intermittent thoughts of suicide. You believe you are helpless to change the course of your life.

E. Externalizer. You believe that most of the events that occur in life happen outside of your control. Life is a problem to be solved.

N. Nightmares or dream repression. You have recurring nightmares, or you never dream. You have occasional memory blips—as if a scene flashes on the screen and then disappears. You never know whether these memory blips really happened or not.

C. Compulsive/addictive behaviors. You are an addict. You are compulsive and impulsive.

E. Extremely split. You experience yourself as having at least two personalities. You are one way on the outside and another way at home. No one can believe you are so different at home. You have several personalities. You are confused about your own identity.

You may be beginning to see the *overlap* in these responses to violence. Being violated is traumatic. The symptoms I have been describing are the symptoms of post-traumatic stress disorder. These symptoms vary in intensity depending on the kind of traumatic abuse the victim experienced, the chronicity of the abuse, and whether there was anyone who truly cared about the child.

Sexual and physical violence are devastating forms of abandonment. The child is left alone. The child is a victim of his parent's or caretaker's shamelessness. The child is used and abused.

SUMMARY

The key points covered in this chapter can be summed up using the letters of the word **PERSECUTED.**

Physical Violation—Our Body as the Ground of Our Being

Physical and sexual abuse violate the ground of a person's being. Our body image is our most fundamental boundary. When our body is violated, the core of the self is injured.

Extent of Incest and Sexual Abuse

Because the common conception of sexual violation is the "horror story" kind, few people are aware of the many other forms of sexual abuse. In this chapter we looked at four categories of sexual violation: physical, overt (voyeurism, exhibitionism), covert (verbal and boundary violation) and emotional (cross-generational bonding).

Responds to Physical and Sexual Violence as Normal Behavior

Because physical and sexual abuse are so traumatic, the dissociation from the trauma is intense. The victim loses the connection between the violence and the response to violence. Victims believe their reactive behavior is their normal behavior. *They condemn their behavior as crazy and neurotic. In reality it is a normal reaction to violence. Learned helplessness and bonding to violence are outcomes of this disconnection.*

Setup for Physical Violation by the Poisonous Pedagogy

The poisonous pedagogy promotes a master/slave kind of ownership relationship between parents and children. This belief in ownership implicitly opens up the possibility of physical and sexual abuse.

Entire Family System Involved in Incest and Physical Violence

There is frequently a collusive role played by the spouse of the offender. The nonabusing parent either consciously or

unconsciously permits the victimization. Every member of the family is severely affected by the abuse.

Checklists

These checklists for sexual and physical violence offer victims a way to connect the violence with the natural reactions to the violence. Identifying the behavioral reactions can help victims determine what happened to them.

Universality of Physical Abuse

In this chapter I pointed out that the battering of women and children is part of an ancient and pervasive tradition. Even with the achievements of the women's movement, the extensive battering of women still goes on.

Typical Offenders

The common characteristics of both sexual and physical offenders are: poor self-image, lack of empathy, shame-based, often abuse victims, unrealistic expectations for children, in delusion and denial, isolated, compulsive.

Ego Defenses

Special emphasis was placed on dissociations and ego defense. This defense allows the victim to leave his body when it is being violated. Victims learn to cut off feelings and physically numb out. This sets victims up for compulsive/addictive behavior.

Denial (Keeping the Secret)

The greatest problem with physical/sexual victimization is that victims cannot express their fear, hurt and anger. The incest victims are in a true catch-22. If they tell, they risk losing their family. Physical abuse victims are abused more if they express their hurt and anger.

SEVEN

The "Bad" Child: Checklist for How Your Self-Esteem Was Damaged in an Emotionally Abusive Family

If a child lives with criticism, he learns to condemn.

If a child lives with hostility, he learns to fight.

If a child lives with shame, he learns to feel ashamed.

DOROTHY LAW NOLTE

The most dominant need that any child has is to gradually move from the complete environmental support of infancy and childhood to the self-support of maturity.

In order to grow, children need their parents' good modeling, attention, time and teaching. Children also need their own feelings affirmed.

In many ways children also offer parents a chance to learn and grow. As children go through each of their developmental stages, their parents encounter their own developmental deficits associated with that stage. Infancy is an opportunity for parents to be aware of how they fared with their own infancy needs. Children offer parents a chance to look at the rich emotional life they once had and could have again. In her book, *For*

Your Own Good: Hidden Cruelties in Child Rearing, Alice Miller writes:

> *Children need a large measure of emotional and physical support from the adult. This support must include the following elements:*
>
> *1. Respect for the child.*
> *2. Respect for his needs.*
> 3. Tolerance for his feelings *[emphasis mine]*
> *4. Willingness to learn from his behavior . . .*
>   *a. About the nature of the individual child*
>   *b. About the child in the parents themselves*
>   *c. About the nature of emotional life, which can be observed more clearly in the child than in the adult because the child can experience his feelings much more intensely and . . . undisguisedly than the adult.*[1]

Instead of learning from our children, the poisonous pedagogy exhorts us to mold and train them like animals. It asks us to crush their vitality, spontaneity and emotional expression.

Anger, Sex and Emotional Energy

At any given moment we are having emotions. While our emotions are not all of who we are, they are our vital connection with life as it is now. Our emotions are one of our basic powers. They are like the gas gauge on our car, monitoring our basic need fulfillment. Our degree of happiness and self-satisfaction depends on getting our basic needs met. When we are out of touch with our emotions, we have no way to know what our needs are or whether we should attend to them. To deny our emotions is to deny the vital energy of our life.

I have been offering you checklists to see how you may have lost your self-esteem. The checklist I now propose should have relevance for everyone. It's my opinion that no one had a "perfect" childhood, since no human parent is perfect. When it comes to

---

[1] Miller, *For Your Own Good,* 100.

emotional development, the poisonous pedagogy is clear. Strong feelings are harmful and weak. They mar rational clarity and they must be controlled. The two emotions that are especially danger-ous are anger and sexual feelings.

Anger is essential as the core energy of our strength. Without the energy of anger, we may become apathetic, a doormat and a people-pleaser.

Anger is an *emotion* that is often confused with *behaviors* like hitting, screaming and cursing. The latter are behaviors based on judgment. They are not emotions. Angry emotions protect and pre-serve the individual.

Sexual emotions, on the other hand, promote and preserve the species. Without sexual emotions and the mature, age-appropriate behaviors based on them, the human race would die out in 100 years.

Emotions are energies in motion. If they are not expressed, the energy is repressed. As energy, it has to go somewhere. Emotional energy *moves* us. We are moved to tears when we've lost some-thing dear to us. We are moved to action when we feel our shame. We are moved to joy when our needs are met.

Because our emotions are forms of energy, we can only stop feeling them by mustering counter energy. We do this with muscle tension, shallow breathing, fantasies of punishment or abandon-ment and critical self-talk. This tensing, internal talking and shal-low breathing are the ways we physically numb out. After years and years of practice, we can literally no longer feel our emotions. Psychic numbness is the soil out of which our addictions are born. Our addictions are a way we can feel alive.

In my drinking days, I felt much more alive and sane when I was drinking than when I was sober. As the chemicals relaxed my muscles, I felt my feelings. I felt high. Being high or euphoric is the way we often feel when we are fully functional. When I was drunk, I felt alive; sober, I felt numb and dead.

Emotional repression is perhaps the most common symptom of our current cultural crisis. Our problems with addiction and family violence are rooted in the denial and repression of our affective life. This repression of emotion is supported to some degree by our schools, our churches and our legal system.

Figure 7. I. Ego Boundaries

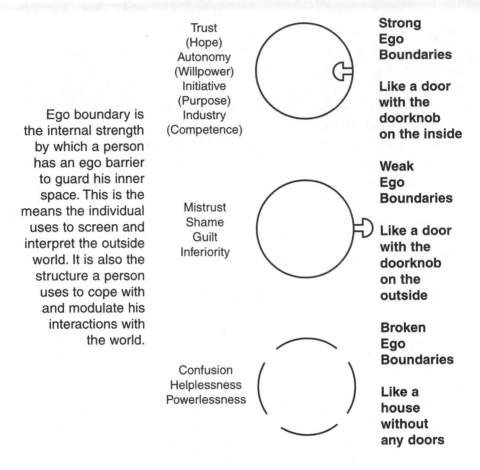

Ego boundary is the internal strength by which a person has an ego barrier to guard his inner space. This is the means the individual uses to screen and interpret the outside world. It is also the structure a person uses to cope with and modulate his interactions with the world.

Trust
(Hope)
Autonomy
(Willpower)
Initiative
(Purpose)
Industry
(Competence)

Strong Ego Boundaries

Like a door with the doorknob on the inside

Mistrust
Shame
Guilt
Inferiority

Weak Ego Boundaries

Like a door with the doorknob on the outside

Confusion
Helplessness
Powerlessness

Broken Ego Boundaries

Like a house without any doors

Epigenetic Development

Human development occurs epigenetically. This means that one stage builds upon the previous one. Nature has her developmental rhythms. There is a time of developmental readiness. At a certain age, humans move toward muscle development, walking and talking. At approximately 18 months, children start saying, "No, let me do it." At three and one-half years, they start asking, "Why?" At six years they get obstinate again. By 15 they have reached puberty and begin moving away from home. Each stage marks a crisis.

Each crisis is a time of heightened vulnerability as well as a time of potential growth.

If the developmental tasks are not accomplished at the proper time and in the proper sequence, we go on without the age-appropriate developmental strength. The strength of our ego is the result of each properly resolved developmental crisis. If the crisis is resolved and the need is met, the ego grows in strength. If the developmental task is not met, the ego does not obtain the structure it needs for the next developmental task. It is weakened, and when the need is not met at all, it is broken.

In figure 7.1, I've tried to show three symbols of ego structure. These ego structures are what I referred to earlier as ego boundaries. A child needs to develop strong ego boundaries to move into adolescence. If we can become solidly a child while we are a child, we then have the foundation to enter adolescence on our way to becoming an adult. If we cannot be children while we are children, we become adult children. Strong ego boundaries are like a door that can only be opened from the inside by the owner of the house. Weak boundaries are like a door that can be opened from the outside and inside, but has no lock. Broken ego boundaries are like a house without any doors.

When an adult abuses a child emotionally, the adult replaces the child's way of seeing, thinking and feeling with his own. This results in the developmental tasks of the child remaining unmet, leading to a weak ego and weak or broken ego boundaries.

Emotional abuse is a form of psychological battering. Psychological battering includes all forms of abuse because victims cannot be physically or sexually violated without also being psychologically battered. Emotional violence is involved in all abuse and causes the neglect of developmental dependency needs.

Mirroring, Echoing, Affirming

Children's earliest needs are for a warm, loving person to be there to mirror, echo and affirm them. This means that in the first 15 months of life (called the symbiotic stage), a child needs a face with accepting eyes to reflect his self. Whatever is in the mothering person's eyes becomes the core and foundation of the child's identity.

Alice Miller has argued that the infant child's inner sensations form the core of the child's self. These earliest sensations come from the mother's feelings about the child. Since the child is non-verbal, everything depends on feelings. These early feelings about the self are the core out of which the child's self-esteem will be formed. This earliest need is called the healthy narcissistic need. If parents never got their narcissistic needs met, they will *use their children* as objects of narcissistic gratification. When this is the case, the children intuit very early on that they must take care of the parents' emotional needs if they are to survive.

Gwenella was born to take care of her mother's grief over her brother, who died one and a half years before she was born. She learned that when she smiled and pretended to be happy, it made her mother happy. The facade of laughter and happiness that Gwenella came to counseling with was truly deceiving. She had been in a terrible marriage for 18 years, taking care of a cocaine-addicted spouse. Both of her children were acting out with drugs. When she finally took off her smiling, "little Mary Sunshine" mask, she wept buckets.

Touching, Warmth, Strokes, Belonging, Attachment

If our mothering figure is defended against her emotions and cut off from her spontaneity and warmth, we will not be touched in the way we need to be. Children need to be touched in order to establish a sense of warm contact. Physical touching is referred to as stroking in some psychological models. Such warm contact tells us that there is someone out there whom we can trust and depend on. Our hope for getting our dependency needs met rests on this. If we can feel the touch and the warmth of an emotionally available person, we can begin our life with a sense of trust. We will believe that the world is friendly and warm. We can depend on what's out there to get our needs met. If our mothering person is not there for us emotionally, we will feel her coldness and mistrust the world. We will have to create a fantasy bond, an illusion of connectedness, in order to go on.

Depriving a child of physical strokes can literally kill the child in the earliest stages of life. As we grow older our need for physical strokes is extended into the need for emotional strokes. Emotional strokes mean getting attention, being prized and valued, and having our growth achievement applauded.

When we cannot get these strokes in a healthy manner, we will do whatever we have to do to get them. Strokes are a *basic* need. Strokes are to the psyche what food is to the body. Children who do not get strokes in a healthy way get them in unhealthy ways. Being *singled out* as bad, causing trouble or being the family failure are all negative forms of recognition.

Selfness, Self-Esteem, Self-Acceptance, Self-Actualization

We need to be valued for the special person we are. We need to see all of our selves in the eyes of our caretakers as we interact with them. All our emotions, all our needs, all our drives need to be echoed back to us so we can get a sense of ourselves and establish an inner unity. If parts of us are accepted (when we giggle and coo) while other parts are rejected (when we have a temper tantrum or cry too loudly), the parts that are rejected split off. Each time we feel those parts of ourselves, our internalized parental eyes and voices reject them. These rejected parts of self (most often our sexuality, anger and aggressiveness) operate underground. They continue to grow outside our consciousness and have a life and power of their own.

Anger, for example, can explode on us without warning. People often say, "I don't know what came over me today" or "I lost it today," meaning, "I lost my temper. I got out of control." The same is true for sadness or fear.

Growing up, I was not allowed to have anger. It was one of the seven deadly mortal sins. A well-meaning Catholic nun passed an X ray of a diseased lung around the room and told us our souls looked like that under mortal sin. I vowed never to get angry again. I was urged to be nice. I was compared (a form of shaming) to a rat fink down the street named B.W. "Why can't you be nice like B.W.?" I was asked. B.W. actually set fires in garages, but he was a saint around adults.

I also grew up, like most males, being told, "Real men don't cry" and "Don't be afraid. There's nothing to be afraid of."

Even when I was joyous, I couldn't be joyous too long because "there are starving children in Latin America." If you can't be glad, mad, sad or afraid, you have to shut down. Your true self indeed shuts down and a false self is created. This false self meets the needs of both the parents and the covert needs of the system for balance.

When a child is allowed to experience his own emotions, he can individuate in the proper developmental sequence. But when a child is used to taking care of his parents' emotions, he loses contact with his own emotions and becomes dependent on others to verify his feelings.

Autonomy, Difference, Space, Separation

Children have a need to be different. They have a need for physical space. In fact, the need for physical space is the foundation for a person's physical boundary. My children never performed a task exactly the way I showed them or asked them to do it. They did it their way. And as frustrating as that often was, it's the way God and nature intended it.

Each person is unique, unrepeatable and incomparable. Each has a basic need for individuality, autonomy and difference. This need emerges at about 15 months. This is the beginning of the long journey of separation. After symbiotic bonding, we start separating.

The Terrific Twos mark the beginning of solid selfhood. In this period, a child learns that his name is "Don't." The child starts saying "No" and this is wonderful. If we allowed children to say no the way nature and God designed it, we wouldn't have as many molested children and we wouldn't have to have a national campaign trying to teach teenagers to "just say no."

Child molesters are like hunters going after prey. A man once convicted of child molestation told me that he learned to look for the most needy and the most obedient child on the playground.

The great danger in the autonomous stage is shame. The child needs to learn a sense of shame and doubt. These are important limits. Shame is the emotion that lets us know we are finite. It tells us we will and can make mistakes. It lets us know we are in need of help; that we are not omnipotent. Shame is what tempers the child's omnipotent willpower. However, too much shaming turns the child's need to exercise his will and manipulate the environment against himself. As the psychologist Erik Erikson writes in *Childhood and Society:*

> *He will over-manipulate himself. He will develop a precocious conscience. Instead of taking possession of things in order to test them by purposeful repetition, he will become obsessed by his own repetitiousness . . . he learns to gain power by stubborn and minute control . . . such hollow victory is the infantile mold for the compulsive neurosis. It is also the source of later attempts to govern by the letter, rather than by the spirit.* [2]

The danger for parents at this stage is over-control and perfectionism. When parents are perfectionistic, the generational cycle takes on a repetitive pattern. The compulsive, controlling parent shames the child . . . who will become an adult with a compulsive, controlling, immature child inside.

Shame results from all forms of abandonment. Actual physical abandonment is shaming. When I was a child, my father was never there. I felt worth-less than his time. We have seen how physical and sexual abuse are shaming. All forms of psychological abuse are shaming: yelling, name-calling, labeling, criticizing, judging, ridiculing, humiliating, comparing and contempting are all sources of shame. Shame-based parents are models of shame. How could shame-based parents possibly teach their children self-love?

The most destructive aspect of shame is the process whereby shame moves from being a feeling to a state of *being,* an identity. (For a full discussion of this process, see my book *Healing the*

---

[2] Erikson, 252.

Shame That Binds You.) The feeling of shame becomes an identity when one's emotions, needs and drives are shamed. I've discussed how one's emotions get shamed. When I'm taught that anger is a deadly sin, I am ashamed when I am angry. My anger gets bound by shame. What this means is that when I feel anger I also feel shame—likewise with fear, sadness and joy.

In the system I grew up in the only emotion you could have without feeling shame was guilt. Guilt is an important emotion. In healthy family systems, guilt is the conscience former. It makes the family members accountable and responsible. Guilt is developmentally more mature than shame. It presupposes the presence of some internalized rules. Guilt is the feeling of regret when your behavior violates a sense of personal value. Shame is a feeling of inadequacy about oneself. Guilt is a guardian of doing; shame is a guardian of being.

When shame is toxic, repair and reparation are closed off. If there is something wrong with my very being—there is nothing I can do about it.

When guilt is toxic, it is a mask of co-dependency. Toxic guilt occurs in dysfunctional family systems that are enmeshed. In such systems each person plays his rigid role in order to keep the closed system in balance, and each gives up his uniqueness in order to perform his false self role in loyalty to the system. Toxic guilt denies us any sense of uniqueness. In fact, in dysfunctional families any attempt to leave the system, to give up your rigid role, to individuate, to differentiate, to be unique and different is met with anger and rejection. Anyone who is in a chronically dysfunctioning family and tries to be his own unique self will feel guilt. It's important to see that this *neurotic guilt is a symptom of the dysfunctioning system.*

Individuals in a dysfunctional family exist for the family. The family does not exist for the individuals.

Internalized shame also results from your drives being shamed. A curious three-year-old will start finding parts of his body. I can envisage the following scenario:

One day little Farquahr finds his nose. He calls it by name, which greatly pleases Mom. Mom invites Grandma over, who promptly asks Farquahr to show her his nose. He proudly responds and receives many strokes. Later on he finds his ear and gets the same response. Likewise with his elbow, fingers and navel . . . and then one Sunday with all the family in the living room (and maybe even with the preacher visiting), he finds his penis. To his little mind, "If the nose got 'em, this is really going to get 'em." Not so. Never has little Farquahr been removed so fast from a room. He has never seen such disdain on his mother's face (not even as bad as when he covered his bedroom wall with shit). He gets it: "There will be no genitals in this family." From that moment on his sexual feelings and drive will be shamed. His sexuality will have to live in secret. It certainly cannot be a part of an open, spontaneous, vibrant family life. And we wonder why Masters and Johnson found 68 percent of marriages sexually dysfunctional. How can we live in a family where genital sex is totally secretive (or banal) for 20 years, and then get married and expect to have an open and vibrant sex life? Many people can only be excited sexually as long as it's illicit. It's when it's licit that many people turn off. What a tragedy! Sexuality is probably the most shamed of all our human drives.

Children also get their aggressive drives shamed. They are curtailed in their rambunctiousness. They are curtailed in their curiosity and desire to explore and learn. Often their drives to eliminate are shamed in potty training so that they wind up like me, having to run water in bathrooms so that no one will know I'm doing the dastardly thing. And God help me if I'm caught in public with a need for number two. That is a catastrophic nightmare. Once the drives are shamed, each time a person feels a natural urge or drive, he will also feel shame.

Likewise with all the needs I'm describing. If no one was there to touch you and you were shamed for wanting to be close and touch, when you felt the need to touch, you also felt shame. Lots of men have been shamed in their need to hug, cuddle and touch. They learn to project or use the ego defense of conversion when that need comes up because they were shamed for being needy. Real men don't need.

A lot of men end up converting the need to be touched and to be close into sexuality. They sexualize their affectional needs. They come home from work. They feel the need to be warm and close so they say, "I'm horny." Women have also been shamed for their sexual needs, maybe even more so than men. So women learn to be ashamed of their sexual needs. They affectionalize their sexual needs. They may be hugging and close and start to feel sexual. Then they feel shame and cut off those feelings. All needs can be shamed. If one cannot be who he is and no one is really there for him, then any feelings, needs or wants he has are not okay.

Pleasure, Pain, Stimulation

Children need pleasure and fun. They need to be stimulated by age-appropriate challenges. Children also need to experience their legitimate suffering. Overindulgent and oversubmissive parents are abandoning and abusing their children by not letting them experience the normal amounts of pain that life brings. Pain is the vehicle of growth and the carver of wisdom. "The deeper that sorrow carves into your being, the more joy you can contain," writes the poet Kahlil Gibran. It is abusive to protect a child from this source of growth, courage and wisdom.

On the flip side of the coin, over-perfectionistic and overly punitive parents deprive their children of the fun, laughter, joy and spontaneity that are our childhood rights. The stern, authoritarian, often somber religious parent cuts off these life-giving and spontaneous emotions. Children growing up in such families are deprived of the joys of childhood.

Dependability, Predictability

Children need dependable parents. They need to count on their parents' presence and support as they test their personal limits. This testing of personal limits is a requirement for identity formation. It demands that a child be able to push against reasonably healthy solid persons.

For example, when the two-year-old toddler ventures out in exploration and autonomy, he needs the mothering person to be there. He may say, "Let me do it," but if Mom leaves the room, he'll follow her and do it where she's in his peripheral vision. He needs to find his boundaries and self-identity within the limits of safety. This will hold true all the way through adolescence. An adolescent needs to test and experiment and have a dad and mom with a pretty firm identity who is there for that teen. If Dad is needy and wants his son to show him how grateful he is for all Dad has done, then the son has to *interrupt his identity formation* to take care of needy Dad.

The need for dependency is the need for predictability and meaning. Children need their parents to be there for them in a reasonably predictable manner. In chronically dysfunctioning families, the children never know what to expect. Dad may be getting drunk—that's why he's not home. Mom may be hysterical or hypochondriacal. The children have to walk on eggshells. They never know what's coming next. The rageaholic father may have an outburst at the most unexpected times.

Parents who are adult children often use their children as a substitute for their own parents. The child can become the object of both adult and childish wishes, which are often contradictory.

In such an atmosphere the children have no time to tend to their own feelings, needs and wants. They are often hypervigilant. They are constantly on alert to what may happen next in the family.

There are *no bad children*. Children are born precious, unique and incomparable. We must fight to protect children so that each child has the right to a good childhood.

I certainly don't believe that everyone always stays good and pristine. I believe that evil is an obvious fact in the universe. People can become vicious—but there would be far less evil in the world if more children had a healthy emotional environment to grow up in.

Children are confused by the moralistic measures imposed on them at an early age. We ask two-year-olds if they've been a "good" boy or a "bad" boy. We call them good boys or good girls when they please us. We call them bad boys and bad girls when they displease us. Such distinctions are parents' projections and come from the moralistic presuppositions of the poisonous pedagogy.

Lawrence Kohlberg, a psychologist at Harvard, has spent the better part of a lifetime researching moral development in children.

His studies are built on the monumental work of Jean Piaget, who spent 50 years studying how children's minds work. Piaget wrote a dozen books and 100-plus articles showing us his researched data on the stages of mental development. Kohlberg's data suggest the following: From birth to seven years old, children are pre-moral. The good is what they want and like. They begin to think logically at about age seven, although their logic is limited to the concrete literal. With proper challenge, they move from thinking that the good is what you want and can get away with, to a kind of concrete reciprocity—you scratch my back and I'll scratch yours. Only in adolescence are they cognitively capable of altruistic thinking. Adolescent morality is dominated by interpersonal conformity. Only later on is the mind capable of thinking that the good has intrinsic value. At this level of moral thinking, the individual does good because good is good to do. He does good because of the principles and beliefs that he adheres to. It takes 25 years for an individual to get to this level of thinking. According to Kohlberg, many adults never make it.[3]

Parents who model goodness and who firmly establish behavioral consequences for antisocial behaviors provide a much more stable moral foundation for their children than do parents who spank and punish them. To label children bad throughout the first seven years does damage to their self-worth. Calling children "bad" and spanking and punishing them for being "bad" causes shame. Shame-based people feel flawed and defective as human beings. If anything sets people up to be immoral, it's shame.

Look at the following checklist for adult children of emotionally violating families.

A Abandonment fears
D Denial and delusion
U Undifferentiated emotions
L Loneliness and isolation
T Thought obsessions

---

[3] Lawrence Kohlberg, *Essays on Moral Development* (San Francisco: Harper and Row, 1981), vol. 1. For an explanation of Kohlberg's stages, see *Educating for Characters* by Thomas Lickona (New York: Bantam Books, 1991), 243.

C Compulsive/addictive behaviors
H High-level anxiety
I Intimacy problems
L Loss of affect and energy
D Drives and needs are shame-bound
R Resentment/guilt cycle
E Emotionally shame-bound
N No expression of emotions, no-talk rule

O Overly controlling
F False self

E Empty and narcissistically deprived
M Manipulating and game-playing
O Overindulged and over-submitted to
T Terrorized and tormented
I Insatiable inner child
O Overly perfectionistic, rigid and authoritarian
N Needy and wanting
A Abused physically or sexually or both
L Lack of emotional coping and communication skills

V Violated emotional boundaries
I Internalized anger, sadness, fear, joy, shame, guilt
O Offender/victim ambiguity
L Loss of inner self-unity
E Enmeshed in caretaking others' feelings
N "Now" phobic
C Corrupted through bad modeling
E Emotional constraint (with or without dramatic outbursts)

A. Abandonment fears. You have great difficulty separating. You stay in relationships long after it is healthy to do so. You hoard things and cannot seem to let go of anyone or anything.

D. Denial and delusion. You are fantasy-bonded to your family of origin. You defend your parents against any suggestion that they did less than a sterling job. You continually try to please your parents and win their love. But no matter what you do, it is never quite enough.

U. Undifferentiated emotions. You never know quite what you feel; you don't know how to express your emotions. You cry when you're angry; you get mad when you're afraid. You somatize your feelings—in other words, you have unusual amounts of sickness. You feel through others.

L. Loneliness and isolation. You are unconnected and things sometimes seem unreal. You feel lonely and never quite feel that you belong.

T. Thought obsessions. You detail your discussions to the point of boring other people. You generalize a lot and often obsess on things that you can't do anything about—the Middle East conflict, the government, inflation. You obsess on little things, you ruminate and worry excessively. You stay in your head (intellectualize, explain, analyze) a lot and discuss your problems, rather than doing anything about them. You are always reading about your problems, learning why you are the way you are.

C. Compulsive/addictive behaviors. You use euphoric-type substances to change your feelings. You use activities to distract you from your feelings.

H. High-level anxiety. You are chronically anxious. You don't know exactly what you fear, but you imagine the worst. You catastrophize.

I. Intimacy problems. When you start feeling close to someone, you sabotage the relationship. You're attracted to emotionally unavailable people. When you could be close to someone, you are not interested. You cling to a relationship once you're involved.

L. Loss of affect and energy. People think you are cold and mechanical. You are incongruent. You say you're happy, excited, angry, etc., but you don't look or sound happy, excited, angry, etc. You are numb.

D. Drives and needs are shame-bound. When you desire sex or are hungry, or need touching or any other basic need, you feel ashamed.

R. Resentment/guilt cycle. You resent your duties to your family of origin or to current family, but you feel guilty when you're not taking care of those duties. You feel resentment because you cannot pursue your own individual interests. And you feel guilty any time you do act differently in your own self-interest.

E. Emotionally shame-bound. When you feel any emotion, you feel shame.

N. No expression of emotions, no-talk rule. You grew up in a family where no one expressed how they felt. You were supposed to read minds. You were supposed to know your parents loved you, even though they never told you. You were expected to know other members of the family were mad, hurt, sad or afraid. It was simply not okay to express or talk about your feelings.

O. Overly controlling. You try to control everyone and everything around you. You try to control other people's behavior. You try to control what can't be controlled. You control your emotions and feel shame when you can't.

F. False self. You pretend a lot. You gauge your behavior by how it looks, by the image you believe you're projecting. You wear a mask, play a rigid role and hide your emotions. You say you're fine when you feel hurt or sad. You say you're not angry when you are.

E. Empty and narcissistically deprived. You feel empty and go from one experience to another, trying to be satisfied. No matter how much you do or how much you get, you never feel satisfied.

M. Manipulating and game-playing. You use your energy to play games with people. You manipulate to get your needs met, rather than being straightforward about it.

O. Overindulged and over-submitted to. You pamper and indulge yourself. You are constantly irritated because people don't respond to your needs. You are demanding and impatient and expect others to see to it that your needs are met. You blame others for everything that goes wrong in your life. You never feel that you are responsible for what's happening.

T. Terrorized and tormented. You feel frightened most of the time. You are easily startled and shaken. You panic easily. You torment yourself with self-judgment. You are self-deprecating.

I. Insatiable inner child. You look like an adult and walk and talk like an adult, but you really feel like a child. You feel remorse about the past and wish you could do it over. You fantasize about the future, saying, "Things will be better when it comes." You live in the past or future but never in the "now." Memory and imagination are ways to avoid your present feelings.

O. Overly perfectionistic, rigid and authoritarian. You endlessly strive to do everything right. You constantly monitor yourself. You are critical and judgmental.

N. Needy and wanting. You feel needy and look to others to fill your needs. You married to be taken care of. Your wants are never fulfilled, or you don't know what you want.

A. Abused physically or sexually or both. (Explored in chapter 6.)

L. Lack of emotional coping and communicational skills. You feel overwhelmed by strong emotions. You are frightened when you are around someone with strong emotions. You can't communicate what you feel or clarify what others are feeling.

V. Violated emotional boundaries. You don't know where you end and others begin. When your friend, spouse or children feel an emotion, you feel the same emotion. You have no empathetic ability because you actually start feeling what others feel. You are intimidated by anger. You are manipulated by fear, sadness and anger.

I. Internalized anger, sadness, fear, shame, joy, guilt. You are an angry person; you don't feel anger. You are a sad person; you don't feel sadness. Internalizing feelings means that they no longer rise and fall like feelings but function like the broken "on" button of a machine. They are frozen; they are a state of being. When shame is internalized, all the emotions are bound in shame.

O. Offender/victim ambiguity. In relationships, you bounce back and forth between being a victim and being an offender.

L. Loss of inner self-unity. You are alienated from some of your feelings. They function autonomously at times. For example, you find yourself exploding with temper at unplanned times. You say, "I don't know what came over me." The same pattern occurs with sadness, fear or sexual feelings.

E. Enmeshed in caretaking others' feelings. You feel others' feelings and continually act in ways that will make others feel better. If they are angry, you change your behavior so they will feel better. If they are sad, you will do things to take away their sadness.

N. "Now" phobic. You feel remorse about the past and wish you could do it over. You fantasize about the future, saying, "Things will be better when it comes." You live in the past or future but never in the now. Memory and imagination are ways to avoid your present feelings.

C. Corrupted through bad modeling. You trust no one. You live in paranoid expectation. You feel you should take whatever you can. You hate blacks, whites, Asians, Europeans, etc. You hurt and shame people whenever you can.

E. Emotional constraint (with or without dramatic outbursts). You are physically numb and you feel and express no feelings. You are psychologically numb and you express your feelings in dramatic outbursts. In the latter way you get them over with quickly.

S U M M A R Y

The key points covered in this chapter can be summed up using the letters of the phrase **BAD CHILD.**

Basic Dependency Needs

All children need someone they can depend on; to have someone to mirror and echo them; to be touched; to have their feelings affirmed; to be taken seriously and to be stimulated and challenged.

Attention, Direction, Time and Good Modeling

Children need caretakers who give them time, attention, direction and good modeling. To do this, parents need to get their own needs met.

Dependency Needs Neglected

When a child's dependency needs are not met at the proper time and in the proper sequence, the energy of that developmental stage gets blocked. This blocked energy arrests emotional growth. The child grows up to be an adult with an unfulfilled inner child.

Checklist for Emotional Violence

The list outlines the range of reactions that normally result from emotional violation and neglect. The list is offered to help victims of emotional violence see that their behavior is more about what happened to them, than it is about them.

House and Doorknob

The house with doorknobs on the inside is a symbol of a person with good boundaries. The house with the doorknobs on the outside is a symbol of a person with bad boundaries. And the house with no doors is a symbol of a person with no boundaries at all. (See figure 7.1.)

Internalized Shame

Shame moves from being a feeling to being a characterological state of being in three ways: (1) through shame-based modeling; (2) by being shamed (neglect, abuse); (3) by having our feelings and drives shamed.

Loss of Affect

When feelings are not affirmed, they are split off from our sense of self. We are beside ourselves. The energy needed for direct coping with the world is lost to the inner warfare of keeping the prohibited feelings in check. We lose all spontaneity.

Developmental Psychology

The work of Erikson and Kohlberg show how emotional and moral development take place.

EIGHT

The Most Common Impact of Chronic Family Dysfunction: Co-dependency

There is nothing so rare as an act of your own.

HENRY THOREAU

You do not need to be loved, not at the cost of yourself. . . . Of all the people you will know in a lifetime, you are the only one you will never leave or lose.

JO COUDERT

Co-dependence is a dis-ease of the developing self causing various degrees of deselfment. I hyphenate the word disease to indicate that co-dependency is not a medical condition. It is a loss of ease with oneself, a feeling of inner emptiness, a state of not being at home with oneself. When we look at the rules of the poisonous pedagogy, it seems clear that selfhood would be a unique achievement for anyone raised with these rules. In other words, achieving selfhood in spite of these rules is a remarkable achievement.

Blind obedience asks a person to give up his own mind and will. It also asks that a person repress all emotions except fear. Monarchies of old disdained anger in their subjects because anger leads to revolution. "Rule by fear" keeps people in their place. It is a way to control people and keep them in conformity. Without a mind and will of our own and without anger, the energy of self-protection, we cannot develop a solid sense of self-esteem.

The co-dependency spawned by monarchial patriarchy was once *a way of life*—a way of ensuring security and survival. In the new world of deep democracy, with its emphasis on holistic thinking, individuality and personal power, what was once a normal adaptation for survival has become a dis-ease.

Co-dependency can be understood as a characteristic of an adult who is contaminated by childish dependency needs. The reason almost everyone identifies with many characteristics of co-dependency is that the monarchial patriarchal rules (the poisonous pedagogy) created an environment wherein children could not get their developmental dependency needs met.

When children are nurtured properly, their developmental dependency needs are, on some level, met. This is never achieved perfectly, but certainly in a manner that allows them to grow into adulthood with a certain degree of autonomy. When these dependency needs are not met, children become adults with a child's "neediness." This is the general meaning of what is described by the words "adult child."

A co-dependent person is an adult with mild to severe developmental deficits. These developmental deficits are the reason adult children experience spontaneous age regressions. These regressions take place primarily in significant adult relationships.

For example, I was feeling quite good about myself when I married at the age of 35. I had been sober for a year and a half and had worked hard on myself during that time. At the time of my marriage, I was teaching high-brow philosophy at Dominican College and a psychology of religion course at Rice University. However, early in my marriage, I found myself frequently pouting and periodically raging.

Pouting and raging are *childish* behaviors, which in my case were age regressions to toddlerhood. I learned to pout and rage because anger was punished in my family and needs were often labeled as selfish. Children need their adult source figures to name their feelings for them and to model functional ways to express their feelings. Children also need to have their basic needs validated. It is the parents' job to show their children how to affirm their needs and how to get them met. I never learned how to recognize and express anger, so I repressed it. What is repressed doesn't go away. Years later my anger came out in bursts of primitive rage.

The Response to Stress

We humans have a built-in protection system that allows us to defend ourselves against stress. When a demand is made that threatens us, we adapt to it in several ways. In the face of the threat, the body prepares to fight or take flight. The heartbeat increases; the muscles tense; the blood is taken from the sections of the body that don't need it; the muscles of the bowels and bladder are constricted or released in order to have greater mobility; the blood is sent to the upper muscles and legs. The person becomes hypervigilant.

This state of readiness was intended by nature to be a *survival state*. In a chronically dysfunctioning family, it is often the normal state. When a threat actually occurs in the forms of abandonment I have described, the person responds with survival *behaviors*. Such behaviors include denial, dissociation, repression, withdrawal (flight responses) or anger, identification with the persecutor, and reactive and reenacting behavior (fight responses). These survival behaviors are the traits I have been describing in the checklists.

Survival Behaviors

Even if the stressor stops (Dad quits raging, drinking, working, being violent), the members of the family still carry the impact of the stress. In chronically dysfunctioning families, the stress often goes on for years, even generations. The degree of stress ranges in intensity from mild (chronic fear) to severe (traumatic events). The child in a chronically dysfunctioning family learns to survive by developing certain patterns of behavior. These behaviors are the survival behaviors that were the *actual* responses to the violence.

As the child from the dysfunctioning family grows up, these survival behaviors continue even though they are now disconnected from the original source of distress. *These survival behaviors feel normal since they are the patterns the family member used every day of his early life in order to survive.* As an adult they are not only unnecessary, they are actually unhealthy. While once they were protective, now they are destructive.

The psychologist Robert Firestone has compared these defenses to the body's physical reaction when it forms pneumonia. In pneumonia, the body's defensive reaction is more destructive than the original assault. The presence of organisms in the lungs evokes cellular and humoral defenses that lead to congestion that can destroy the organisms. In a similar way, the ego defenses created by the vulnerable child to protect against abuse become, in adult life, more troublesome than the original trauma. One's ego defenses literally become the core of one's co-dependency.

Survival behaviors are hard to give up. They are old friends that served us well. *We did survive.* But we survived by developing a kind of power that resulted from sacrificing ourselves. We learned to control people by becoming Caretakers, Stars, Heroes and Heroines, or by being Lost Children, Perfect, the Problem, the Rebel, or the Scapegoat. We were Surrogate Spouses, our Parent's Parent, Little Parents, etc. In these early role decisions, we developed a dependency on things outside ourselves to the point of self-neglect. We gave up our own reality in order to take care of our parent(s) or the needs of the family system. In short, we survived by abandoning our true selves. We survived by not being there. We learned all our defenses in order to cover up the pain of being toxically shamed.

In the end our survival behaviors left us powerless and spiritually bankrupt. Co-dependency is a set of survival behaviors we learned in order to have some control over the chronic distress that was threatening us.

According to Dr. Timmen Cermak in his book, *Diagnosing and Treating Co-dependence,* co-dependence is now clearly definable enough "to warrant the diagnosis of mixed Personality Disorder as outlined in DSM IV." This means that co-dependence has enough significant clinical status to be recognized and labeled as an emotional disease entity in its own right.

Another way I like to describe co-dependency is with the word "otheration," as used by the Spanish existentialist José Ortega y Gasset. In describing the essence of man, Ortega y Gasset contrasts the life of man with the life of animals. Man, he says, lives from within himself *(ensimismamiento)*, while animals live constantly on guard against the outside. Their lives are dominated by the outside. They constantly guard against the threats from the outside. They must guard against the ever-present dangers to their lives. They must constantly stalk and look for food. If they cease their endless vigilance, they will die. The life of an animal is "otheration" *(alteration)*. "Otheration" is a good description of co-dependence.

The discussion and labeling of co-dependence has an interesting history. Originally the word co-dependence was limited to the study of alcoholic families. It was first used to label the spouse of the alcoholic. As the definition of addiction was expanded to include the wider range of addictions (activities, feelings, thoughts), the awareness dawned on observers that *any type of dysfunctional family exhibits the same co-dependent structure.* Co-dependence is the most common impact of chronic family dysfunction because when there is constant and chronic stress in a family, no one can attend to his own needs. Each member of the family adapts to the distress in an attempt to control it. *Each becomes co-dependent on the stressor.* Each becomes outer-directed. This outer-directedness prohibits family members from focusing on their own feelings or needs. Without awareness of these internal cues, there is no way for the family members to know what they need or what they are feeling.

In my television series, I extended the discussion to include our entire society. With our new awareness of deep democracy, we see that the rules of the poisonous pedagogy naturally create co-dependent families.

As society is modeled after the monarchial patriarchal families we grow up in, society itself becomes a dysfunctioning family system.

Society can become a closed system. Like the individual families we have examined, when society becomes a closed system, it dictates the roles (sex roles) and behaviors the individual can choose from. Society as a closed system calls forth certain characteristic behaviors and processes in the individuals who make it up. Our current society encourages co-dependence. Many of the traits that have emerged as components of co-dependency are traits that in one way or another are culturally normal. Sociologists have clearly outlined the process of "consensus reality" formation. They have shown how we create what is normal by our social consensus.

For example, Erich Fromm pointed out that during the Vietnam War, it was normal to hear someone say that the way to end the war was to drop a hydrogen bomb on Hanoi. If the same person suggested that the way to end air pollution was to level all the factories, most would think of him as crazy. The two suggestions are actually identical.

Societal Regression

One of the components of The Bowen Theory is a concept called societal regression. Societal regression refers to the way that emotional problems in society are similar to the emotional problems in the family. I don't know which taught the poisonous pedagogy first, the family or the society. But our society bears the mark of many normal co-dependent traits. We will discuss them now.

Our Notion of Marriage

I once watched a man play a $25 slot machine in Las Vegas. His very obedient wife coyly stood next to him. Every once in a while he reached in his pocket, grabbed a handful of nickels and generously gave them to his wife. He saw me watching him and introduced himself to me, then asked if I'd like to meet his "better half." It was hard for me to believe that he believed she was his better half!

This notion of two halves making the perfect marriage is an extremely dysfunctional notion. Two incomplete people cannot make a good relationship. A good relationship demands that there be two whole people who *choose* to be in the relationship and know that *each can live without the other*. The opposite of this is an enmeshment or entanglement, wherein both persons involved are convinced they cannot make it without the other. We are taught at an early age to call this inseparable relationship true love. Women especially are taught that their destiny is to find their true love and give their life to him. *What is described as true love could be viewed as an addictive relationship.* Enmeshment takes the place of intimacy. Two people come to believe that they can't live without each other. Such a relationship is jeopardized if either partner grows or changes.

Our popular music also reinforces that two halves make one whole notion. These songs glorify suffering and promote the idea that happiness and completion lie in the other person. Some examples are songs like *Stand By Your Man, She's the Sunshine of My Day, Lord She Took Me In and Made Me Everything I Am Today; Good-Hearted Woman* who "loves him in spite of his wicked ways" and *Last Blues Song* where it says, "I'm getting high on feeling low." We could go on and on. We grew up with these songs. We heard many of them during our adolescence, when our identities were forming.

Music has a profound impact on the nonverbal unconscious part of our brain. Just at the time when love and relationships are focusing, our unconscious is being grounded in beliefs that we are nothing unless somebody loves us or that we can't survive without a love partner.

The marriage relationship is the foundation and architect of the family. Little wonder millions of adult children have been robbed of their childhood because they were enmeshed in their family system's intimacy vacuum.

Our Notion of Love

Our beliefs about marriage condition our notion of love. Our cultural beliefs about love are often forms of addiction. (I expand on this in my book, *Creating Love.*) Many religious preachers teach a form of passive-dependent love. They teach that the highest act of love is self-sacrifice. The highest love is to set aside one's own physical, emotional and intellectual needs to serve and take care of others. They teach long-suffering and martyrdom as two of the major ways to attain goodness. Acting good and acting righteous are more important than actually *being* good. Acting loving is more important than being loving.

Helping and giving up ourselves for others can often be a way to attain moral superiority. Helpers are always helping themselves. Taking care of others is a way to feel powerful, and in the moment of helping, we can overcome our feelings of emptiness and powerlessness. The feeling of goodness or righteousness is a euphoric feeling. Feeling righteous is a powerful way to alter our mood. I have some personal experience with this.

I was in a seminary for a number of years, studying to be a Catholic priest. I wore a Roman collar and a black robe. I preached goodness and righteousness. I was a counselor and spiritual advisor. Certainly, I would not discount *all* that I did. I acted out of the best awareness that I had.

Nevertheless, it was a rude awakening for me when I realized *how helping and caretaking can be a subtle disguise for self-gratification.* My shame-based inner self could feel as though I was really okay when I was preaching and helping. I ultimately had to realize that this was a counterfeit form of love.

Being in love is perhaps the most addictive of all. "In love" is not "love." It is a state of biological bonding. When we are "in love" our boundaries collapse and there is a profound mood alteration.

M. Scott Peck has written brilliantly about our culture's various forms of counterfeit love. His book *The Road Less Traveled* offers an enlightening, and for many, surprising discussion of this matter. Love, according to Peck, is a form of work. It involves commitment and overcoming laziness and fear through the courage to risk exposure and rejection. Love is therefore not a feeling—it is an act of the will and a decision. *All true love begins with self-love.* The work and discipline of love flow from a true sense of self-value. We have to know how to value ourselves before we can value others.

Rationalism—the Denial of Fun, Emotions and Spontaneity

The family, schools and churches that I experienced growing up taught me to control myself when it came to fun, spontaneity and emotions. The schools I went to taught me not to talk, to stand straight in line, not to ask too many questions, to memorize great quantities of material, to learn a number of things I've never used again (solid geometry, years of Latin, diagraming sentences). I was discouraged from laughing exuberantly at school and certainly never in church. To be excited, noisy, happy, full of energy was reprimanded as bad behavior. When I was sick (especially at home)—quiet, depressed, obedient, orderly—I was rewarded and called good. Children were good and well-behaved when they obeyed silently and promptly.

Our schools and churches are still highly rationalistic. Reason and logic are desirable; emotions are weak and suspicious. We do not educate the right hemisphere of our brain. Right hemispheric activities include intuition, music, creativity and holistic thinking. Our logic is still characterized by black and white kinds of thinking and judgment. If you believe in one thing, you must by that fact reject its opposite. There is no synthesis—no gray area.

Rationalism has been attacked for 150 years. The philosophers Kant, Whitehead and the entire existentialist movement, as well as countless others, have convincingly argued that the rationalistic bias that favors logic and linear left-brain thinking at the expense of felt thought (poetry), intuition and creativity is polarized and out of balance.

Existentialism has offered a whole corrective model based on right-brain thinking and the phenomenology of human experience. Einstein, Heisenberg and others have exposed the mechanistic universe of Isaac Newton as simplistic.

Dishonesty and Pretending as Correct Behavior

The poisonous pedagogy promotes obedience without content. We should pretend to be grateful, rather than to be honestly ungrateful. We should pretend to be loving, rather than to be honestly unloving. We are taught as children to accept the family's "vital lies." We are not to notice what is happening. We must pretend it is not happening. Rather than asking directly for what we want or saying what we think and feel, we are to play roles and pretend.

We are taught to be nice and polite. We are taught that these behaviors (most often lies) are better than telling the truth. We are taught above all to pretend we are not feeling the things we are feeling. Our churches, schools and politics rampantly teach dishonesty, encouraging us to say things we don't mean and pretend to feel ways we don't feel. We smile when we feel sad; laugh nervously when dealing with grief; laugh at jokes we don't think are funny; tell people things to be polite.

Glad-handing and lying politicians have basically destroyed most people's trust in our national leadership. Presidents, politicians and so-called religious leaders often succumb to their sexual and adrenaline addictions. If not those addictions, they often model other addictions and eating disorders. All in all it's not a pretty picture.

My belief is that co-dependence is the dis-ease of today. All addictions are rooted in co-dependence. We are co-dependent because we've lost our solid sense of self.

Co-dependency as Addictiveness

When I put the cork in the bottle, I still had to face what Vernon Johnson calls the *ism* of alcoholism. I was still a compulsive personality. I worked the 12 Steps on my alcoholism, never on my co-dependency. Consequently, I soon developed other addictions. I smoked and drank 12 cups of coffee a day. I became addicted to the adrenaline rush of working and making money. I struggled with sugar binges and dieting. My belief is that our overt addictions are diseases of a dis-ease. The dis-ease is co-dependency or addictiveness.

The psychiatrist Carl Menninger described alcoholism as "a man on fire running into the sea to put out the fire, but drowning." The alcohol is the substance used to deal with the loneliness and pain. It is like a fever. But fever is a symptom of an organic disorder, and when the fever gets to be 107°, it will kill you. The alcohol that alcoholics use to heal the shame and loneliness can itself become the killer. In this sense alcohol is a disease of a dis-ease.

In the case of alcohol and other chemical abuse (drugs and food) we have to stop using the ingested substances in order to even get to the underlying disorder—the addictiveness or co-dependence. The co-dependence is the dis-ease underneath any substance addiction.

In the activity addictions it is easier to see the co-dependence. Severely co-dependent people have internalized shame and strong feelings of low self-worth. Co-dependents try to make themselves indispensable by taking care of others. They are willing to do whatever it takes to be loved or worthwhile. Co-dependents often choose professions of caretaking and financial achievement, throwing themselves into their work to the point of workaholism and burnout.

Co-dependence as Spiritual Bankruptcy

Co-dependence is the core addictiveness. It is a dis-eased form of life. Once someone believes that his identity lies outside himself in a substance, activity or another person, that person *has found a new god, sold his soul and become a slave.*

Someone has called co-dependence a "conflict of gods." The more co-dependent a person becomes, the less inner life he has. *Co-dependence is at bottom a spiritual problem. It is spiritual bankruptcy.*

In all the families we have examined so far, all the members lack solid selfhood and are co-dependent to some degree. Emotionally dysfunctional families, as we have seen, have certain structural similarities. Those similarities are as follows:

1. A dominant dysfunction causes a threat to which all other members respond. The adaptations to the threat cause the system to close up in a frozen, rigid pattern.
2. The frozen pattern is maintained by each member playing one or more rigid roles.
3. There is a high level of anxiety and confusion.
4. Members are shamed-based, and shame is the dominant trait of chronically dysfunctional families.
5. Because the family's coping strategy is inept, the more the system tries to change, the more it stays the same. Mother covers up for Father's drinking. She calls his office and lies for

him when he is too hung over to go to work. She teaches the children to do the same. The whole family over-functions to solve the problem of Dad's under-functioning.

6. Chronically dysfunctional families are held together by variations of the rules of poisonous pedagogy. Chronically dysfunctional family members have lost their own reality. Each is out of touch with his own feelings, needs and wants. Each maintains a false self and gives up his individual uniqueness for the sake of loyalty to the system.

Adult Children of Dysfunctional Families

In the checklist that follows, see if you identify yourself in *several* of the following traits. If you do, it's likely that you are co-dependent and are carrying your family dysfunction. I use the phrase, *Adult Children of Dysfunctional Families,* to present these traits. This checklist is a kind of summary of all that we have discussed up until now.

A Abandonment issues
D Delusion and denial
U Undifferentiated ego mass
L Loneliness and isolation
T Thought disorders

C Control madness
H Hypervigilant (high-level anxiety)
I Internalized shame
L Lack of boundaries
D Disabled will
R Reactive and reenacting
E Equifinality
N Numbed out

O Offender with or without offender status
F Fixated personality

D Dissociated responses
Y Yearn for parental warmth and approval
S Secrets (dark)
F Faulty communication
U Underinvolved
N Neglect of developmental dependency needs
C Compulsive/addictive behaviors
T Trance—carrying the family spell
I Intimacy problems
O Overinvolved (otheration)
N Narcissistically deprived
A Abuse victim
L Lack of coping skills (underlearning)

F False self—confused identity
A Avoid depression through activity
M Measured, judgmental and perfectionistic
I Inhibited trust
L Loss of own reality—damaged and weak boundaries
I Inflated self-image
E Emotional constraint (with or without dramatic outbursts)
S Spiritual bankruptcy

A. **Abandonment issues.** You were physically abandoned by one or both of your parents. Your parents were there, but not emotionally available to you. You were physically, sexually or emotionally violated by someone in your family. Your developmental dependency needs were neglected. You were enmeshed in your parents' neediness or in the needs of your family system. You stay in relationships far beyond what is healthy.

D. **Delusion and denial.** You believe everything is okay in spite of the facts that say things are not okay. You are unconscious and oblivious about the dysfunction that is going on.

U. **Undifferentiated ego mass.** You carry the feelings, desires and secrets of other people in your family system.

L. Loneliness and isolation. You have felt lonely all or most of your life. You feel isolated and different.

T. Thought disorders. You get involved in generalities or details in order to avoid your painful feelings. You worry, ruminate and obsess a lot. You stay in your head to avoid your feelings. You read about your problems, rather than taking action.

C. Control madness. You try to control yourself and everyone else. You feel extremely uncomfortable when you're out of control. You mask your efforts to control people and situations by "being helpful."

H. Hypervigilant (high-level anxiety). You live on guard. You are easily startled. You panic easily.

I. Internalized shame. You feel flawed as a human being. You feel inadequate and hide behind a role or an addiction or character trait, like control, blame, criticism, perfectionism, contempt, power and rage.

L. Lack of boundaries. You don't know where you end and others begin physically, emotionally, intellectually or spiritually. You don't know what you really stand for.

D. Disabled will. You are willful. You try to control other people. You are grandiose. With you it's all or nothing.

R. Reactive and reenacting. You react easily. You feel things unrelated to what is happening. You feel things more intensely than the event calls for. You find yourself repeating patterns over and over.

E. Equifinality. No matter where you begin, your life seems to end at the same place.

N. Numbed out. You don't feel your feelings. You don't know what you feel. You don't know how to express what you feel.

O. Offender with or without offender status. You are actually an offender, or you are not an offender, but in fact play that role sometimes.

F. **Fixated personality.** Your personality was arrested at an early developmental age. You are an adult, but your emotional age is very young. You look like an adult but feel very childish and needy. You feel like the lifeguard on a crowded beach, but you don't know how to swim.

D. **Dissociated responses.** You have no memories of painful events of your childhood; you have a split personality; you depersonalize; you can't remember people's names or even the people you were with two years ago. You are out of touch with your body and your feelings.

Y. **Yearn for parental warmth and approval.** You seek it in other relationships. You still try to gain your parents' approval and you yearn for the "perfect relationship." You have an exaggerated need for others' approval. You fear offending others. You find emotionally unavailable partners (just like your parents were) and try to make them love you. You will go to almost any lengths to care and help your partner. You find people who need nurturing and take care of them.

S. **Secrets (dark).** You carry dark secrets from your family of origin. You've never talked to anyone about how bad it was in your family, and you carry lots of secrets about your own life. You also carry sexual secrets that you would not want to tell anyone.

F. **Faulty communication.** You have had trouble communicating in every relationship you've been in. Your partners frequently tell you that they do not understand what you say. You feel confused when communicating with others. When talking to people, no matter how good your intentions are to be sane and clear, it winds up the same, conflicted and confused.

U. **Underinvolved.** You stand on the sidelines of life wishing you were a participant. You don't know how to initiate a relationship, a conversation, an activity. You are withdrawn and would rather bear the pangs of being alone than risk interaction. You are not spontaneous. You allow yourself very little excitement or fun.

N. Neglect of developmental dependency needs. You never seem to be satisfied. No matter how much you anticipate something, soon after it is over, you feel restless and unsatisfied. You are childish and feel like a child a lot of the time. You cry when someone says really beautiful things about you. You feel as though you don't really belong much of the time. You are immature. You refuse to be responsible. You goof off and act childish.

C. Compulsive/addictive behaviors. You have been or are now in an active compulsive/addictive behavior.

T. Trance—carrying the family spell. You still carry the family trance. You are fantasy-bonded and still idealize your parents. You still play the role(s) you played in your family system. Nothing has really changed in your family of origin—same dialogue, same fights, same gossip. Your significant relationship is just like the one you had with one or both of your parents.

I. Intimacy problems. You have trouble in relationships; you've been married more than twice; you choose partners who embody the same emotional patterns of your primary caretakers. You are attracted to seductive sociopathic partners; you avoid partners who are kind, stable, reliable and interested in you. You find "nice" men/women boring. When you start getting too close, you leave a relationship. You confuse closeness with compliance, intimacy with fusion.

O. Overinvolved (otheration). You are drawn to needy people. You confuse love with pity. You are drawn to people who have problems that you think you can fix. You are drawn toward people and situations that are chaotic, uncertain and emotionally painful. You are dying and you see someone else's life flashing before your eyes.

N. Narcissistically deprived. You feel empty inside. You compensate with addiction to chemicals, food, prestige, money, possessions, heroism, sex, power, violence, passive-dependent persons, children, etc., as a way of feeling important and worthwhile. You constantly seek admiration from others. Much of your energy is spent trying to impress others and get their approval.

A. Abuse victim. You were physically, emotionally or sexually abused as a child. You are a victim in life and play that role in most areas of your existence. You feel hopeless about changing anything. Your identity comes from being a victim. You expend lots of energy impressing people with details of your victimization. Or: You were abused and have become an offender. You identified with the abusing parent or caretaker and act just like he or she did.

L. Lack of coping skills (underlearning). You never learned how to do many things necessary for a fully functional life. Your methods of problem-solving do not work, but you continue to use the same ones over and over. You learned ways of caring for your wounds that, in fact, perpetuated them. You have no real knowledge of what is normal. Your bottom-line tolerance is quite abnormal.

F. False self—confused identity. Your self-worth depends on your partner's success or failure. When you're not in a relationship, you feel an inner void. You feel responsible for making your partner happy. You take care of people to give yourself an identity. You wear masks, calculate, manipulate and play games. You act out rigid family roles and/or sex roles. When your partner has a stomachache, *you* take the antacid.

A. Avoid depression through activity. You get actively involved in fixing unstable relationships. The more you are active and in your head, the more you can avoid your depression. You have an activity addiction like gambling, working or sexing.

M. Measured, judgmental and perfectionistic. You have unrealistic expectations of yourself and others. You are rigid and inflexible. You are rigid and judgmental of yourself and others. You're stuck in your attitudes and behavior, even though it hurts to live the way you do.

I. Inhibited trust. You don't trust anyone, including yourself. You doubt the validity of your own feelings, perceptions and judgments.

L. Loss of own reality—damaged and weak boundaries. You take more than 50 percent of the responsibility, guilt and blame for whatever happens in a relationship. You know what others feel or need before you know your own feelings and needs. Any change in the status quo of a relationship is experienced as a threat by you. You feel embarrassed by what others do and take responsibility for their behavior. Or rather than risk abandonment, you withdraw and refuse to get involved.

I. Inflated self-image. You live according to an ideal image of yourself, rather than what your true identity is. You have a grandiose and exaggerated notion of yourself.

E. Emotional constraint (with or without dramatic outbursts). You control your emotions. You have dramatic outbursts of emotions that have been repressed for long periods of time. You have inappropriate outbursts of emotions. You go to great lengths to verbalize every feeling as soon as it enters your awareness. You do this so that you won't have to feel them for very long.

S. Spiritual bankruptcy. You live totally oriented to the outside, believing that your worth and happiness lie outside of you. You have no awareness of your "inner life."

Taking Action

In order to do something about your co-dependency, you must experience the feelings of powerlessness and unmanageability that result from your co-dependent behavior.

A high percentage of the following 12 traits (table 8.1), if practiced regularly, will progressively lead you into a state of powerlessness and unmanageability in your life.

As you read each trait and the behavioral examples that go with it, I invite you to reflect on your own life and see if you identify with any of these behaviors. If you do, I invite you to write out specific examples of a time when this behavior cost you something in your own life.

By writing out your examples in detail, you connect with the *emotions* involved. "You cannot fail with detail," is a therapeutic slogan. The emotions are what move you to change. Feeling the pain of your co-dependent behavior will *move* you to do something about it. The more behaviors you identify with, the more likely you suffer from the dis-ease of co-dependency.

Table 8.1. 12 Essential Traits of Co-dependency That Lead to Powerlessness and Unmanageability

Traits	Behavior
1. Core of Self Is Shame-based This is experienced as being worth-less, flawed and defective.	a. You try to be perfect and to control everyone, or you are a slob living out of control. b. You are guarded about feelings and needs, never depending on anyone so that you will never be caught off guard and show your neediness. c. You are a people-pleaser (nice guy or sweetheart), or difficult and obnoxious (raging and shaming).
2. "Otheration" Experienced as overreacting to people and things outside of you and underreacting to your internal signals.	a. Your self-worth comes solely from others' approval of you. You spend all your energy on "impression management"—feeling excessively responsible or taking care of other people's needs. b. You find people who are needy and can't leave them, or you get excitement for your passionless, apathetic life by finding those who are passionate and exciting and living through them. c. Happiness lies outside yourself. Your decisions are based on what others think, want and expect of you.

Traits	Behavior
3. Denial, Delusion and Defensiveness Experienced as denying or minimizing your pain, your problems and the impact of the problem on you and on others.	a. You overeat, get sick, are chronically depressed and tell yourself that these things are not happening. b. You feel helpless and hopeless as far as doing anything about your problem(s). c. You believe what you want to believe in spite of the facts; you stay isolated so that you receive no feedback.
4. Extremes (Polarization) Experienced as not knowing what normal is—also as grandiosity. You are more than human (special/arrogant) or nothing—less than human (a hopeless slob).	a. You trust everyone or no one. You have no limits. b. You are all or nothing—can't initiate, but once you do you can't stop. You're super-sweet or abusive. You're over-responsible or under-responsible. c. You have no mind of your own or you're rigid, critical, opinionated and judgmental.
5. Primary, Progressive, Pervasive Experienced as tolerating more and more intolerable behavior. You're growing more addicted to something or someone. You feel you are losing yourself.	a. You do things you said you would never do. b. You stay in an abusive relationship for a long duration without help. c. You violate your own values—you become physically sick, depressed or suicidal because of an unhealthy relationship you are in.
6. Emotional Repression Experienced as being numb—not knowing or expressing what you feel, or having dramatic outbursts like rage or frequent crying or panic attacks.	a. Your fear of anger determines what you do or say. b. You feel ashamed when you are happy, angry, afraid or sad. c. You rage and frighten those around you.
7. Noetic Disorders Experienced as being in your head all of the time. Life is a problem to be solved. You're always trying to "figure" things out.	a. You can't arrive at a clear position. You read about and discuss problems rather than taking action. b. You worry about everything—even about things you have no control over. c. You obsess on details and trivialities— what they said, what you said.
8. Disabled Will Experienced as willfulness and "self-will run riot," grandiosity or apathy.	a. You try to will what cannot be willed. b. You try to control everything and everyone. c. You have trouble making a decision.

Traits	Behavior
9. Enmeshed Boundaries You need to be in a relationship at almost any cost. You don't know where you end and another begins—or you isolate and avoid any relationship.	a. You don't know when you are tired, hungry or wanting sex. b. You give up yourself or try to live up to others' expectations of you. c. You expect others to know what you need, feel or want.
10. Narcissistic Deprivation Experienced as insatiability. Nothing ever seems like it's enough—especially praise, admiration and attention.	a. You use your children to give you admiration and love. b. You need money, possessions and public acclaim in order to feel worthwhile. c. You have relationships with very needy people who adore you and feel as though they can't leave you.
11. Communication Problems Experienced as continued relationship problems. No one seems to understand you or give you what you need. You are confused by others' verbal and nonverbal signals.	a. You talk too much or not at all. You don't say what you mean or mean what you say or know what you mean. b. You apologize all the time, believing that what you say is unimportant. You take a long time getting to the point. c. You talk indirectly. You say, "It's cold in here," rather than, "Please raise the thermostat." You rarely ask for what you want.
12. Emptiness You feel like you're standing on the sidelines watching your life go by. You rarely feel connected to people and events around you.	a. You're frequently depressed and feel as though life has no meaning. You resent what you are doing—feel like a victim. b. You feel powerless to change your life. You don't like to be alone for very long. c. You're in an act most of the time, therefore you never feel really connected with others.

SUMMARY

The key points in this chapter can be summed up using the letters of the phrase **MOST COMMON DIS-EASE.**

Major Family Problem—Co-dependence

The most common family problem is co-dependence. In a family system the whole is greater than the sum of the parts. Therefore, if the family is dysfunctional, all the members share to some degree in that dysfunction. They are described as co-dependent.

Otheration

The word "otheration" is used to describe the core problem in co-dependence. All members of a dysfunctional family live in reaction to the major distressor. Since the distress is a threat to the members' existence, they must be alert and on guard all the time. They therefore have no time to go inward and care for their own feelings, needs or wants.

Survival Behaviors as Symptoms of Abandonment

Co-dependence is a set of normal reactive survival behaviors. Co-dependence is a symptom of the abandonment you have gone through.

Typical Structure in Any Dysfunctional Family

Any dysfunctional family will have common structure. The adult children of such families will embody similar behavioral traits.

Cultural Phenomenon

Our culture defines co-dependence as normal. The whole society is built on the poisonous pedagogy and in many ways operates like a dysfunctional family.

Outer-directed

Our society has been described as conformist and self-image actualizing rather than self-actualizing. Books like The Lonely Crowd *and* The Organization Man *describe this with great thoroughness.*

Marriage as Co-dependence

Our ideal of marriage in American society is actually a co-dependent relationship ($\frac{1}{2} \times \frac{1}{2} = \frac{1}{4}$).

Manipulative Lifestyle

Manipulation, pretending (lying) and playing the game are not only socially acceptable, they are positively encouraged.

Other-Directed

People-pleasing and being nice are looked upon with the highest regard in our current social life. Acting *selfless is more important than* being *selfless.*

Normal = Neurotic

What was once considered normal (monarchial patriarchy) is now seen as neurotic (deep democracy). It is now clear just how life-denying and uncreative many of our accepted social norms are.

Deselfment

The core of co-dependency is the lack of solid selfhood, or deselfment. I like to define it as "a dis-ease of the developing self resulting from the failure to achieve ego strengths at the age-appropriate developmental stages that is manifested as intimacy dysfunction in adult relationships."

Incest Families as Identified Patient

The high incidences of incest and sexual abuse uncovered in recent years point to incest families as the identified patient in a sexually addicted and sexually shameless society.

Step One

I've presented an outline for taking a written first step in doing something about your co-dependency.

Emotional Numbness

When we are numbed out emotionally, we are set up for addictions. Some addictions keep us numb and unable to feel our shame and loneliness. Some addictions distract us from our numbness—gambling, sex and work are addictions that distract through excitement.

Apathetic Relationships

Because of our low self-esteem, we allow ourselves to settle for mediocrity and lack of excitement. Apathetic relationships are predictable and safe.

Spiritual Bankruptcy

The spiritual life is an inner life. Shame-based people become what Terry Kellogg calls "human doings" rather than "human beings." In co-dependency, we lose touch with our inner life. We live from the outside, making persons, activities or substances our whole life. Co-dependency has been referred to as a "conflict of gods."

Emotions Subjugated to Logic

"Don't be so emotional" is a commonplace saying in poisonous pedagogy households. Emotions are considered weak and should be ruled by reason. Being rational and intellectual are a cover-up for emotions.

Road Map for *Recovering* Your Disabled Will: Stage I—Finding a New Family of Affiliation

In the midst of winter, I found within me an invincible summer.

ALBERT CAMUS

At some point in our lives, we have to grow up if we want to be our own authentic selves. The natural place for this transition to begin is adolescence. Adolescence is characterized by what Erik Erikson calls the Identity Crisis. Each of us needs to answer the question, "Who am I?" Adolescence calls us to leave home, find our own values and create our own destiny.

Leaving home includes both physical and emotional leaving. Leaving home means becoming your own person. Even in the most functional family, leaving home is a painful and difficult task. Saying good-bye to parents and choosing our own values are parts of a long and arduous process.

Those of us with damaged self-esteem, who identify ourselves as adult children, never really negotiated adolescence. Some of us may have never fully negotiated pre-adolescence.

For many of us, our autonomy was not balanced by a healthy sense of shame. We internalized our shame and lost contact with it as an emotion that provided a good framework of limits. Once internalized, shame was no longer available to us to monitor *the limits* within which our will could healthily function. Without our shame, we became *shameless and grandiose.*

For adult children to grow up and find our identity, we have to give up our delusions of grandeur and our need to control. Our wills have gone astray. We are *full of will.* We've lost our true freedom of choice in our willfulness. We have to give up being absolutizing and willful children and become willing adults. A willing adult lives life within the "limits" of finitude and human possibility. An adult child lives life in polarized grandiosity, either feeling hopeless (a symptom of grandiosity) or feeling godlike.

As a drinking alcoholic, I often felt unique, sometimes to the point of being extraordinary. I can remember believing that I was the most sensitive of all men. I told myself that I drank because I experienced human suffering in a way few others knew. Then after drunken episodes, I experienced myself as the most screwed-up person I knew. I felt degraded and wormlike. I was worthless. Both polarities—being extraordinary to the point of arrogance and being worthless to the point of being a worm—are forms of grandiosity. In my recovery, I learned that I was an "extraordinary worm." For co-dependents, hopelessness can be a manifestation of grandiosity. Hopelessness declares that I am so unique among humans that *there is no possibility of recovery for me.* A truly hopeless person is frozen in apathy and despair, saying nothing and doing nothing.

Grandiosity accounts for the cycles of control and release that all addicts go through. For 12 years I quit drinking every Lent. I've been on a hundred diets and have lost 5,000 pounds. When I smoked, I'd cut down to six cigarettes a day and do that for a month or two. The control phase is a part of every addiction. It is only an illusion and feeds the addict's grandiose belief that he can control his addiction.

Recovering Our Disabled Wills

The first stage of recovery from co-dependence is recovering our disabled wills. This involves letting go of any attempt to control the issues in our lives we've been trying to control. I asked you to write out a first step for co-dependence, and to pay attention to details because writing out concrete, specific, behavioral details about co-dependency helps us to feel the powerlessness and unmanageability of our lives.

Without experiencing my powerlessness and the unmanageability of my life, I stay in the grandiose delusion that *I can control* my husband's drinking, children's grades, parents' abuse, booze, work, eating, smoking, etc. The first decision adult children who want to grow up need to make is to surrender.

Dr. Harry Tiebout, who was Bill W.'s (the founder of AA) therapist, made a great contribution to our understanding of how to break the denial of an addiction by distinguishing between "compliance" and "surrender."

Compliance is motivated by guilt. In the last year of my seminary days, I asked to see a psychiatrist because of my sense of hopelessness. I told him I thought I was an alcoholic and that I needed help. He spent considerable time with me discussing my relationship with my mother. During this period he gave me prescriptions for sleeping pills and tranquilizers. I started feeling a lot better. I even *cut down* on my drinking! I enjoyed our visits and felt a sense of relief about my life. At the end of about three months, I terminated my treatment. But soon my drinking got worse and worse. One and a half years later, I committed myself to Austin State Hospital for alcoholism. On December 11, 1965, I surrendered.

Surrender is motivated by the acceptance of shame. For an addict, surrender is the first true act of freedom since beginning the addiction. It certainly was for me.

Dr. Tiebout wisely understood that denial and delusion can continue in spite of the acknowledgment of guilt. Guilt can even be a way to distract yourself from the real problem. For example, it's not at all uncommon to hear a smoker or an overeater condemn themselves for creating a dangerous threat to their health with their addictions. *Talking about it is certainly preferable to stopping smoking or overeating.* As an alcoholic, I frequently felt guilty for the things I did when I drank. It was a lot easier to admit to these harmful consequences than to admit my drinking was out of control. By being guilty, I could deny that my life was unmanageable and out of control. Guilt was a useful way to continue my denial. Compliance and guilt are ways that many an unwary therapist has been hoodwinked by an addict.

Shame-based people tend to seek and even embrace punishment. The two therapists I went to before joining a 12-Step group praised my honesty and commitment. They said that by my acknowledging what drinking was doing to my life, I was being responsible. Both therapists were psychiatrists and both put me on chemical medication. Admitting my guilt and paying for it enhanced the denial of what I most deeply feared, which was to quit my drinking. To quit drinking would necessitate my feeling as badly as I really felt about my drinking and my life. I would have to feel my shame.

The only way out of the compulsive/addictive shame cycle is to *embrace the shame.* Embracing the shame means that we actually feel ashamed. We feel the limits that shame imposes. We acknowledge that we are powerless to control our problems and that we need help. That is what it means to surrender.

The problem of the disabled will is the problem of denial and the pain that denial ultimately brings. By the time most of us are ready to do something about our lives, our pain has reached a point of great intensity. As my shame-based self went deeper and deeper into hiding, the intensity of my false self increased proportionately. My addiction to hiding my shame created the chronic pain of knowing that I was not the person I pretended to be (hiding in priestly robes) or was supposed to be. I literally was beside myself. Tolstoy once said, "Men often act unlike themselves." Animals cannot become deanimalized. Tigers don't become detigered. But we humans can become dehumanized. The "otheration" of co-dependence is dehumanization.

For me the dis-ease (co-dependence) had to wait until I dealt with its cover-up, my alcoholism. This point is crucial. For any acting-out substance abuser, the use of the substance has to be stopped before you can treat the co-dependence (the disease of the disease). Alcoholism is caused by drinking alcohol. Alcoholism is a primary disease. That means it has to be treated first. The same is true for other drugs and chemicals.

Food, sex, work and people addictions are somewhat different. You can't just stop eating, drinking, sexing, working or relating to people completely. Total abstinence would bring death to self and the species. Each addiction has its own particular nuances for recovery, but there are some commonalities. One commonality is surrendering the grandiose will.

Identify Formation

Whether you've identified with co-dependency or not, *everyone must go through a self-recovery, uncovery, discovery process*. Those of you graced by growing up in a well-functioning family must go through identity formation. In the natural life cycle, unencumbered by dysfunction, this process may take 40 years. Socrates said, "The unexamined life is not worth living." The Jesuit poet Gerard Manley Hopkins wrote, "What I do is me: for that I came."

For those of us who are adult children, the journey is not qualitatively any different from that of a person from a functional family. We just got started a whole lot later.

The journey to wholeness is a process made up of disenchantment and grieving. Our layers of defense must be collapsed one by one. The Buddhist Masters speak of enlightenment as progressive disillusionment.

We must break through our delusions. Figure 9.1 gives you a way to visualize the layers of defense.

Stage I Recovery details the outer layers. The outer layer defenses comprise our self-indulging habits and painkillers (our addictions) and our characterological strategies of defense against shame. Stage I deals with our compulsive/addictive behaviors and our control madness.

There are many ways one can begin the process. Most often it begins with new awareness. Shame keeps us so rigidly in hiding that *we spend most of our energy on our defenses.* Our mind is narrowed by emotional repression and our awareness is vastly limited.

Figure 9.1. Layers of Defense Hiding Shame Core

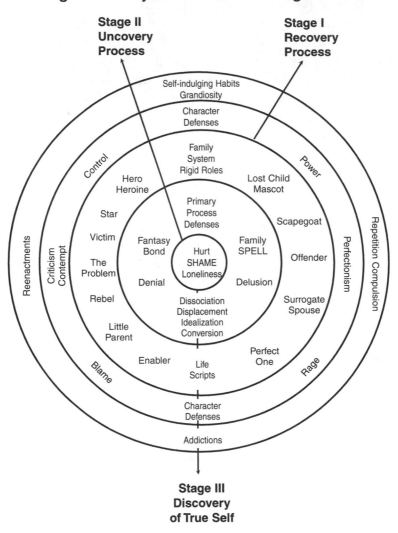

Awareness can come from hearing a lecture or reading a book. It can come from a friend sharing his experience with us. I've received thousands of letters in response to the television series, which prompted this book.

The first time I drew a five-generation family map, I was comforted by a new awareness. For the first time I could see that there was something bigger than me or any one person in my family. I saw that I was carrying multi-generational hurt and pain. This is one of the positive aspects of family systems theory—*it removes causality and blame.* Everyone is responsible and accountable, but no one is to blame. If you want to use the genogram to probe your own family system, see my book *Family Secrets.*

Family systems theory also challenged me to do something about myself. It suggested that if I quit playing my role in the family system, the system would change. In fact, systems thinking puts the responsibility squarely on our individual shoulders.

Another way that the walls of defense are collapsed is through a confrontation process called intervention. We can literally intervene and confront another person's defenses. This form of confrontation needs careful planning and consideration.

It is important to be aware of our own motives when considering intervention. We need to ask ourselves, "Am I doing this to help this person? Am I really willing to be there for them?" Some of the pioneers working with addiction developed methods of intervention that have proved to be highly successful. I heartily recommend that if you are living in a dysfunctional family and are thinking about confronting the primary addict in your system, you seek some professional advice before you do it. This means going to someone who knows how to set up an intervention.

The most powerful ways that our shame defenses crumble are through actual pain and suffering. Pain is a teacher that we cannot argue with. Our defenses are there to cover up the pain. Their purpose is to avoid suffering. When we start experiencing suffering and pain that is greater than the pain we are trying to avoid, the walls start tumbling down. We can no longer control our defenses against our deep inner pain.

There is an old slogan in 12-Step programs that says, "No pain, no gain." Another therapeutic slogan says, "The way out of our pain is to go through our pain." Personally, I needed the pain before I was *willing to risk* doing something about my life. If you took the first step for co-dependence and experienced your powerlessness, you may *be willing to take action.*

Talking about our problems and mapping out our families' dys-function is not the same as taking action. Action means that I've let go of control and I'm willing to listen to others and *do it their way,* rather than my own way.

I dabbled with doing something about my alcoholism for a year before I surrendered. I tried to find an easier way, believing I didn't have to do what others had to do to get their alcoholism arrested. Finally, I reached an excruciating level of pain and vol-untarily committed myself to Austin State Hospital. I didn't like it there and I thank God I'll never forget it. In six days I was released and headed for a 12-Step program.

In my earlier attempt at quitting drinking I felt the 12-Step pro-gram was too simple for me. I had degrees in theology and phi-losophy and had taught both of these at the university level. I felt that my problems were more complex than those of most of the people I met at the meetings. I felt that my drinking was a symp-tom of a deep and profoundly sensitive soul. This, of course, was all hogwash. Intellectuals create the most grandiose denials.

I thank God there were some other intellectuals around when I went back to the 12-Step program. One man especially was impor-tant for me. His name was Fran and without him, I don't know what I would have done. He was the instrument of God's grace for me.

Going back to the 12-Step group after leaving the state hospital was the most important experience of my life. There was warmth, kindness and great patience, tempered by firmness and rigorous honesty. My Hero and Superachiever roles continuously got in the way. I was used to being in control and distinguishing myself. I needed to be the *best* drunk seeking recovery. I needed to do the 12 Steps perfectly.

My Surrender and Recovery

I quietly learned that control and perfectionism had reduced my life to shambles. I had to surrender and acknowledge my power-lessness. I had to feel as bad as I really felt. My use of alcohol and pills kept me from my feelings of deep shame and loneliness. My control and good-guy act kept me away from my fear and sadness. Now I was losing both my masks and the shame was starting to break through. For years I had been addicted to my shame. I lived my life guardedly so that I would never be caught off guard. During the years of studying to be a priest, I hid behind my Roman collar and black robe. I was beside myself for so long, I didn't even know how lonely and empty I was. Coming out of hiding was terrifying, but the love and warmth of the group made it bearable. In fact, I couldn't believe it. The more I shared my truest feelings, the more acceptable I was to them. I found that being myself was easy. Trying to control and doing my act—that took energy. This was the first step in recovery.

My New Family

The group was my new family. It was my family of affiliation. I was experiencing being mirrored and accepted by the group. We were a network of friends sharing our common problems. There was social equality and mutual respect. Each time I went to a meeting, I felt better. I couldn't understand it. Nothing was really happening. All we did was share our experiences or talk about one of the 12 Steps.

I now understand what was happening then. I had found *a new family. The rules were different in this family.* It was not only okay to make mistakes, it was a requirement for membership. Everyone was equally vulnerable. There were no leaders. The group was based on mutual respect, social equality and rigorous honesty. People talked about their feelings.

I was accepted just for me—not because of my performance or achievements. This helped me recover my self-esteem. Each time I went to a meeting, I was coming out of hiding and *reducing my shame.* Each time I talked about myself in an honest way (this was a gradual process), I broke old family rules. I started being real.

My own belief is that adult children need to find a new family of affiliation. Our co-dependence was fostered by broken relationships. It is a product of social dysfunction. Therefore, we need a social context for healing.

The new family can be one of the numerous 12-Step groups. It can also be: an ACoA or co-dependency group; a therapy group; an honest, nonshaming church group; a therapist or a good friend that you can be honest with without being shamed. A group is crucial because of the shame. The only way out of the toxic shame is to embrace the toxic shame. Since toxic shame loves darkness and isolation, we must expose it to the light.

Recovering Self-Esteem

Only through this honest, truthful, sharing and mirroring can we recover our self-esteem. My shame said that I was flawed, defective and unacceptable. The pain of my addiction finally forced me to show myself. When I showed myself, I found that I was accepted and loved. I recovered my sense of self-esteem. I started accepting myself. As I accepted myself, I accepted my feelings. As my trust grew, I came out of hiding more and more. I broke the no-talk rule: I shared my secrets, I was willing to be vulnerable, to be scared, awkward or embarrassed over the state of my life. As I felt and expressed those feelings, my three-trillion circuited computer began to function better and better. My group called this "getting your brains out of hock." It was true: After I expressed my emotions, I had clearer insight. I started trusting my own judgment and perceptions. Consequently, I started making decisions. I chose to live one day at a time.

I also started recovering my own sense of values. As an alcoholic studying to be a priest, I lived a double life. One self was the young seminarian praying and meditating daily. The other self hid pills and whiskey in my room, using these chemicals late at night when the others were asleep. That double life caught up with me. I felt split. I was living a life unlike myself. I was doing things I did not really value. When we give up our compulsive/addictive behavior and begin a recovery program, we can start to clarify our own values.

The First Stages of Recovery

However, the early stages of recovery are painful. You have nothing to substitute for the pain. As you get honest, there is often anger and hostility at yourself for messing up so badly and for so long. If you were addicted to a euphoric chemical substance, there is the actual physical withdrawal. There is emotional withdrawal in other addictions. There is obsession and preoccupation with the addiction itself and a grieving over its loss. With addictions like work, food, religion and sex, there is confusion over how much of it is safe, since you can't stop working, eating or worshiping, and you can't become celibate. These are hard questions and need time and trial and error. You need lots of patience and it's a great help to get a sponsor. A sponsor is someone who has walked before you, who is working a successful program and who is *modeling* the quality of life that you desire.

All this takes time. Recovery is a process, not an event. For those of you who are not addicts, growing up is a process and not an event. We didn't get messed up overnight, and it will take energy to modify our troubled behavior. *We need to learn to live one day at a time.*

Living one day at a time is a way to relativize the absolutizing and grandiose will. For 30 years I've quit drinking one day at a time. I've never quit forever. Precisely because you cannot quit forever. Quitting forever is grandiosity. The paradox of all this is that as I became willing to accept my limitations, I actually gained control over my life. Living one day at a time is a discipline that confronts our willfulness. The new willingness to be in pain, to be confused and to accept the fact that recovery is a long process goes a long way in changing the grandiosity of the old willfulness. Living a day at a time means that we are willing to let go of trying to control things. It means that we have stopped looking for the grand salvation experience—the visitation by God that heals everything.

The will is the most dis-eased part of any adult child's co-dependence. I believed for years I could stop drinking anytime I really wanted to. I pointed to my times of abstinence as proof of this. It was a fact that I could stop. But I couldn't *stay stopped.*

All of us adult children have a distorted relationship to our will. We are willful and believe we can exercise control over all kinds of things—like other people's emotions, our relationships and our own emotions. My self-will ran riot.

When our will can only will itself, it loses all contact with reality. It is blind. When I was not able to resolve the problems of my life through sheer willpower, I became hopeless. It was all or nothing.

What I learned from my new family of affiliation was that there were many things in life that I have *no control over.*

Early on I was taught a prayer that said, "God grant me the serenity to accept the things I cannot change, give me the courage to change the things I can and the wisdom to know the difference." This prayer clearly makes a distinction between being willing and being willful. The willing person accepts limited freedom and human finitude. In fact, willingness is rooted in healthy shame. Healthy shame posits a Higher Power. By turning my will over to a Higher Power (which I call God), I got my willpower back.

The 12-Step Programs

The 12-Step programs are unsurpassed in helping arrest compulsive/addictive behaviors. I'd like to briefly comment on the 12 Steps.

The first three steps state:

1. We admitted we were powerless over *whatever the compulsive/addictive behavior was* and that our lives had become unmanageable.
2. We came to believe that a power greater than ourselves could restore us to sanity.
3. We made a decision to turn our wills and our lives over to the care of God as we understand him.

These steps embody the unequivocal acceptance of limitation. They profess that the only way to deal with the addiction is to surrender. All attempts to *control* the addiction lead to the addict's life becoming unmanageable. The steps then address the spiritual bankruptcy created by the internalized shame.

Internalized shame has an absolutist quality. If I am a mistake, if I am flawed and defective as a human being, then *repair and reparation are not possible.* This hopelessness is grandiosity. This grandiosity is created by shame itself. Shame binds all feelings. This in turn mars reason and judgment. All that is left is blind willpower. The will to will is playing God. So the steps immediately address this idolatry and spiritual emptiness by first calling on a power greater than ourselves and then calling that power God. The steps are clear about not trying to *control* anyone else's conception of God (as if we could).

Winning by Losing

Steps 1 and 3 offer us the chance to embrace our shame and vulnerability. Only by embracing the shame can we come out of hiding and give up trying to control the shame. Paradoxically, the only way we can win is by losing. The steps also offer a restoration of the interpersonal bridge. Realizing that a shame-based person trusts no one (why would I trust any person when I couldn't trust my own father?), the steps ask us to trust someone or something greater than anything human.

Steps 4, 5, 6 and 7 begin the process of moving us from shame to guilt. These steps say:

4. We made a searching and fearless moral inventory of ourselves.
5. We admitted to God, to ourselves and another human being the exact nature of our wrongs.
6. We were entirely ready to have God remove all these defects of character.
7. We humbly asked God to remove all our shortcomings.

By embracing our shame, we can look at our shame. We can take a fearless moral (not immoral) inventory of ourselves. We can honestly and squarely face our selves.

By taking these steps, I became aware of how my character defects were strategies I used to transfer my shame to others. My perfectionism, for example, was a great way not to feel shame. How could I be vulnerable if I never made a mistake? And since I felt exceptional, those around me were usually one down.

My rage was another way I kept people away from me. While in a rage, I was mood-altered and didn't have to feel my shame. Below all the character defects was a fear of exposure. That fear flowed from my shame.

The admission to self, others and God in Step 5 is a way to come out of hiding. Shame loves secrecy and darkness. To come out into the light is a way to overcome it. Steps 6 and 7 focus on becoming willing. I was entirely willing. I was vulnerable and asked for help and forgiveness. Asking for help is something no shame-based person would do. *Shame believes that it doesn't have any right to depend on others and therefore ask for help.*

Steps 8 and 9 are action steps. They take us into healthy guilt. Healthy guilt is moral shame, the feeling that safeguards our conscience and the need for reparation:

8. We made a list of all the people we have harmed and became willing to make amends.
9. We made direct amends to such people, whenever possible, except where to do so would injure them or others.

Relativizing Shame

Internalized shame feels irreparable. Therefore, it must be externalized. This means relativizing its grandiose claims.

Steps 1 through 7 do precisely that. As shame is externalized and relativized, I can *feel shame* over some things I've done without concluding that I'm defective as a person. Shame as an emotion moves me to do something about what I've done. Shame triggers my guilt, which triggers my conscience. I can then take action to repair the damage that I had done. With guilt I made a *mistake* and I can correct it wherever possible. Steps 1 and 9 restore me to respectability. I become a self-responsible person with a conscience.

Step 10 says, "We continued to take personal inventory and when we were wrong, we promptly admitted it."

This is a maintenance step. It asks us to stay in touch with the healthy feeling of shame. Such a feeling tells us we are limited, finite and human. It tells us that *we will make mistakes* and that it is healthy to acknowledge them. With the restoration of healthy shame, we have accepted our humanness and our limitations. We can stop playing God. Our wills are restored.

I will discuss Steps 11 and 12 in chapter 11. My own belief is that they are generally not a dominant part of this first stage of recovery.

I don't wish to impose my experience of the journey to wholeness on anyone else. No one can tell others how to find their own authentic selves. Everyone's journey may look different from the outside. Many readers may not have any experience with the 12 Steps or any other recovery program. Yet even the most functional persons need to examine and update their childhood, emotionally separate from their family of origin and grieve the all-too-human wounds that come from life's hurts. Some form of this journey is required if you are to achieve your own solid self-esteem.

For those of you who identify with compulsive/addictive problems, the stages I'm outlining are more in the order of logic. In actual experience, things are not quite so neat and tidy. People may enter different stages at different times and by different doors.

Having said that, there is still some value in offering you ordered stages of recovery. I've seen several people jump to Stage III and do higher consciousness work without going through their ego work. I've seen people who have purported to have spiritual healings but who have never done any of the painful shame-reduction work I spoke about in this chapter. I have seen them maintain this spirituality for a while, only to go back to their compulsive/addictive lifestyle later on. And I've seen them become spiritually addicted.

I believe I went through this spiritual addiction. I was in a monastery at 21 years of age. I meditated every morning. I prayed (sometimes six hours at a time) and fasted. I was celibate for nine and one-half years. My own evaluation of that experience is that I was totally unprepared for the spiritual discipline that such spirituality demands (I hope God chalked up the nine and one-half years of celibacy).

We need strong ego boundaries before we are ready to let go of our boundaries (Stage III work, discussed in chapter 11). Adult children who were abandoned through sexual, physical or emotional violence need to do repair work on their ego boundaries before they are ready to soar into higher consciousness. What I've described as Stage I work does not yet repair those ego boundaries. More work needs to be done for that to occur.

The Dark Side of Stage I

One can become addicted to Stage I work. I know people who quit drinking and drugging and became addicted to their guru, a religion, even the 12-Step program itself. This happens because Stage I recovery is a first-order change. A first-order change is a change in behavior within a given way of behaving. In the case of Stage I, people are still *dependent* on the group. They have not yet achieved a solid sense of self-esteem. They have not yet grieved their childhood wounds. They are dry and abstinent but they are still compulsive. They frequently act out compulsively with something other than alcohol. The 12-Step program of Alcoholics Anonymous calls this kind of acting out a "dry drunk."

All in all, Stage I brings one a better sense of balance (yin/yang). Life is no longer all or nothing. The peaks are lower and the valleys not as deep.

S U M M A R Y

Let me summarize Stage I using the phrase **STAGE I RECOVERY.**

Surrender to Pain

Surrender means I give up trying to control my compulsive/ addictive behavior. I am willing to let others help me and do it their way. I'm willing to go to any lengths to get well.

Trust Others with Your Secrets

As you seek help, you are willing to label yourself an alcoholic, co-dependent, drug addict, sex addict, etc. You are willing to trust enough to ask for help. The labeling is crucial. You can't heal what has no name. An old 12-Step program slogan is, "We are as sick as our darkest secrets."

Affiliation Needs

As you surrender to a recovery group, you come out of isolation. You are willing to let people care for you. You receive new mirroring, warmth and trust. You start believing that you can depend on the group.

Group Support

You now belong to a new family. There are good models here for your journey toward wholeness. You receive education on the nature of addiction and raise your awareness. You pick someone to be your sponsor who can model how to walk the walk for you.

Experience Powerlessness and Unmanageability

You experience this out of your pain. You come to see the power-lessness more and more as you get your "brains out of hock."

Ist-Order Change

Stage I is a first-order change because you have not done your work on your family system. First-order change is a change of behavior within a given way of behaving. You are no longer acting out, but you are very dependent on the group. You are not yet your own person. You have to be careful that you do not become addicted to recovery. I've seen people embrace spiritual programs, make a god out of the religious guru. They stop drinking and drugging, etc., but they become addicted to the guru. One can be dry and abstinent and still be compulsive. In AA this is known as a dry drunk. *Recovering people frequently get addicted to recovery because they have not done the second-order change work.*

Relativize the Absolute Will

You live one day at a time. You are learning to delay gratification. You accept the things you cannot change and change the things you can, and you are learning the difference. You accept limitations.

Experience Emotions

You are no longer psychically numb. You are starting to experience your emotions. You feel awkward, like a teenager who is having emotions for the first time. You grieve the good times. You feel shame and embarrassment. You grieve over the loss of control and over a past you wish had been different and often seems wasted. Healing demands that you experience these emotions. You can't heal what you don't feel.

Collapse of Grandiosity

You have given up your denials about being able to control your compulsive/addictive behavior. You have given up your grand expectations. *You are more realistic and have more realistic expectations of yourself and others. You can laugh more at things. They are not so dramatic or serious.*

Oneness with Self

You see yourself as acceptable in the eyes of your group. You are starting to accept yourself. You are accepting responsibility for your life and know that your happiness will depend on you. You're starting to trust your feelings, perceptions and wants.

Values Restored

Even amid confusion and painful feelings of shame, you feel a sense of cleanness about yourself. You experienced yourself as split for a long time—living in opposition to your own values. Now you feel good about clarifying and living your values.

Externalizing Shame

You have come out of hiding. You are committed to self-actualization and/or some recovery type of program. You are willing to be vulnerable and ask for help. As you embrace your shame, you see that you are not so bad. You're starting to grasp that 95 percent of your shame is about what happened to you and is not about you. Shame is now a feeling and not a state of being.

Rigorous Honesty

You are being confronted by your teacher, therapist, sponsor or other group members on your character defects—such as perfectionism, judgment, rage, criticalness, manipulation and power-seeking. You are confronted when you are dishonest. You are becoming aware when you are being dishonest.

Yin/Yang Balance

Your life is becoming balanced. It's not all or nothing. The peaks and valleys are not as dramatic.

Road Map for *Uncovering* Your Lost Self: Stage II—Breaking the Original Spell

I saw the angel in the marble and I just chiseled til I set him free.

MICHELANGELO

Growing up means leaving home and becoming a self-supporting adult. I think this is the hardest task any human being has to face. It means breaking the fantasy bond and facing separation and aloneness.

Growing up means leaving home and giving up our family system roles. It means bringing our primary ego defenses into conscious focus so that we can use them more appropriately. These last layers of defense cover the most precious core of our selves. To get at this part of ourselves involves emotional pain. This is the legitimate suffering we fear most.

For those of you recovering from compulsive/addictive behavior, Stage I was a *sine qua non* for survival. It's hard to imagine anyone doing Stage II work well without the achievements of Stage I. In Stage I, I found a new family with new models of maturity. I began to trust and share my vulnerable inner self. I experienced acceptance in the eyes of others and began to accept myself. I felt like I *truly belonged* in my new network of relationships. I worked on my defensive character defects. I started feeling my emotions. I quit trying to control my relationships. I gave up the grand adventure and settled into the "terrible dailiness," living one day at a time. I lost all conscious desire to drink or use chemicals. I recovered my disabled will and self-respect.

I did this for some 10 years before I became aware of my co-dependency issues. I had behavior-modified my alcoholism. My disease was arrested.

Co-dependence—the Core of Compulsivity

Despite 10 years of recovery, I hadn't yet dealt with the *dis-ease of my disease*. Vernon Johnson called it the *ism* of alcoholism. It's what I am calling co-dependence—the core and root of any and all compulsive/addictive behavior.

After 10 years of recovery, I found that I was still highly compulsive. Perhaps that's a good guideline for Stage II work. How compulsive are you still? Can you take a first step on co-dependence and honestly not identify with it?

Stage I allows us to see what Michelangelo called the angel in the marble. Once we've accepted that we are an angel, we still have the job of chiseling to set ourselves free. Stage I was a first-order change. We modified our behavior. We stopped using, eating, sexing, obsessing on relationships, buying, gambling, smoking, etc., and joined the human race. We accepted limitations. Two layers of our defensive shell were gone. But we still remained dependent. Many of us transferred our compulsivity to something else. Work addicts quit working and started drinking; smokers quit smoking and started eating; alcoholics quit drinking and started working addictively.

Stage I recovery can become an addiction itself. We can use the program to avoid dealing with the problems of everyday life.

When I worked as counselor-consultant for the Palmer Drug Abuse Program (PDAP) in Houston, person after person came to me who was using the program to avoid real honest responsibilities. Almost all had money problems caused by compulsive spending. In many cases, they were working a frantic program, but refused to go to work.

Dispelling the SPELL

We have to treat our co-dependence if we are to uncover the core problem. This requires uncovering the delusions of the original family trance—the SPELL. Stage II is disenchantment. Children are magical and make gods out of their parents. Disenchantment is a natural process. Many primitive tribes construct situations of disenchantment to mark the entry into adulthood.

The initiation rite for Hopi children is a good example. The rite centers around kachinas, masked gods who visit the village. During the rites of passage, the kachinas tell the children secret stories and dance to entertain them. The kachinas frighten them with ogre masks. As the ceremony reaches its climax, the children are taken to huts to await a kachina dance. As they wait, they can hear the dancing gods calling as they approach the hut. But to the children's amazement, the kachinas enter without their masks. The initiates learn, for the first time, that the kachinas *are their parents impersonating the gods.*

The experience of disenchantment is the beginning of mature consciousness. We have to move from the delusions of childhood fantasy to the disenchantment of adult life. I once heard the psychologist-theologian Sam Keen say, "We have to move from the illusion of certainty to the certainty of illusion."

The family SPELL is powerful. My friend Howard Trush compares it to instinct in animals. He writes:

It is learned outside of one's awareness, it becomes just as much second nature to us as the spoken language.[1]

---

[1] Howard Trush, *Close Encounters of the Intimate Kind; or How to Stay a Couple by Really Trying* (New York: Vantage Press, 1985).

Stage II involves breaking this SPELL. This is a second-order change. First-order change involves the change of one behavior to another within a given way of behaving. Second-order change involves a change from one way of behaving to another. In second-order change, we give up our compulsivity. That certainly does not mean that we can go back to using chemicals at this stage. *The ingestive addictions have their own inherent addictive properties.* Current research suggests that once you have passed over a certain line of tolerance, you cannot return to using in a normal way.

Stage II is the process of going back and uncovering the original pain that occurred as a result of our abandonment. We have to make the feelings about our abandonment real. This means giving up the primary process ego defenses. These include the denial and delusion about our parents and family.

Externalized Shame

By embracing this deep internalized shame, we can begin to externalize it. We began the externalization process in Stage I. It is a long process (it will probably go on until death for some of us). The externalization process is a process by which we (a) transform the shame back into a feeling (internalization made our shame into a state of being); (b) reduce the shame; (c) give the shame back to those "shameless" source figures who interpersonally transferred it to us; (d) transform the energy of the shame into positive action.

Giving the shame back to "shameless" caretakers involves dealing with our carried shame. This was the shame our source figures dumped on us through their control, perfectionism, critical judgment, power trips, contempt and rage. This was the shame we carried whenever our caretakers acted "shameless" and played God. This was the shame resulting from the poisonous pedagogy.

Induced shame doesn't mean that it isn't our feeling of shame. It *is our feeling of shame.* But much of it resulted from our caretakers covering up their shame with one of their defense strategies against shame.

For example, Mom feels shame over the state of her life, her children's suffering and her alcoholic, nonintimate marriage. When the pain is too intense, she yells at the kids to clean up their rooms or do the dishes. In her verbal shoulds, oughts and condemnation, she shames her children. She shames her children as a way of defending against her shame. The children carry the shame. The transactional theorists call this "passing the hot potato."

Externalizing the shame is the process of owning the shame and then uncovering the sources from whence it came. Much internalized shame *does not belong to the person who carries it*. Therefore, it must be reduced and given back. Realizing how we were abandoned and expressing our feelings about it are the beginnings of Stage II. Alice Miller writes:

> *The greatest of all narcissistic wounds—not to have been loved just as one truly was—cannot heal without the work of mourning.*[2]

Mourning is the ultimate work of the externalization process. Mourning is the only way to heal our unmet developmental dependency needs. Since we cannot go back in time and be children and get our needs met from our very own parents, we must grieve the loss of our childhood self and our childhood dependency needs. Grief is a complex process that involves a range of human emotions.

Grief work begins with shock and denial. It proceeds to a kind of bargaining, then to hurt, sadness, anger, guilt, remorse and finally, acceptance. In truth, many of us have been stuck in the grief process all our lives. We have been stuck at the levels of shock and denial.

Stage II work builds on the work begun in Stage I. It was there you began to feel again. You can't do the grief work if you can't feel. You can't feel if you are psychically numb.

The grief work is sometimes called the "original pain work." Alice Miller writes:

> *The achievement of freedom . . . is hardly possible without the felt mourning. This ability to mourn, i.e., to give up the*

---

[2] Miller, *The Drama of the Gifted Child*, 85.

illusion of a happy childhood, can restore vitality and cre-
ativity. . . . if a person is able to experience that he was never
loved as a child for what he was, but for his achievements,
success and good qualities . . . and that he sacrificed his
childhood for this love, this will shake him very deeply.[3]

This work is painful and that's why we hold onto our denials and delusions. Why go back to the past? Why go through all that pain again? The fact is, *we really never went through the pain.* We developed a fantasy bond and used our primary ego defenses to avoid the anger, hurt and pain of our abandonment. Then we avoided our avoidance with our rigid roles and characterological defenses. We missed expressing the feelings at the *crucial time.*

We missed it because our caretakers would not allow us to be angry or sad. They justified this with the poisonous pedagogy. We also missed it because it was so painful. Your emotions can only be your emotions by expressing them. Denying our emotions is a way that causes us to lose control over them. Once repressed and denied, *you no longer have your emotions—they have you.*

The repressed emotions form a frozen energy core that *uncon-sciously runs your life.* Compulsive/addictive behavior is by definition *outside our control.* Emotional energy has to go somewhere. You either repress emotions (act them in); project them onto others (say others look needy when you feel shame over your own neediness); or "act them out."

My addiction was an acting-out of my shame. My drunken episodes, which started as a way to feel better and overcome shame, escalated into shameful behaviors. Hanging over the commode after a drinking bout (a fitting place to celebrate toxic shame), I felt deep shame and remorse. What started as a way to cover up shame ended with more shame. This vicious cycle is referred to as a squirrel cage. Alice Miller calls this cycle "the logic of absurdity."

The only way out of this self-destructive style is to embrace our legitimate suffering. *You can only heal what you can feel.* Alice Miller writes:

---

[3] Miller, *The Drama of the Gifted Child,* 56-57.

Only the mourning for what he has missed, missed at the crucial time [emphasis mine] *can lead to real healing.*[4]

There are many ways to do this work. No one way is the right way. Almost all major therapeutic schools offer some help along these lines. My only caution here would be to avoid a therapy that stayed only on the level of "cognitive insight." I agree with Alice Miller when she says:

Problems cannot be solved with words, but only through experience, not merely corrective experience as an adult but . . . Through a reliving of early fear (sadness, anger) . . . Mere words, however skilled . . . will leave the split from which he suffers unchanged or even deepened.[5]

I don't wish to imply that cognitive therapy is not effective and useful. I just do not find it effective at this stage.

I covered my pain with cognitive insight. I was in my recovery for 10 years before I began any *feeling* work. I believed that because I no longer used any mind-changing chemicals, I had arrested my addiction. However, I was still enormously addicted. I was still controlling, out of touch with my feelings, grandiose and compulsive. My marriage grew progressively less intimate and I basically had no close friendships. When a marriage counselor confronted me with my "act," my grandiosity and my loneliness, I was shaken. Being a successful public speaker, TV personality and counselor was a great defense. I received great adulation and praise. I was "helping" all kinds of people. *I was a professional co-dependent.*

The disease of my disease was the insatiable wounded child that ruled my life. *I had to experience that child's pain.*

My belief is that all of us who identify ourselves as co-dependent will have to go through some kind of grief process if we want to be free of our compulsivity. When we are in touch with our true feelings, the energy to act them out is gone. Again, Alice Miller writes:

---

[4] Miller, *The Drama of the Gifted Child,* 43.
[5] Ibid., 99.

It is very striking to see how . . . acting out ceases when the patient begins to experience his own feelings.[6]

The Need for Therapy

While I don't believe everyone needs to be in formal therapy, I believe that many people do. Therapy provides the kind of modeling and mirroring that most of us did not receive from our major caretakers. The kind of therapy is less important (as long as it's feeling work) than the therapist who is doing the work.

Martin Buber, the great Jewish existentialist, studied all the available therapies and concluded that what heals is not so much the theory or the specific technique of the therapist, but the *relationship between the therapist and client*. Our co-dependence resulted from, and ended in, pathological relationships. So a good relationship with a primary caregiver can be a healing phenomenon. Actually, a good loving relationship with anyone is healing. Eric Berne, the founder of transactional analysis, once said, "Love is nature's psychotherapy."

In choosing a therapist, you have every right to ask lots of questions before beginning. You can ask them about their success in treating co-dependency. You can ask about their belief in group therapy.

Why this question? I believe that the most effective therapists working with co-dependency believe in moving their clients into groups. The groups may be 12-Step groups, support groups or interactive therapy groups (ideally, a combination of all three). Co-dependent issues are basically about *relationship problems*.

Dr. Timmen Cermak writes:

> *The primary purpose of a long-term interactive group is to provide a setting in which the issues of co-dependency emerge spontaneously. . . . Interactive group therapy works best when members discover themselves behaving inside the group much as they do in real life—being distrustful, controlling their feelings,*

---

[6] Miller, *The Drama of the Gifted Child.*

sacrificing their own needs to ensure that others are taken care of, revealing only carefully chosen parts of themselves . . . then they finally understand that those behaviors reflect habitual and unconscious patterns, the group can become a laboratory for experimenting with alternative behaviors.[7]

In choosing a therapist or group, I recommend that you use simple criteria. Do you feel safe with this person or group? And can you reveal yourself *without being shamed?* I know people who have been shamed by therapists and by groups. Feeling work can also be done in workshop intensives.

While it certainly is conceivable that one could do this feeling work without formal therapy, it's very difficult. The difficulty lies in the fact that the denial system that has to be broken is the primary ego defense system. The primary ego defenses are activated in early life and function automatically and unconsciously. We can't know what we don't know.

In Stage I, we needed echoing mirrors; in Stage II, we need confronting mirrors. We need confrontative feedback that reflects how we avoid or deny our feelings.

"Containment" is the therapeutic term for keeping a person in his feelings. Containment is done through confrontation. Confrontation is a form of mirroring. We show a person how he looks or sounds to us.

For example, a man in a share group I used to be in described how he had totally accepted his wife's recent affair. As he spoke, *his fist was clenched and his voice tone was shaky.* I simply said to him, "Herbert, when you said you had accepted your wife's affair, I saw that your hand was clenched and I heard your voice crack. It doesn't look to me as though you've accepted your wife's affair." This is confrontation. He can use what fits in that feedback or reject it. Two other men in our group gave him similar feedback. In this way, he has the opportunity to become aware of what he was not aware of.

---

[7] Cermak Timmen, *Diagnosing and Treating Co-dependence: A Guide for Professionals Who Work with Chemical Dependents, Their Spouses and Children* (Minneapolis, Minn.: Johnson Institute Books, 1986), 88-89.

I remember a time in my own uncovery process. I was sharing some details of my self-destructive behavior during my drinking days. I evidently had a smile on my face as I talked about some very painful stuff. One of the members of the group asked me to retell the experience, but to consciously avoid smiling. I started retelling the experience without the smile and within a few minutes, I was crying. My face muscles were part of the defense I set up to avoid my sadness. Without mirroring eyes to see what I could not see, I would have had no way to confront my own unconscious defenses.

Corrective Experience

The work of Stage II needs to move past reexperiencing the early feelings. This step is necessary as part of the shame reduction work. But there is need for *corrective experience*. This involves uncovering the lost child that hides within us. As adults, many opportunities arise for us to embrace the child within us and do the work of reparenting ourselves. We can also learn, as adults, to let the nurturing we get from others be parenting.

The important phrase I want to emphasize here is "as an adult." The grief work was not a "corrective experience." I reexperienced what I felt at the beginning and during my abandonment. The solution to acting-out behavior is to experience what we are acting out. This is what the grief work accomplishes.

Once the grief work is done, it is possible to have corrective experiences. All our experience is encoded and imprinted in our memory banks. Our developmental stages are like the circular rings of a tree. Each developmental stage is left intact.

Hypnotic age regression work clearly suggests that each of these developmental stages remains intact. There are an infant, a toddler, a preschool and a school-age child in each of us. We can age regress and feel just as we did when we were children. There is an adolescent in us who feels and thinks just as we did in adolescence.

The neurosurgeon Wilder Penfield corroborated some of this hypnotic work with experiments he made during open brain surgery. When he stimulated parts of the brain, the subject experienced the exact sensations and memories of a certain age level.

This work formed the foundation of Eric Berne's famous model of personality as composing three distinct ego states.

Berne theorized that we have an Adult Ego State (our current thought life); a Parent Ego (our recorded and unexamined life—an exact copy of our own parents'); and a Child Ego State (our felt life, especially as we experienced it as a child).

There is strong agreement that the children we once were live in us as a complete energy state of feelings, thoughts and desires. If our developmental dependency needs were not met, the energy that would have accrued in the resolution of each developmental stage is blocked.

The basis of the corrective experience used in inner child work rests on the fact that we can age regress and rework this blocked energy. Another presupposition of inner child work is that our developmental needs are recycled over and over again throughout our life.

In infancy, for example, the emotional need is basic trust. If that need is not met, we move onto the next stage in a wounded manner. It will be much harder to experiment and separate from the mother in toddlerhood if we do not have basic trust. Later in life, every time we go into a brand new situation, the issues of infancy will come up.

I have developed a workshop that I'm now conducting in several places in the country. My design is taken from several sources (most notably, Pam Levin's *Cycles of Power*). The workshop allows participants to go through the developmental stages of childhood and offers them corrective experiences relating to each developmental stage. This is done by creating small groups that serve as nurturing mini-families. Each person receives from the group various kinds of mirroring and feedback appropriate to the age-specific developmental need.

For example, in infancy, we all needed to be touched and nurtured. We needed to feel warmth and have the feeling that we could trust someone. We needed to hear words like: "Welcome to the world"; "I'm so glad you are here"; "You can count on me being here for you"; "You can take all the time you need to get your needs met, I will not rush you"; "I'm glad you're a boy"; "I'm glad you're a girl"; "I want to touch you, I want to hold you"; "I will accept you exactly as you are"; "Everything about you is okay with me."

When I facilitate the workshop, I ask one person at a time to move to the center of the group. The group members then move as close to that person as their boundaries permit. Each person in the group communicates one of the verbal affirmations while patting, stroking or just gently touching the subject. I have them go around the group several times amid lullaby music. The person in the center keeps his eyes closed and listens.

The first time I facilitated this exercise, I couldn't believe the intensity of feeling that emerged. Within seconds after beginning, some people in the center began sobbing deeply. As many of them were my clients, it suddenly dawned on me that almost all the ones sobbing so deeply were in the family system role of Lost Child. They never felt the primal trust an infant *needs to feel.*

When we touch the hurt places in ourselves, we feel it deeply. Watching Jack Nicklaus' son embrace him when he won his fifth Masters title immediately brought tears to my eyes. Any time I see a father and son embrace, I feel a tinge of pain and sadness.

In my workshop we go through all the developmental stages of childhood, allowing each person to test whether he got those needs met or not. We offer corrective experiences in the workshop and we suggest other ways a person might work on getting those needs met.

For example, Lost Children who are starting any new adventure as an adult need to have a friend, a sponsor or a support group who will hug them, stand by them, or maybe take them out to eat (figuratively feed them). They can wrap up in a blanket or eat several snacks (nutritional, of course) the day before they start something new. Massages and bubble baths are also effective. These are other ways, as an adult, they can take care of the child inside them.

Later in the workshop we make contact with the child within through inner imagery and meditation. I have each person bring a picture of himself before age eight. By experiencing the child in internal imagery, a contact is set up. I suggest that each person tell the child within that he is from their future and that he knows better than anyone what the child has been through. I further suggest a line from Jo Coudert's book *Advice from a Failure*. I suggest each person tell his inner child, "Of all the people you will ever know in your life, I'm the only one who you will never lose." Then I ask each person if he is willing to add, "and I will do my best never to leave you." The latter is important because out of our shame we have given up on our self and abandoned our inner child.

This experience is one of the most powerful I have ever witnessed. I began doing it with my clients about 17 years ago and have adapted it over the years.

I strongly suggest that each adult child set aside a few minutes each day in order to meditate and make contact with his inner child. I recommend that each one keep a picture of his child in his wallet or on his desk. I have found this to be very healing. When I'm frustrated or in a hypervigilant stage, I like to look at my picture of myself as a four-year-old boy and talk to the little frightened boy within me. I have found this very helpful.

There is much more that can be said on inner child work. For more detailed information, read my book, *Homecoming: Reclaiming and Championing Your Inner Child*.

My work is not original. I have simply made a synthesis of many kinds of therapies that are going on in the field right now. I would especially recommend the work of Dr. Charles Whitfield called *Healing the Child Within*. Wayne Kritsberg, a therapist in Seattle, was also a pioneer in this work.

When we contact this vital, spontaneous, natural child who was abandoned by the rules of the poisonous pedagogy, we can begin restoring our inner life. Restoration of the inner life is the foundation for Stage III, the Discovery Process. Once we go back and contact our lost self, we can discover our true self.

Leaving Home

We cannot nurture our lost self *unless we leave home*. We leave home by giving up our scripts and rigid roles. They denied us our authenticity. We played these rigid roles out of loyalty to our dysfunctional family systems. We got power and control from these roles, but they have cost us dearly.

Each of us is an unrepeatable and incomparable precious child of God. We were born to be ourselves. This can only be done by separating from our family systems designations and from our parents' beliefs and opinions about us. Jesus Christ was strong in affirming the impossibility of finding God, much less ourselves, unless we left home. Matthew quotes Jesus as saying, "I have not come to bring peace, but a sword. For I have come to put sons against fathers and daughters against mothers . . . And a man's foes shall be those of his own household."[8]

Leaving home means separating from our family system. It means giving up the idealizations and the fantasy of being forever protected by our parents. Only by leaving and becoming separate can we have the choice of having *a true relationship* with our parents. Relationship demands separation and detachment.

Once we've done this work, we may need a lot of distance from our family at first. For those who've been badly abused, you will have to make a prudent evaluation of how close you can get to your original family without violating your own boundaries. I encourage you to work toward forgiveness and reconciliation.

Forgiveness

Stage II is a forgiveness stage. We forgive ourselves and we forgive our parents. Forgive means to *give as before*. It means that we give up the resentments and release the energy that has *kept us in bondage*. We can love our parents as the really wounded people they are, not as a magical child's absolutized and mythological gods. Only by becoming separate can we have a relationship with them. Only by breaking the SPELL with our family of origin can we have a life of our own. If your parents are still abusive, you may have to choose to physically separate from them and the forgiveness process may take longer. You can still forgive them.

Doing the work of Stage II often leaves us with what has come to be called "survivor's guilt." I can remember saying to a therapist during this stage of my work that I felt like a rat deserting a sinking ship.

---

[8] Matt. 10:34-36

My mother, brother, sister and I had been through trauma and I was escaping from it. For a long time I put lots of energy into trying to get these members of my original family into therapy. I felt guilty for every good fortune that came my way. I felt I should split it four ways. It took me lots of therapeutic work to realize that I had a right to my own life. I came to see that I had a right to self-actualize and become my own, unique, individual self.

The guilt is a symptom of the family system dysfunction. Guilt in dysfunctional systems is a cover-up for co-dependency. Guilt is the symptom of the family's enmeshment. As a frozen undifferentiated ego mass, no one in a dysfunctional family has a right to any autonomy and separateness. This lack of differentiation means that *no one has the right to be different.* Therefore, to be autonomous and different is to feel guilty.

There is nothing wrong with helping one's family as a caregiver, provided it's a choice and not a family system duty. I loved my mom. I held my father on his deathbed and told him that I loved him. I had no unfinished business with him. I love my sister and brother and because of that, I refuse to play my Caretaker, Little Parent or Hero Role with them. I can't really love them if I don't love myself. To play these roles without any real relationship would continue the same old family dysfunction. Happily, my brother and sister have found their own recovery programs.

Breaking the family SPELL means breaking the bonds of enmeshment. It means separating and focusing your energy on *your own life problems* (crucial for co-dependents). Some parents have never dealt with their neediness. They have never taken on the responsibility of their own lives. If you gave up your childhood to take care of your needy parents' emotions, you have a right (I would say a God-given duty) to focus on your own life.

Reexperiencing the original pain and embracing our lost child are the core of Stage II work. In order to secure and enhance the gains of this work, we must continue to do maintenance work.

Maintenance on Shame

Maintenance work is especially crucial in regard to shame. Maintenance work on shame requires a continuous monitoring of the internal source figure voices. These voices come in the form of drivers like Be Perfect, Be Strong, Please Me, Try Hard and Hurry Up. We have to learn how to dramatize these voices and answer them. We also have to learn how to create new affirmations to confront our shame voices.

Shame is also maintained by internal imagery. The images of ourselves as flawed and the actual memories of being shamed are encoded as neurological imprints in a part of the brain called the amygdala. When we have experiences that in any way resemble these imprinted memories, we respond as we did when we were first shamed.

There are powerful remapping techniques that can affect a healing of these memories. These techniques can also change our internal images. I have presented these techniques in detail in my book, *Healing the Shame That Binds You.*

In conclusion, let me remind you again that recovery is a process and not an event. "It ain't over 'til it's over," Yogi Berra is quoted as saying. The grief work can start in a therapy group or a workshop, but it usually needs to be continued for many years. Once you've connected with your inner child and committed to be there for her or him, there's ongoing work to do. Love is the work of overcoming inertia and the courage to risk giving our time and attention to ourselves. To embrace your lost child is the beginning of the work of self-love. It's a lifelong commitment and it requires courage. Remember, of all the people you will ever know, you are the only one you'll never lose!

S U M M A R Y

I'd like to sum up **STAGE II UNCOVERY** by using this phrase to organize the ideas we've been discussing.

Separation Process

In order to achieve an individuality and solid sense of self-esteem, we must separate from our family of origin.

Trance Breaking

Breaking the family SPELL can be done by refusing to play your rigid role or by breaking your family of origin rules. The most dramatic way to break the SPELL is to become aware of your abandonment and grieve it.

Anger and Resentment Work

Part of the grief work is to symbolically express the anger and resentment resulting from childhood abandonment. It is important to give up the resentment and come to forgiveness.

Group Therapy

Group therapy is the therapy of choice for co-dependency, since the issues of co-dependency emerge spontaneously in the setting of group interactions.

Embracing Your Inner Child

Once the deep grief work is accomplished, corrective work should follow. Corrective work involves embracing the wounded inner child of the past at the various stages of development. Inner child work is symbolic. The wounded inner child is a metaphor for our most vulnerable feelings and needs related to hurts and traumas of the past.

II. Second-Order Change

Second-order change involves giving up primary process ego defenses and rigid roles. When we truly achieve a second-order change, we stop our compulsive addictiveness.

Uncovering Your "Carried Shame"

"Carried shame" is the result of the interpersonal transfer of shame (passing the hot potato). When a shame-based person in authority projects his shame onto a person subject to his authority, if the person in the underlying position is immature and without strong boundaries, that person will carry the authority's shame. Because children are extremely vulnerable, they are subject to carrying their parents' shame.

Normalcy and Averageness

As we mature, we come to realize that the environment we grew up in may not be normal even though we thought it was normal when we were growing up. Adult children often confuse love and abuse. Our whole society has accepted the rules of the poisonous pedagogy as normal. As our new consciousness of deep democracy emerges, we are realizing that these rules discourage the formation of solid self-esteem.

Corrective Experiences Concerning Developmental Deficits

Once we embrace our wounded inner child, we need to learn the tasks appropriate to our childhood developmental stages. Unmet infancy, toddler, preschool and school-age developmental tasks can be learned as an adult. These learnings are called "corrected experiences."

Original Pain Grief Work

The majority of the symptoms of childhood abandonment in all its forms are caused by delayed grief. Grieving our childhood grief is called "original pain grief work."

Values Clarification

The poisonous pedagogy legislates values in an authoritarian way and uses methods based on shame, fear and punishment. Such values are not internalized. Once we break the SPELL, we must re-form our own values. The process of maturity asks each of us to critically examine and internalize the values we were given as children so as to make them our own.

Ego Boundary Work

Boundaries are the guardians of our self-esteem. Once we break the original SPELL and realize how the poisonous pedagogy damaged our physical, emotional, intellectual and spiritual boundaries, we have to work to rebuild them. This is part of Stage II work.

Recycling Childhood Developmental Dependency Needs as an Adult

We can learn as adults to reparent ourselves and to mutually reparent each other. We can choose to let adult nurturing be enough.

Yearning for Family Health—Survivor's Guilt

Once we break the family SPELL, we see the family realistically. We see how our rigid role really didn't help anyone. We feel a new freedom and vitality. We are no longer caught up in the reactive family feedback cycle. We want the whole family to experience this new vitality and may feel very guilty that we have new freedom and other family members do not.

Road Map for *Discovering* Your True Self: Stage III—Spiritual Awakening and Compassionate Social Action

The Spiritual life is . . . part of the human essence. It is a defining characteristic of human nature, without which human nature is not fully human.

ABRAHAM MASLOW

Our lives are limited by our beliefs. In my active addiction, I believed that my life and happiness depended on external forces. I made decisions according to that belief. My false belief led me to make wrong choices. I ultimately created the kind of world I believed in.

Some years ago I had a great example of how beliefs shape our world view. During the Christmas season I went to the Galleria Mall with a friend of mine and his uncle. The Galleria is the most crowded shopping center in Houston during the holidays. The traffic is terrible. It often takes 40 minutes to get there from my house, which is only six miles away.

My friend is a warm, loving person. He has an infectious smile. He loves people and *believes* in their goodness. He was driving the car and we got to the Galleria in 20 minutes. His smile was captivating as he asked people to let us get through traffic lines. He created the kind of world he believed in.

His uncle wanted to drive on the way back. His uncle is rather somber and believes people are "no damn good." It took us 20 minutes to get out of the Galleria parking lot! His uncle gave people dirty looks, yelling aggressively at other drivers. No one let him in line. Finally, a sweet little old lady signaled for him to get ahead of her. He shot her the finger! Not only did he create the kind of world he believed in, when data emerged that could change his belief, he refused to look at the data.

Our beliefs create the kind of world we believe in. We project our feelings, thoughts and attitudes onto the world. I can create a different world by changing my belief about the world. Our inner state creates the outer and not vice versa. It took me 42 years to grasp this rather simple spiritual principle. Co-dependence is at bottom spiritual bankruptcy because co-dependents believe that happiness lies outside of ourselves.

Stage III begins as we change our old belief systems. Our addictive false gods have failed us. By embracing our shame, we were able to accept our feelings about ourselves and start building solid self-esteem.

Stage III starts us on the journey to discover our inner life. This involves the work of spiritual disciplines. Such disciplines demand the same attitude that the previous stages involved: resolve, commitment and working one day at a time.

Just as we needed a sponsor in Stage I and a support group or therapist in stage II, so also we may need a spiritual director in Stage III. You may find such a person in your new family of affiliation. You may know a spiritual master that you wish to approach and ask to be your sponsor or guide. You may know a pastor, priest, rabbi or spiritual friend whose life and teachings appeal to you.

Guidance is important in the beginning. Almost no one has been taught how to meditate. Most people continue their childhood methods of prayer and have no idea about expanding their prayer life. Spiritual diaries and journal writing are not common practices for most people. Few people know anything about dream interpretation or dream integration. A spiritual director is most useful in Stage III.

The 12-Step programs lead us directly to the development of an inner life. The 12-Step programs grew from the six tenets of the Oxford movement. These six tenets were themselves the result of a minister named Frank Buckner's spiritual experience. The founders of AA were participants in the early Oxford movement in the United States. They built upon the tenets of the Oxford movement in forming their 12-Step program.

The founders of the AA movement, Bill W. and Dr. Bob, were clear about the ultimate problem of alcoholism. For them it was "spiritual bankruptcy." This is what I have described as the problem of co-dependency. This *ism* of alcoholism or any addiction is the inner self-rupture called, variously, internalized shame, self-will run riot or co-dependence. Each is a way to describe spiritual bankruptcy.

The 12th Step speaks of a spiritual awakening. The 11th Step speaks directly of prayer and meditation. It says:

> 11. *We sought through prayer and meditation to improve our conscious contact with God as we understand Him, praying only for knowledge of His will for us and the power to carry that out.*

The spiritual quest is not some added benefit to our life, something you embark on if you have the time and inclination. We are spiritual beings on an earthly journey. Our spirituality makes up our beingness. We are the kind of spiritual beings who, in order to adequately be spirit, need a body. We are not earthly beings trying to get spiritual. We are *essentially spiritual*. This is why the abandonment I have described is a spiritual problem.

If we humans are essentially spiritual, then when we are abandoned, abused or enmeshed, we are spiritually violated. Indeed, when our caretakers acted shamelessly, they were playing God. Healthy shame tells us we are finite, limited and prone to mistakes. When our caretakers acted shamelessly, we were forced to carry their shame. Our self-esteem was wounded by that shame. Co-dependence is the outcome of this abuse.

The False Gods of Addiction

As a form of spiritual bankruptcy, co-dependence sets us up for false gods. The addictions that are the diseases of the co-dependency are little idolatries. They are aborted quests for God. Every addiction is spirituality gone awry.

Every addiction has its professed moment of salvation, its atonement. The mood alteration and adrenaline rush provide a moment when all self-rupture and alienation are overcome. We are high, ecstatic. We are one with ourselves. We are enthused—from the Greek, *en theos*—one with our God. But unlike the permanent bliss taught by the spiritual masters, this high is a dud.

Spiritual Awakening as Discovery

Stage III is Spiritual Awakening. In Stage III we begin a true journey of *discovery.* We enter places we have never been before. Our past egoic meaning rests upon our doings and our accomplishments. In Stage III, we move beyond ego and egoic-type meaning.

The new meaning is less about doing and more about being. We come to know our own beingness—our true self. This awareness is historical. It is timeless and originates from within us.

The psychologist Dr. Abraham Maslow spent his life studying the highest potentials of human nature. He wanted to know about human greatness. He spent much time studying what he called self-actualized people and peak human experiences. Out of these studies Maslow concluded that we human beings have a hierarchy of needs. Our most basic needs he called deficiency needs. I've called these dependency needs, and I've been discussing the problems resulting from not getting those needs met.

Maslow believed that once the dependency needs are met, we can move on to a higher level of needs, which he called *being needs.* The being needs have to do with identity, individuality, justice, truth, goodness, beauty, ultimate meaning, wisdom and a relationship with a higher power. The two sets of needs are connected. It's hard to imagine seeking justice and truth if you are starving; or being concerned with issues of individuation and identity if you are starved for love and affection.

Maslow believed that each set of needs had a certain kind of consciousness or cognition governing it. The lower order needs are the domain of ego. The higher order needs are the domain of a more expanded consciousness. Higher consciousness constitutes the realm of our soul, our *true self*. In the figures in chapter 4, I visually presented this theory of human consciousness. From these drawings you can immediately see that the pathway to the *true self* rests upon the resolutions of one's ego issues.

Unfinished Ego Needs

Jacquelyn Small, in her book *Transformers* states: "The ego will continually draw us backwards, toward the level where the unmet need exists, until the need is met." The lack of fulfillment of childhood dependency needs creates the problem of the adult child. As an adult with unmet childhood dependency needs, we are continuously drawn backwards in an attempt to get those needs met. Stage I uncovers these needs and provides a context to get these needs met as an adult. As the ego is reconstructed, we become free to move beyond ego.

The ego represents our limited or narrowed consciousness. Ego is to the true self what a flashlight is to a spotlight. The purpose of ego is adaptation, coping and survival. We cope with the world and get our basic dependency needs met by means of ego. To live life adequately we need strong ego boundaries. As hypervigilant co-dependent survivors, our life is dominated by distress and threat. We cannot even think of Stage III, where our task is discovering our *true self*, as long as our boundaries are weak and our life is an unending hypervigilant defense against pain.

When our ego boundaries are strong, the world is less threatening. We know we can take care of ourselves. We know we have the inner resources to make it. We do not have to live in hypervigilance any longer. Our ego is now available for the work of expanding and moving beyond itself. Moving beyond ourselves is both an inward journey and an outward reach toward community.

The Journey Within

Moving within is the journey of unfolding spirituality. Since we humans are essentially spiritual, there is no other way to discover our essential selves except through deepening awareness. My soul as my ultimate identity lies in a realm beyond my family or cultural roles. But paradoxically, I can only discover it through my family and culture.

The spiritual writer Chögyam Trungpa says, "Spirituality is completely ordinary . . . it is the most ordinary thing of all."

Most of us think of spirituality as extraordinary because our inner life has been so damaged.

Once we reconnect with ourselves, we can find spirituality everywhere. There are three dimensions of spiritual awakening that I'd like to focus on in the rest of this chapter.

1. The growing body of data pointing to a life beyond our ordinary consciousness.
2. The spiritual disciplines that help us achieve and maintain a life beyond ordinary consciousness.
3. The importance of our living in a compassionate way. Living in a compassionate way involves finding and/or creating a community that fosters social harmony and world peace and that has deep respect for nature. Giving of ourselves in social service and caring for others expand our capacity to love and allow us to know ourselves in a new and deeper way. When we live with compassion, we create "deep democracy."

Transcending the Ego

Recently a number of researchers have looked into the phenomenon of higher consciousness. People like Ken Pelletier at the Langley Porter Psychiatric Institute in San Francisco, Elmer and Alice Green at Menninger's, Russel Targ, Gerald Puthoff, W. Brugh Joy, Karl Pribrim and Fritz Capra have reached a surprising consensus about the powers available to us at the heights of consciousness. The Greens and Pelletier are research psychologists. Karl

Pribrim is a brain physiologist. Targ, Puthoff and Capra are physicists. Brugh Joy is a medical doctor.

Psychics like Olga Worrell and my friend Jack Schwarz have also verified some of the great possibilities of higher consciousness. Olga Worrell did weekly healing services. Her healing powers have been acknowledged by many. Schwarz eats sparingly (three meals a week) and sleeps only two hours a night. Jack can put 12-inch knitting needles through his veins while maintaining alpha brain wave consciousness. He can then heal the wounds. Jack has voluntary control over so-called involuntary processes. (See his book, *Voluntary Controls.*)

The central conclusion arrived at by all the people I've mentioned is that our full human consciousness is much more than our narrow ego consciousness. All agree with the perennial spiritual wisdom that there is a higher consciousness that transcends ego.

There is also some suggestive evidence that this consciousness is connected to all other created consciousness. The early telepathy studies of J. B. Rhine at Duke University pointed clearly in this direction. The more recent work of Puthoff and Targ at Stanford Research Institute (SRI) on Remote Viewing ESP has offered powerful new data suggesting that once in higher consciousness, we have a *higher power* available to us. Their belief is that this power results from being connected to all other created consciousness.

There are also ancient traditions supporting a higher power through expanded consciousness. The American Indian medicine healers believe there is greater power available through the use of meditation and the fusion with power animals. Jesus told his followers that there were powers available to them that were greater than the powers he manifested.

The remote viewing experiments at SRI have corroborated some of the conclusions of quantum physics. These experiments suggest that we are not limited by space and time. People in sealed rooms can see what someone else is seeing 30 miles away. This research is recorded in books like *The Silent Pulse* by George Leonard and *Mind Reach* by Harold E. Puthoff and Russell Targ.

When we are in the highest moments of consciousness, we are *one* with the universe. We are a hologram of the world. The world is a *system* and we are partly a whole and wholly a part. *Each of us in our own way is the universe.* Many great spiritual masters have taught this for centuries. The ego creates separation and illusion. Once beyond ego there is no separation. We are all one. Modern science is catching up with the perennial wisdom.

Modern science makes it clear that mind and body are not antagonists. Mind and body are two different forms of energy. Our consciousness is now understood as high-frequency energy. As forms of energy, mind and body influence each other.

If mind and matter are the same stuff, we can learn to use matter in more powerful and profound ways. Learning to let go of ego control and turning it over to higher consciousness are powerful ways to get results. A slogan in AA says, "Let go and let God." People speak of powerful things happening in their lives when they turn it over to their Higher Power.

I will now summarize the findings I've been describing.

We are more than our ordinary ego consciousness. To find our true self we have to transcend our ordinary ego consciousness. This conclusion:

1. Is compatible with a growing amount of behavioral science data;
2. Is integral to almost all the world's religious traditions; and
3. If fully believed at the personal level, would totally transform our lives.

The propositions leading to this central conclusion are:

1. Much of our significant mental activity goes on outside of conscious awareness. Examples include biofeedback, dreams, intuitive knowing, family systems and ego defenses.
2. The powers of suggestion and autosuggestion are far greater than we typically assume. We all operate in a posthypnotic SPELL induced in early infancy. The major elements of this SPELL come from our family of origin and the culture we are born into. This SPELL operates unconsciously.
3. We will resist the knowledge we most deeply desire. Language, ego defenses, denials, delusions, family systems and cultural roles keep us from higher consciousness.

4. Each of us has access to a supra-conscious, creative, integrative, self-organizing, intuitive mind whose capabilities are apparently unlimited. This is the part of our consciousness that constitutes our God-likeness.

5. Higher consciousness is connected to all other forms of consciousness.

6. There is no reason to doubt that my creative/unconscious mind may have a *plan* for me. As we look back over our lives, it often seems clear that there was such a plan. We are free to follow or disregard it.

7. Acting in accordance with my Higher Power's plan, I can expect my actions to be in harmony with the ultimate well-being of all those around me. I will be moved toward compassionate social action.

8. There seems to be no reason to doubt that the necessary resources for actualizing the plan will be available whenever needed. Einstein has shown that mind and matter are both energy. There is copious evidence that proves the power of mind energy over matter energy (psychokinesis, etc.).

9. It appears that a healthy life is one in which the act of choosing is given over to the creative/intuitive mind. One way this is accomplished is through the conscious contact resulting from prayer and meditation.

10. One of the conditions for hearing an undistorted inner voice is the willingness to perceive differently. This involves a number of spiritual disciplines in which the ego is bypassed.[1]

These propositions fill me with hope. In order to actualize what they promise, let's look at prayer and meditation.

Spiritual Disciplines

The 11th Step spoke of prayer and meditation. These are the two fundamental tools for opening up our higher consciousness and making conscious contact with our Higher Power.

---

[1] These propositions are adapted from a lecture by Willis Harman.

Every religion and spiritual tradition teaches its devotees to pray and meditate. There are many ways to approach prayer and meditation. No way is the *right way* and no prayer or meditation technique is in itself the goal we are seeking. We can get stuck trying to find the best technique. Prayer and meditation techniques are like the booster rocket stage of a spacecraft launch. The booster's job is to get the spaceship out of Earth's gravitational pull so that it can reach outer space. Techniques for prayer and meditation are ways to reach beyond ego so that we can reach the expanded spaces of our higher consciousness.

Once we have reached that altered state, we can have a more intimate and immediate contact with our Higher Power. Reaching the experience of conscious contact is what is important. Once we are at this level of awareness, our more essential self becomes visible. To know and be who we really are is our destiny. If we fail to achieve this, we have missed the mark. Perhaps only the greatest saints fully achieve what I am describing. But full self-awareness (sometimes called enlightenment) and oneness with God are the most profound callings of our being.

There are many other approaches to inner spiritual life. Many believe that dreams are not only a direct way to access our unconscious, but also the most direct way that our higher power encounters us. I point to the many sacred scriptures of various religious traditions that record direct encounters with God through dreams. In my own experience, dreams have been valuable sources of self-understanding. I've described what the psychologist Carl Jung called a "big dream" in my books *Healing the Shame That Binds You* and *Homecoming: Reclaiming and Championing Your Inner Child.*

Big dreams help us break through stuck places in our lives. Some people describe achieving inner peace and conscious contact with their Higher Power through journal writing. They contend that writing out their dialogue with their Higher Power is a form of prayer and that it focuses and expands their awareness of the reality of their Higher Power.

Worship services, spiritual rituals, fasting and mortifications of one's appetites are other forms of spiritual discipline. The form itself seems less important than the sincerity of one's intentions.

Compassionate Social Action

I spoke of the 12th Step earlier. This step describes the fruit of the first 11 Steps as "spiritual awakening."

The last of the 12 Steps states:

> 12. *Having had a spiritual awakening as a result of these steps, we tried to carry this message to other addicts and to practice these principles in all our affairs.*

The 12th Step is a call to social action. It asks recovering alcoholics to do two things:

1. To carry the message to other suffering alcoholics; and
2. To practice the principles of the 12 Steps in all their affairs.

I understand the 12th Step as a call to compassionate social action. Alcoholism is the tip of the iceberg of addictiveness. Any type of ultimate concern (making money, being well-liked, etc.) can become an addiction. Many spiritual masters contend that any form of life without God-consciousness is a form of addiction.

In this book, I have tried to show you the vast extent of destruction caused by addictive behaviors. But even if you don't identify with the addictiveness I've been describing, the call to compassionate social action is a part of finding your true self. We humans are by nature social. Our lives were shaped by the mirroring eyes of our source figures. The foundation of our solid selfhood was formed in the matrix of our earliest source relationships. As we develop a solid sense of self-esteem and experience the goodness of our own being, we want to reach out to that same goodness in others. Goodness is diffusive of itself. It is part of the fullness of our being to care for others. Once our ego-dependency needs are met, love and care are the personality strengths that our nature calls us to develop. Love and care are higher-order "being" needs—we need to love and care for others if we want to be self-actualized. As our self-actualization progresses, our values are more and more concerned with being.

The specific social action we take is less important than the commitment to social action itself. Erik Erikson describes this commitment as *generativity*. When we are generative, we reach outside ourselves in productive, creative and socially valuable ways. One person may be an environmentalist. Another may work with the dying or homeless. The specific action is less important than the reaching outside of oneself.

George Bernard Shaw once suggested that the true meaning of life is to live for something defined by yourself as a mighty cause. He said:

> *I want to be used up when I die. . . . Life is not a walking shadow . . . rather it is a splendid torch that I want to set afire and hand onto the next generation before I die.*

The danger for those who reach middle adulthood feeling some sense of mastery is that they can become obsessed with themselves and stagnate. I consider self-stagnation a sign that you have not fully regained self-esteem. Because when we have a full sense of self-love and self-value, we will of necessity want to expand and grow. That happens by developing a deep inner life and by expressing the richness and goodness of that inner life in compassion for others.

If we experience a blissful contact with a Higher Power, that power cannot be less than good and loving or else it wouldn't be a Higher Power, since goodness and love are our highest human values. And if it is good and loving, our Higher Power cannot be less than a personal being since we've never experienced goodness and love except in interpersonal relationships. Thus the conscious contact that is created in inner stillness desires to be expressed in outer compassion toward others. The fruit of spiritual awakening is to carry the graceful goodness and love we have received and give it to others.

Deep Democracy

Full human self-actualization demands that we care for the planet we live on. For me this is a call to compassionate social action extending to nature and world peace.

The evolution of our present consciousness makes human self-actualization even more urgent. We have arrived at a point of consciousness where we realize for the first time the dynamics of human evolution and the evolution of the universe. This new stage of consciousness has revealed some of the fundamental laws governing all life, and we are beginning to see how these laws relate to families. The law of differentiation tells us that the differences in the world are part of the dynamic process whereby the universe is becoming conscious of itself and unfolding. The differences in the world are part of the solution—not part of the problem. The law of differentiation, in particular, has relevance to the formation of individual self-esteem and identity. The law of differentiation is also important when trying to understand the differences between cultures and nations of the world. When people grow up enmeshed in their family systems, they tend to project that enmeshment onto their national system. Enmeshed nations become closed and prejudicial systems. A closed system sees any other system that is different from it as the enemy. This is the cause of wars and the violent destruction that goes with it. Hitler and the Nazi system created a trance-like belief that Aryans were a master race of people. That belief ushered in a reign of violent murder and destruction unlike any the world had ever known. We can never forget this and we must never cease trying to understand how Hitler's Germany could have happened.

That was one of the questions that I began my PBS series with and one of the questions I posed in this book. I hope some awareness about the destructive potential of closed systems has emerged from the content of this book. Closed systems are extremely dangerous because they deself their members and deprive them of self-esteem. Closed systems are dangerous because they allow no feedback. When no new information can be integrated into a system, it feeds upon itself and becomes an absolutizing agent. Its own beliefs become sacred laws; its own rules infallible; its own leaders all-powerful. This is exactly the problem with monarchial patriarchy and the poisonous pedagogy it spawns.

How are we going to accept each other's differences? How can we come to believe that every culture, with its unique mythology, religion and ethnicity, is necessary for the survival of life on our planet? I don't profess to have a full answer to these questions. I know that our ultimate survival depends on how we answer them. I do believe that by each of us developing a rich inner life in which we find the stillness that reveals the interconnectedness of all life and a loving Higher Power, we can engage in responsible, compassionate and loving social action. If we can find our own inner peace and express it outwardly, we can develop a sense of *deep democracy*. Deep democracy is the internalization of the timeless feeling of compassionate love for *all* life. Every great religious tradition has deep democracy at its core. With the feeling of deep democracy, we respect every part of the system we live in and we also give every part a voice. In a family, this means that power is shared and each person's viewpoint is respected. It means that each person in the family, from the unborn fetus to the oldest person, is respected and honored as a unique, unrepeatable and sacred person.

If we can create families that are deeply democratic, we can expect that our societies and nations will be deeply democratic. Carl Jung once said that at bottom, all great historical events are the result of some individual person or persons. It is in individuals that transformations first take place. So what is most important is the spiritual awakening of each individual.

Taking Action

When I first started in my 12-Step recovery program, I found a little green card that asked me to do two things each day to help some fellow suffering human beings. The card said to do them in a way that no one would know what I had done. The card was a call to virtuous action. Doing morally good works is a private matter and loses its goodness if it is made public. I found this very hard to do. I realized how much I wanted my good works to be acknowledged and praised. I wanted credit for doing them. I followed that card's suggestions in a human, not perfect, way. I found the experience incredibly rewarding.

I cannot tell anyone else exactly what to do in terms of community building and social service. I can only urge you to do something (two things each day that no one will find out about).

Doing works that help rebuild our social harmony are ways to expand our souls. Do good works because good works are good to do if you can. Probably only saints do good without some ulterior motive. Rather than letting their grand achievements deter us, we can let them inspire us. After all, nothing human is foreign to me. It is possible to love as they have shown us.

But even with ulterior motives, you gain a great deal. Love and compassion expand our being and allow us to transcend ourselves. In loving others we become more than we were because when we truly love, we become the other. We experience what it means to be them. The consciousness that results from loving is an expanded consciousness. It potentially connects us with every living thing. And the more we love, the more we expand our consciousness of others.

Being Ordinary

Each of us is unique in the sense that there has never been anyone like us before and never will be again. In this regard we are truly special. But it's also important to be *ordinary* in the sense that I am the same as all other human beings on this planet. I struggle with the same vulnerabilities. I am subject to the same fate and live with the same fear of death, "The undiscovered country, from whose bourn / No traveller returns," as Shakespeare said. No one is above the limits of human finitude. But the more I love and give myself in social service, the more I feel a sense of belonging. When I believe I am special or too good for common social action, or when I simply let others do it, I experience isolation and closure.

Wisdom

The great spiritual master Sri Aurobini says, "You must know the highest before you can truly understand the lowest." The third stage of our journey toward wholeness gives us a new perspective on all that has gone before. Stage III leads to wholeness itself. In becoming complete we see more clearly what is important.

Wisdom may be defined as knowing what is and what isn't important. With wisdom we see the whole picture. This is why it takes a long time to truly grow wise. It is only in the evening that we can evaluate the whole day. Wisdom allows us to know the parts by knowing the whole. When we are wise, we see the interconnectness of all things. With wisdom, we unify our vision. We see how paradoxical polarities fit together. We understand that life and death are part of the whole.

Bliss

Once we find comfort inside ourselves, tremendous transformations take place. First, a new kind of peace and calm come over us. Our inner life belongs to us alone. It depends on us, not on something outside of us. We can depend on this inner world because we actually experience it. It will never go away. By having an inner life we are no longer dependent on the outside for our good feeling; we can engender peace and calm from within.

As we advance in meditation, a new mental faculty emerges. The spiritual masters call it intuition or enlightenment. But it is not like a perceptual intuition or intellectual intuition. It only emerges from silence and stillness.

Moving into the silence is what the spiritual disciplines are all about. Learning how to quiet the conscious mind (the ego's incessant chatter and self-talk) requires practice. The practice is done one day at a time. We need to be very careful of grandiosity in pursuing skill in meditating. Grandiosity looks for the big experience—the visitation by God. Learning to meditate is more like the dripping of water on a rock. Over the course of time the rock will be eaten away. Co-dependents want to turn the water on full blast. That has little effect on the rock.

As we advance into silence, the intuitive faculty becomes more and more available. The intuitive faculty is the power of immediately experiencing God. "Be still and know that I am God," the Bible says.

To have immediate conscious contact is to experience bliss. Once experienced, bliss has no opposite. We want more and more. We hunger and thirst for such peace and oneness with all things. The desire and longing for bliss are signs that we are advancing in the inner kingdom.

The deep peace and calm that conscious contact brings also transform our vision of our whole life. Since the new self is a new state of consciousness, we start seeing our whole life from this new point of view.

Seeing Your Life as Perfect

In my own case, I'm beginning to see that everything that I have gone through had to be. From the perspective of my unity consciousness, I see that my parents were perfect. I needed to become a drunk so that I could understand the kind of suffering addiction causes. Coming out of a dysfunctional family, I learned about the rules that create dysfunction in families. All of this is part of my self's purpose for being here.

Had my dad not been a drunk and my family system not been dysfunctional, I could not have created a television series about dysfunctional families and wouldn't be writing this book. My life was just what it needed to be for me to evolve and expand my consciousness through suffering. The French novelist Léon Bloy once said, "There are places in the heart that do not yet exist; pain must be in order for them to be."

Without my suffering, I would not be able to bear witness to an addictive society and the pain it causes its people. I could not be in the system enough to understand it, and at the same time be in recovery enough to stand outside of it and confront the rules of the poisonous pedagogy that our society encourages and authorizes. From my true-self point of view, my life has been perfect.

Growth in true selfhood comes from becoming more and more who I am. I struggle less with myself. It has less to do with anything that I do. The only thing I do not have to struggle with is being myself. Stage III transformation is effortless because as Jacquelyn Small says, "There is nothing that has to be done—there is only someone to be."

Years ago when I was in the monastery, I read and studied the things I'm writing about now. I felt very afraid. I remember reading Abraham Maslow's description of how self-actualized people are no longer concerned about the impression they are making, and how they love their solitude. He described self-actualized people as being interested in listening to other people's opinions of them, but being very little affected by those opinions. Maslow's self-actualized people had united their consciousness.

Work and play merge for the self-actualized person. The more innocent and childlike they become, the more mature they become. The more individuated they become, the more they can belong to the group and be intimate.

At the time I read about Maslow's self-actualized persons, it all seemed terribly confusing to me. I remember reading the great philosopher-mystic Krishnamurti and being perplexed by his statement, "We must be extraordinarily capable of standing alone." Being alone triggered my abandonment issues.

Today, I'm getting small glimpses of what all this means. Today I belong to my Higher Power and to myself. I'm willing to accept full responsibility for my life and my creations. What I do is me— for that I did come. And it's a long way to come—from being laid out on a stretcher in a state hospital to delving into higher consciousness. It's a long way to come, and yet *it was all there in my compulsions and addictions. I was seeking God, but I didn't know it.* I wanted ecstasy, oneness with self, oneness with the world and transformation. And now I have it.

I'm happy that God writes straight with crooked lines.

For those of you still struggling with compulsivity and addictiveness, let me remind you of the *promises* that will come to you if you thoroughly work a 12-Step program. I can assure you that they will come true. In the *Big Book of Alcoholics Anonymous* it says:

> *We are going to know a new freedom and happiness.*
> *We will not regret the past nor wish to shut the door on it.*
> *We will comprehend the word serenity and we will know*
>   *peace.*
> *No matter how far down the scale we have gone, we will see*
>   *how our experience can benefit others.*
> *That feeling of uselessness and self-pity will disappear.*

We will lose interest in selfish things and gain interest in our
*   fellows.*
Self-seeking will slip away.
Our whole attitude and outlook upon life will change.
Fear of people and economic insecurity will leave us.
We will intuitively know how to handle situations that used
*   to baffle us.*
We will suddenly realize that God is doing for us what we
*   could not do for ourselves.* [2]

---

[2] *Alcoholics Anonymous,* 3rd rev. ed. (New York: Alcoholics Anonymous World Services, 1976), 83-84.

SUMMARY

The salient points in this chapter are summarized by using the letters of the phrase **STAGE III DISCOVERY.**

Spiritual Awakening

You have a rich inner life. You're no longer a feverish clod of grievances and ailments. You want to be a force of nature and one with your creator.

Transpersonal—Beyond Ego

You have let go of control. You trust your own resources and your network of friends to get your needs met. You practice prayer and meditation.

Aloneness as Solitude

You look forward to your time alone. The relationship with yourself is ongoing and enjoyable. You use your solitude for self-discovery.

God Consciousness

You pray and/or meditate daily. You have conscious contact many times a day. You feel less lonely or frightened.

Expanded Consciousness

You see your whole life differently. You are conscious of your purpose in life. You see your family system from the perspective of a higher purpose. You are evolving rather than revolving.

III Third-Order Change

You are becoming transformed. You are not getting better; you are a different person. You are discovering yourself from the inside. You have transcended all the rules.

Deep Democracy

You know how differences make a difference. You love and affirm yourself and extend that love to others in a compassionate way.

Intuitive Vision

You experience moments of powerful insight and enlightenment. At times you have an immediate knowledge of God's presence. Being in contact with God allows you to know yourself.

Spiritual Disciplines

You practice meditation. You put aside time every day to make conscious contact with God. You pray to acknowledge God's glory. You spend time on your spiritual life. You study spirituality.

Compassionate

You are more creative in your love. You often go beyond any kind of giving to get. You're committed to social service. You perform kind acts no one will find out about.

Oneness (Unification of Polarity)

You do not see the world in black and white. You see that there is no joy without sorrow; no pleasure without pain; no light without darkness; no life without death. The more individuated you become, the more intimate, mature and childlike you are.

Values Concerned with Being

You are most concerned about truth and honesty. You see beauty where you had never seen it before. You see goodness where you had never seen it before. You are less possessive and attached. Your life is less complex and more simple.

Energized and Empowered

You have more energy than ever before. You feel one with yourself and have ceased using energy for inner warfare. You have a powerful impact on those around you.

Reverence for Life (Peacemaking)

You feel concerned about generating life. You want to leave the world better than when you came. You work for interpersonal and world peace.

Yearning for God (Bliss)

You experience high moments of oneness with God and all things. You've felt the unity and seen the illusion of separation. You have an urge for more peace, love, truth, goodness and beauty. You hunger for personal love and oneness with God.

Revising Traditional Values

S ince I first wrote *Bradshaw On: The Family,* modern social life has grown more chaotic and violent. Schoolyard squabbles are now knifings. There is a growing incidence of very young children beating up and even murdering younger children. The divorce rate continues to climb higher. Deadbeat fathers are giving up their parental responsibilities and abandoning their families. People are buying guns in record numbers—even forming neighborhood vigilante groups. Many politicians preach about family values but are accused and often caught up in webs of vicious behavior. We do not know for sure whether we can trust our president and first lady. TV evangelists have been exposed and criminally indicted for their avarice and lust. Sexual acting-out among the clergy of all denominations has reached epic proportions.

There is a dire lack of true virtue and morality. Traditional values like strong families, intimate and committed marriages, responsible parenting, discipline, honesty, moral virtue and character, commitment, perseverance, hard work, love of God and country, true friendships, and respect of the elderly seem to be slipping away from modern life.

There is a loud cry to return to traditional values. But it mostly comes from the polarized right wing, which, because of its rigid polarization and overt violence (the murdering of doctors at abortion clinics), turns many people off. I am conservative, but the right-wing version of traditional values that I most often hear sounds exactly like monarchial patriarchy and calls for a reinstallment of the poisonous pedagogy.

If we are to embrace traditional values, we must take into account our new "deeply democratic" self-awareness and revise these values with the aid of our new knowledge about family systems. We must also take into account the new-found evidence for the primacy of the emotional brain. The old way repressed emotions. We need our emotions if we are to be emotionally intelligent. We also need to understand the advances in developmental psychology and the crucial role that natural shame plays in the formation of self-esteem.

My first suggestion for revising traditional values is to change the whole educational approach to their installation. We must also change our approach to teaching values and inculcating virtue. The monarchial, patriarchal way of teaching values and forming character has clearly failed. The German families of the early 1930s embodied the old way as perfectly as one could imagine. The monarchial patriarchal approach was based on authority and blind obedience.

The poisonous pedagogy taught children to be good by using scare tactics like verbal shaming and corporal punishment. Children were often shamed when they acted in ways that were completely in accord with their normal level of development.

When I review my own moral education, I can see how these ways failed to achieve what they set out to do. No child knew his catechism better than I did, nor was any child more obedient or helpful than I. But as I grew up I found myself rebelling against these values, and in my early adult life I discovered that I had glaring character defects and holes in my conscience.

As I grappled with raising my own children, wanting them to be people of high moral character, I had to find a new model for teaching virtue and values. I came to see that goodness is dependent on appetite, that a truly moral person *wants* to be good. Virtuous people seek goodness for its own sake. They are not driven by rigid laws that spawn feelings of guilt-laden duty and fear of punishment.

In revising traditional values, we have to learn better ways to internalize virtue and help ourselves and our children learn a *process* for forming and clarifying values. People learn to be virtuous by doing virtuous acts. And the motivation for doing virtuous acts begins by experiencing the virtue of the people we interact with. By watching and experiencing our source figures acting virtuously, we develop an appetite for virtue. The ancients called an appetite for virtue a "right" appetite. Right appetite results from habituated experience. It cannot be legislated. Blind obedience allows no alternatives. In monarchial patriarchy you do good acts because an authority tells you to. "Do it because I said so" was a statement I heard frequently as a child.

Values must be prized and cherished. A person with strong values has a passionate attachment to what he believes and will even publicly proclaim it if necessary. And values must be acted upon and acted upon repeatedly. When a value is acted on repeatedly, it is internalized as a constituent of a person's character.

Children can only learn in age-appropriate stages. Childhood is characterized by very specific stages of emotional, intellectual, moral and spiritual readiness. Understanding these developmental stages makes it clear that we cannot stuff values down children's throats. They can only learn in ways that take their cognitive and emotional capacities into account. Our new knowledge of this developmental material has taught us that the past approach to moral education must be reformulated. This new knowledge tells us that the *process* of forming values is equally as important as the content in the terms of internalizing values. The contrast between learning a process and learning content is aptly illustrated by the old Zen story:

Feed a person a fish dinner and they are satisfied for a day
. . . teach them to fish and they will be satisfied for a lifetime.

Making people memorize the Ten Commandments, coercing them to obey with the use of punishment, and telling them what they must believe do not really create a person of moral character. But teaching people a process that shows them how to form values allows them to know how to internalize their own values. This is precisely what the philosopher John Dewey taught.

The work of Dewey and his disciple Louis Raths has been popularized by a group of educators led by Sidney B. Simon, Leland Howe and Howard Kirschenbaum. Raths' work clearly differed from the old monarchial, patriarchal way in that he was concerned with the *way* people formed values. Valuing according to Raths is composed of seven subprocesses:

Prizing One's Beliefs and Behaviors

1. Prizing and cherishing
2. Publicly affirming, when appropriate

Choosing One's Beliefs and Behaviors

3. Choosing from alternatives
4. Choosing after consideration of consequences
5. Choosing freely—acting on one's beliefs

Acting on One's Beliefs

6. Acting
7. Acting with a pattern, consistency and repetition

The goal of this approach is to avoid coercing or commanding people into accepting someone else's values and to help them utilize these seven processes in their own lives as a way to form their own values. To accept someone else's values and to act on them out of blind obedience, guilt-laden duty and fear of punishment hardly constitutes a freely chosen act.

The empirical data done on this new process-focused approach and the reports by thousand of teachers indicate that children and students exposed to this approach are less apathetic, less flighty and wishy-washy, less conforming and less rebellious. They are more zestful and passionate, more critical in their thinking and more likely to follow through on decisions.

A second overarching context for revision is our new consciousness of deep democracy. Power must be shared; it cannot be hierarchal. We may need to study tribal partnership cultures more extensively and glean new ways of parenting from them. Our so-called primitive ancestors, the American Indians, never saw value in hitting or spanking their children. How ironic! We pride ourselves on our civilized achievements and have for centuries resorted to physical violence to discipline our young.

Deep democracy as a new form of consciousness has emerged from many sources. Its obvious beginnings stem from the French and American Revolutions. The 19th-century movement in philosophy called existentialism also aided its development. The existentialist philosophers prized emotion and argued that the will was equally as important as reason. They attacked the philosophy of rationalism, which placed will and emotion under the control of reason. Deep democracy has grown as a reaction to the Nazi debacle, which clearly exposed the inherent potential in *any* monarchial patriarchy to abuse and destroy human life.

General systems theory, the core of this book, aided the growth of deep democracy by validating an earlier philosophical movement led by Henri Bergson, Alfred North Whitehead and Martin Heidegger, which emphasized dynamic process over static essence. The information revolution, which Alvin and Heidi Toffler called the Third Wave in Social Consciousness, has played a crucial role in helping us understand the common humanity of the peoples of the Earth. Because of the instantaneous communication that technology provides, Planet Earth has become a global village. Today our kids can play Monopoly on the Internet with Iraqi children.

Instantaneous communication has brought us face to face with the diversity of cultures on the planet. We now know that there are many religions with differing beliefs and devotions. There are myriads of etiological stories, some quite different from others, telling about the origins of Earth—how goodness and evil came about—and giving guidelines for the right ways of behavior.

Modern physics describes a universe that is far more chaotic and less measurable than we have previously understood. It underscores the importance of giving expression to every element in an energy field.

Evolutionists tell us that the process of forming this planet and human consciousness was governed by several laws. One of the most important of these is the law of differentiation, discussed in chapter 11. This law tells us that the universe grows, balances and regulates itself because it continually *differentiates*. In this book we have seen that the goal of good functional parenting is the healthy self-differentiation of children. Evolutionists tell us that we have now reached that point in self-reflecting consciousness where the population of the planet—5.82 billion people and growing—is the Earth thinking. We not only need every species of animal and marine life, we need to accept every political, cultural and religious difference if the evolutionary process is to continue. The conclusion the evolutionists ask us to understand is that the differences are not the problem, they are the solution. Accepting and honoring all differences and giving them voice is the way we will get to the next stage of evolution. This is precisely what deep democracy calls us to do.

Earlier I listed several items that I think of as traditional values. How could we revise these values in light of our new deeply democratic consciousness and the new knowledge we have available to us? What follows are a few cursory remarks pertaining to the revision of the 12 traditional values listed below. I am currently writing a book in which I discuss these issues in depth. When it is available, you may want to peruse that work for a more detailed discussion of these matters. The 12 traditional values are:

1. Love and Devotion to God (Higher Power)
2. Law and Order (Natural Law Morality)
3. Human Rights
4. The Preservation of Human Liberty
5. Loving Families
6. Strong Marriage
7. Responsible Parenting
8. Discipline
9. Perseverance and Hard Work
10. Virtue and Character
11. Love of Country and Respect for Traditions
12. Piety—Care and Respect for the Elderly

Love and Devotion to God (Higher Power)

There was a time when the word "God" had common meaning for most people in our country. Today that is not the case. When I use the word God, I refer to my own unique understanding of a higher power. My Higher Power is the fruit of my subjective search for meaning, coupled with my spirituality and religious faith.

As our new deeply democratic consciousness is internalized, we accept the vast plurality that makes up our human culture. Our future survival and true peace on Earth are matters of ultimate concern to us. The evolutionary law of differentiation must now be applied to the evolution of consciousness. This means that the Judeo-Christian God is one among many. This should not deter Christians from a passionate love and devotion to Jesus Christ. It could be a wake-up call for Christians to love the strangers—the ones who are different. It is a call to break out of the closed system of religious provincialism, which cannot help us in building a community of love and tolerance on the planet Earth.

The expansion of knowledge resulting from the information revolution makes us painfully aware of the relativity of our religious thinking. Who among us would claim to *know for sure* anything about the ultimate human questions? Where did we come from? Where are we going? Is there a personal God who cares about us? Are there a Heaven and Hell? No one *knows* the answers to these questions. This is why the response to God and the knowledge of the nature of God (as your own Higher Power) is a matter of faith and not the result of logic or reason. It is certainly reasonable to believe that there is some higher power, whatever you call it.

The love of God (higher power) is rooted in healthy shame. The German philosopher Friedrich Nietzsche wrote, "Shame is the source of spirituality." The feeling of shame tells us we are finite, that we need help and are prone to mistakes.

Shame has always been an appropriate response to the reality of God. Healthy shame literally means modesty, awe and reverence. Our nature is rooted in healthy shame, which is an emotion that distinguishes us from other living beings on Planet Earth. Without shame, we become shameless and *idolize* ourselves, our money or our power. They become our gods. When we have a true sense of shame we know that there is something greater than ourselves.

A revised traditional value that calls us to love and worship the god of our choice must be the cornerstone upon which we create our deeply democratic culture in the new millennium.

Law and Order (Natural Law Morality)

When we nourish healthy shame, it grows into guilt or moral shame. Guilt safeguards our conscience and insures that we will live within the boundaries of whatever moral laws our family and culture develop. The presence of healthy shame, then, is the foundation for moral accountability.

Once we've established healthy shame as the foundation for conscience and spirituality, the belief in a natural law morality easily follows. There is no place in human history where we find human beings who do not believe in something they consider good and something they think is bad. All people believed that good is to be done and evil avoided. The ancients believed that this was a self-evident first principle. They believed it was the foundation of natural moral law.

Moderns have argued that there are no self-evident truths; there are no absolutes.

It seems to me that it *is* self-evident that there are more people who seek goodness and peace than there are people seeking evil and war. Even terrorist groups believe they are on the side of goodness, fighting for their rights—often their god. Their actions are motivated by their belief that they are right and their enemy wrong. The people who blew up the Federal Building in Oklahoma believe that the government is so evil that they must take innocent lives to prove their point. I think they are evil. I think this because I believe there is a moral absolute that says that murdering innocent people is *never* morally good, even if you believe that the federal government is evil.

More good people emerged at Oklahoma City than bad ones, and we watched in awe as people overcame self-interest and self-preservation to save others. Moral goodness is far more desirable than moral evil. No one would truly debate this. While the content of most of our moral values may be subject to discussion, no one would really argue that we do not need moral values. The very argument would be self-defeating, as would saying that having no moral values is *good*.

In revising our moral values we will have to be tolerant of those who see things differently than we do, unless it has to do with one of the few areas where we believe the matter in question is an absolute.

Human Rights

In order to bring this traditional value up to date we need to begin with the rights of children. The abuse of children is our greatest social problem. We have no right to do to children many of the shaming things that our ancestors proscribed, often in the name of God. While we can acknowledge our ancestors' good intentions and lack of awareness of deep democracy, we have to say that some of their methods and beliefs were and are abusive. Our human rights list would certainly have to include the rights of people of color, women, children and those of different sexual orientation.

The Preservation of Human Liberty

One of our basic human rights is freedom. There are still millions of our fellow human beings who do not enjoy the fullness of human freedom and large parts of humanity who have been enslaved throughout most of human history. And even in our own country, which prides itself as the guardian of human rights, we deprive many of our citizens of their freedom. This needs to be changed.

The traditional value of freedom has always been understood in the context of law. It is a right that was rooted in reason and natural law. Freedom was denied to those who transgressed the natural law.

Freedom has also been understood as the opposite of irrational and undisciplined license. I don't know the source of the saying, "Of all the masks of freedom, discipline is the most difficult to understand," but it makes sense to me. There is no freedom with discipline.

My discussion of the meaning of discipline in this epilogue will expand on this matter. Suffice it to say that freedom has nothing to do with irrational whim or license. Because we are free, we can't just do anything we feel like doing. No civilized society could survive if such were the case.

In revising the traditional value of freedom, we will have to expand our vision of human nature to include the rights and freedom of gay, lesbian, bisexual and transgendered people. Their sexual lifestyles have been judged as violations of the natural law and were legally prohibited in the past. Newly found *genetic* evidence is clearly contrary to that traditional belief. It is astonishing to me that such genetic studies were not even considered in the past. A growing number of people see nothing wrong with a gay, lesbian, transgendered or bisexual lifestyle. Such people were born that way. Our revised commitment to the values of human freedom would therefore have to include the liberty of gay, lesbian, transgendered or bisexual people. They are a part of the great diversity by which the Earth expands itself and evolves.

The awareness of deep democracy also calls us to validate and expand our tolerance of those who think and teach differently than we do. We must continue to support the rights of those who hold opinions that differ from the socially accepted consensus reality of the majority, especially when the majority is supported by strong religious faith.

Deep democracy goes far beyond representative democracy. Deep democracy demands a radical form of participatory democracy, where every voice has the freedom to be heard and expressed, no matter how far it departs from commonly held opinions. The planet as a social system cannot be balanced until every voice has equal freedom to express itself.

Loving Families

The family is the foundation of social life. Whatever we teach about families in the future must be grounded in systems thinking. The family as a social system has awesome power over the individual members and is more than the sum or the total of its membership, The one law that should be absolute in the family is the law of love. Paradoxically, this law cannot be legislated; it can only be modeled.

Strong Marriage

Family systems theory promotes marriage as the chief component in the family. As the marriage goes, so goes the family. Marriages will need to be based on equality and shared power. Individuals who do not have a solid sense of self-esteem will have trouble forming intimate bonds with a mate. They will also have trouble loving in a free and uncontaminated way. On the one hand, unless we love ourselves *to some degree* we cannot really love anyone else. But on the other hand, self-love is aided by the love of another. We begin our life dependent on the love of our source figures. Without their love, we cannot develop properly.

I believe we need better understanding of the developmental stages that form our solid self-esteem. Couples who marry carrying unresolved developmental dependency needs will have the opportunity to work them out in their marriage because their marriage will, to some degree, recapitulate each partner's developmental stages and bring out those needs.

The most important way to revise the traditional belief in a strong marriage is to give couples better education as a preparation for marriage. The legal requirement for marriage is a blood test. Imagine what changes might occur if we gave high-school students information on how developmental deficits in their childhood could affect their marriage. These "hot issues" from the past cause many people to divorce. We could spend some of the many hours of high school working on repairing our developmental deficits. Those deficits themselves are due to the poor relationships we had with one or both of our source figures. Instead of a blood test, we might do the following:

- Offer a communication course
- Introduce a sampler of "hot issues" that couples have to deal with in therapy

- Offer a life skills course, teaching things like expressing anger in a contained and nonshaming way and assertiveness training
- Present learning about basic needs and how to express them
- Teach people about naming and expressing feelings
- Offer courses on parenting skills

Such a preparation might strengthen marriage and stop the upwardly spiraling divorce rate.

Responsible Parenting

To revise our grasp of what it takes to be responsible parents, we need to clearly grasp the scope of parental responsibility. Parents need to:

- Work on updating their own childhood developmental dependency needs—having children will offer parents the opportunity to work on these
- Model a functional marriage
- Be there for their children, to give them their time, to teach them both by instructing and by modeling, to give them physical nurturing, to give them attention
- Be in their healthy shame, which tells children that parents do not know it all and that they are not always right, that parents will make mistakes and that they are not gods and that the parents have a Higher Power themselves
- Be willing to take the time to get the information that will teach them how to parent
- Be in agreement about the bottom-line family rules and boundaries and to support each other in firmly enforcing these
- Be self-disciplined disciplinarians

Discipline

As far as I'm concerned, the psychiatrist M. Scott Peck, in his bestseller *The Road Less Traveled,* wrote the basic revision of the traditional value of discipline. I cited his outline on discipline in chapter 3. Peck makes it clear that the purpose of discipline is to reduce life's pain. This is a refreshing way to revise the lugubrious duty-bound suffering associated with the monarchial, patriarchal type of discipline. A revised notion of discipline should include a primary emphasis on developing a sense of responsibility as well as on the ancient virtues of temperance, justice, fortitude and prudence. I would suggest the following as an addendum to Peck's work:

Parental discipline needs to be nonshaming and inventive. The goal of that discipline is empowerment. The methods of discipline need to be evaluated in terms of whether they produce people who have a solid sense of self-esteem. In this model, natural consequences of behavior are enough punishment for misdeeds. These consequences need to be related to developmental age and maturity. In my revised notion of discipline, parents who use physical punishments, such as threats, scare tactics, spankings, pinching, punching or pushing, would be subject to fines and/or legal action. How that would be enforced is problematic, but the very existence of the law and/or fines would be an advance in the humanization of parenting.

Perseverance and Hard Work

I do not want to suggest that work is valuable just because it is work. Working for work's sake can be addictive and tends to diminish one's solid sense of self-esteem. Our work needs to have meaning and enhance our self-esteem. When work enhances self-esteem it becomes a value. Ideally, our work will also give something of value to others.

Perseverance is valuable when it evidences a purposeful self-determination. It is not valuable as a kind of long suffering. Buddha suggested that perseverance in work is valuable when:

1. Our work helps our human potential;
2. It enables us to overcome ego-centeredness and expand ourselves spiritually; and
3. It affords us enough money to live a becoming life.

Virtue and Character

We need to revise our whole approach to the development of character and virtue. The moral crises we are presently experiencing are signs that the obedient ethics of the poisonous pedagogy have failed to produce truly virtuous people. Look at the corruption in politics and religion, and the violence in our cities as proof of this.

In order to revise our educational approach to virtue and character, we might well reconnect with the ancient tradition represented by the philosopher Aristotle and the medieval theologian Thomas Aquinas. Their ethics were a prudential ethics. We have completely lost the meaning of prudence today. For Aristotle and Aquinas, prudence was the "soul" of virtue. All virtues insofar as they were truly virtues were prudent.

Prudence is a virtue of the practical intellect. It is defined as right reasoning in things to be done. Prudence is moral "know-how." A prudent person *does* good without necessarily knowing all about goodness. The development of prudence depends on parts who *model* goodness rather than preach about it. Prudence also depends upon "right appetite." Right appetite develops as a person does good acts and experiences the joy of being good. Prudence is also related to what is today being called emotional intelligence. I discussed E.Q. earlier. To revise our approach to teaching virtue in our families and our schools, we need to educate our emotions.

The fruit of a virtuous life is the ability to love in a compassionate way. When we act virtuously, we love and respect ourselves. We cannot truly love ourselves without wanting to love others. Goodness is diffusive of itself. With love, we reach out to others and expand ourselves; we become more. Our being is expanded and we become more fully who we are. We become persons of character.

Compassion comes close to being a synonym for deep democracy. A compassionate commitment and a responsibility to all life extend to caring for the poor, the sick, the homeless and those who are vulnerable. Compassion also extends to loving and caring for our planet.

Love of Country and Respect for Tradition

When we grow up in deeply democratic families, our need for sharing power and feeling a deep connection with other family members will extend to our cities and our state and overflow into love for our country. Our country is an extension of our family, and while many of us do not want our government to be too strong and interfere with our personal lives, we need to value our country's government. Once the voice of our participatory democracy has spoken, we need to get on board and make it work.

The current political practice of ridiculing and shaming one's political opponents is an alarming sign of degeneration. It is even more degenerative to continue to ridicule and shame our opponents after they have won the election. The radio host Rush Limbaugh's daily attacks on the president of the United States evidence a marked disrespect for our country.

Deep democracy asks us to learn the meta skill of radical synthesis. This demands we step into our opponent's shoes, experience their motivation, and for a while act as if their position is true. If political opponents were capable of doing this, a stronger position embodying the strengths of both sides would emerge. To some degree this already happens, but more by accident than by conscious design. I would like to see a day when the possession of this meta skill is the reason we elect leaders.

Another alarming trend is the emergence of the various armed militia groups. Their paranoid fears are rooted in the methods espoused by the poisonous pedagogy. Monarchial patriarchy calls for the repression of all human emotions except *fear.* Fear of authority is considered good. It enhances blind obedience. The militia takes the fear of authority to a rebellious extreme.

If we would use our anger (even rage) constructively, we could take positive action (not arms) and do something to change what we do not like about our government. If we truly experienced deep democracy in our families, we would move beyond a mere representative democracy and work to create a truly participatory process of government. Democracy is optimistic and wants everyone to have some voice in what is going on. Apathy and hopeless inactivity would never appear if we revised our traditional values in these ways.

Deep democracy also demands that we honor past forms of government, or past stages of our evolving democratic consciousness. These stages were valuable differentiations, and they allowed our deeply democratic conscious to evolve. Great Britain has maintained the monarchy in a symbolic way as an honoring of the past.

Our country's traditions are not just archaic remnants from the past; they are living forms that have, in the process of differentiation, become the resources for the strengths that we now have as a country. Traditions are our living past. We must be sure to love our traditions, yet not succumb to a rigid traditionalism. I once heard a talk by the theologian Martin E. Marty. In it he said that, "Traditions are the living faith of dead people, whereas traditionalism is the dead faith of living people." We could well use this as a slogan for revisioning our love and respect for our country and its traditions.

Piety—Care and Respect for the Elderly

The ancients spoke of the virtue of piety. It referred to the care and respect for the older members of the society. They honored their elderly in gratitude for all they had done. They also cared for, honored and respected them because of their wisdom. In chapter 11, I spoke of wisdom. I suggested that it most often comes in the evening of life because it is only then that our whole life comes into view. To the ancients, wisdom was vital because it comes from experience and cannot be learned in books. When a wise person dies, it is like losing the only copy of a book from a great library.

It is also a fact that all old people are not always wise. When an old person has failed to learn anything from life, we see him as foolish. But foolish or not, our parents deserve our gratitude because they participated in the miracle of our life. If we hold that life is precious, then no matter how we feel they may have failed us, they still gave us our life.

The manner in which we are personally involved in caring for our elderly parents may be quite different, depending on the level of friendship we have achieved with them. If they were abusive, we can still help them while keeping strong physical boundaries in relation to them. Piety is a virtue and should be part of our revised traditional values.

Our traditional values have made us the greatest nation the world has ever known. Each of us is responsible for revising and recreating these values in our lives. That is the task before us. Shakespeare's words sum it up:

> *There is a tide in the affairs of men*
> *Which, taken at the flood, leads to fortune;*
> *Omitted, all the voyage of their life*
> *Is bound in shallows and in miseries.*
> *On such a full sea are we now afloat.*
> *We must take the current when it serves,*
> *Or lose our ventures.*[1]

---

[1] *Julius Caesar,* 4.3.217-223.

REFERENCES

The author gratefully wishes to acknowledge the following books, articles and tapes as sources for this book. I heartily recommend them to the reader.

_____. *Alcoholics Anonymous.* 3d rev. ed. New York: Alcoholics Anonymous World Services, 1976.

Berger, Peter L., and Thomas Luckmann. *The Social Construction of Reality: A Treatise in the Sociology of Knowledge.* Garden City, N. Y.: Doubleday Anchor, 1966.

Bohr, Neils. *Atomic Physics and the Description of Nature.* New York: Cambridge University Press, 1964.

Bowen, Murray. "A Family Concept of Schizophrenia," in *The Etiology of Schizophrenia.* Dan Jackson, ed. New York: Basic Books, 1960.

_____. *Family Therapy in Clinical Practice.* Northvale, N. J.: Jason Aronson, 1985.

Bradshaw, John. *Healing the Shame That Binds You.* Deerfield Beach, Fla.: Health Communications, Inc., 1988.

_____. *Homecoming: Reclaiming and Championing Your Inner Child.* New York: Bantam Books, 1990.

_____. *Creating Love: The Next Stage of Growth.* New York: Bantam Books, 1992.

_____. *Family Secrets: What You Don't Know Can Hurt You.* New York: Bantam Books, 1995.

Carnes, Patrick. *Out of the Shadows: Understanding Sexual Addiction.* Minneapolis, Minn.: CompCare, 1992.

Cermak, Timmen. *Diagnosing and Treating Co-dependence: A Guide for Professionals Who Work with Chemical Dependents, Their Spouses and Children.* Minneapolis, Minn.: Johnson Institute Books, 1986.

Coudert, Jo. *Advice from a Failure.* Lanham, Md.: Scarborough House, 1987.

Dossey, Larry. *Space, Time and Medicine.* Boulder, Colo.: Shambhala Publications, Inc., 1982.

Erickson, Milton H., et al. *Hypnotic Realities: The Induction of Clinical Hypnosis & Forms of Indirect Suggestions.* New York: Irvington, 1976.

Erikson, Erik. *Childhood and Society.* New York: W. W. Norton & Co., 1963.

Farber, Leslie H. *The Ways of the Will.* Houston: Colophon House, 1987.

Firestone, Robert. *The Fantasy Bond: Structure of Psychological Defenses.* New York: Human Sciences Press, 1985.

Foley, Vincent. *An Introduction to Family Therapy.* Philadelphia: W.B. Saunders Co./Grune & Stratton Incorporated, 1974.

Forward, Susan. *Betrayal of Innocence: Incest and Its Devastation.* New York: Penguin Books, 1979.

Fossum, Merle A., and Marilyn J. Mason. *Facing Shame: Families in Recovery.* New York: W. W. Norton & Co., 1986.

Frederickson, Renee. *Repressed Memories: A Journey to Recovery from Sexual Abuse.* New York: Simon & Schuster, 1992.

_____. Tapes can be ordered from Frederickson & Associates, 821 Raymond Avenue, St. Paul, MN 55114.

Goleman, Daniel. *Emotional Intelligence.* New York: Bantam Books, 1995.

Harper, James, and Margaret Hoopes. *Birth Order Roles and Sibling Patterns in Individual and Family Therapy.* Gaithersburg, Md.: Aspen Publishers, Inc., 1987.

Hoffman. *No One Is to Blame: Getting a Loving Divorce from Mom & Dad.* Palo Alto, Calif.: Science & Behavior, 1979.

Jackins, Harvey. *The Human Side of Human Beings: The Theory of Re-Evaluation Counseling.* Seattle, Wash.: Rational Island Publications, 1978.

Kaufman, Gershen. *Shame: The Power of Caring.* 3d rev. ed. Rochester, Vt.: Schenkman Books, Inc., 1992.

Kellogg, Terry. Tapes can be ordered from 20300 Excelsior Boulevard, Minneapolis, MN. 55331.

Kohlberg, Lawrence. *Essays on Moral Development.* 1st ed. San Francisco: Harper and Row, 1981.

Leonard, George Burr. *The Silent Pulse: A Search for the Perfect Rhythm That Exists in Each of Us.* New York: E. P. Dutton, 1978.

Levin, Pam. *Cycle of Power: A User's Guide to Seven Seasons of Life.* Deerfield Beach, Fla.: Health Communications, Inc., 1988.

Lynch, William F. *Images of Hope: Imagination as Healer of the Hopeless.* Notre Dame, Ind.: University of Notre Dame Press, 1987.

McCall, Cheryl. "Special Report: The Cruelest Crime." *Life* 7, no. 13 (December 1984): 35-62.

Mellody, Pia. *Permission to Be Precious.* Tape series can be obtained by writing P.O. Box 1739, Wickenburg, AZ 85358.

Midelfort, Cristian. *The Family in Psychotherapy.* New York: McGraw Hill, 1957.

Miller, Alice. *The Drama of the Gifted Child.* New York: Basic Books, 1981.

_____. *For Your Own Good: Hidden Cruelties in Child Rearing and the Roots of Violence.* New York: Farrar, Straus, Giroux, 1983.

Mindell, Arnold. *The Leader as Martial Artist: An Introduction to Deep Democracy.* San Francisco: HarperSanFrancisco, 1993.

Omar Khayyàm. *The Rubaiyat of Omar Khayyàm.* Translated by Edward FitzGerald. New York: Doubleday & Co., Inc., 1879.

Peck, M. Scott. *The Road Less Traveled: A New Psychology of Love, Traditional Values & Spiritual Growth.* New York: Simon and Schuster, 1978.

Peele, Stanton. *Love and Addiction.* New York: Taplinger Publishing Co., 1978.

Puthoff, Harold E., and Russel Targ. *Mind Reach: Scientists Look at Psychic Ability.* New York: Delacorte Press/E. Friede, 1977.

Putney, Snell, and Gail Putney. *The Adjusted American.* New York: HarperCollins Publishers, Inc., 1986.

Rilke, Rainer Maria. *Letters of Rainer Maria Rilke,* vol. 1: 1892-1910, vol. 2: 1910-1926. Translated by Jane Barnard Greene and M. D. Herter Norton. New York: W. W. Norton & Co., 1969.

Satir, Virginia. *Conjoint Family Therapy.* 3d ed. rev. and expanded. Palo Alto, Calif.: Science and Behavior, 1983.

——————. *Making Contact.* Millbrae, Calif.: Celestial Arts, 1976.

Schwarz, Jack. *Voluntary Controls: Exercises for Creative Meditation & for Activating the Potential of the Chakras.* New York: NAL-Dutton, 1978.

Small, Jacquelyn. *Transformers: The Artists of Self-Creation.* Marina Del Rey, Calif.: DeVorss & Co., 1994.

Targ, Russell, and Keith Harary. *The Mind Race: Understanding and Using Psychic Abilities.* New York: Ballantine, 1984.

Targ, Russell, and Harold E. Puthoff. *Mind-Reach: Scientists Look at Psychic Ability.* New York: Dell Publishing Co., 1977.

Toffler, Alvin. *The Third Wave.* New York: Bantam Books, 1980.

Trush, Howard. *Close Encounters of the Intimate Kind; or How to Stay a Couple by Really Trying.* New York: Vantage Press, 1985.

Verny, Thomas R. *The Secret Life of the Unborn Child.* New York: Summit Books, 1981.

Walker, Lenore E. *The Battered Woman*. New York: Harper & Row, 1979.

Whitfield, Charles L. *Healing the Child Within*. Deerfield Beach, Fla.: Health Communications, 1987.

Wilber, Ken, ed. *The Holographic Paradigm and Other Paradoxes: Exploring the Leading Edge of Science*. Boulder, Colo.: Shambhala Publications, Inc., 1982.

Wynne, Lyman C. *Exploring the Base for Family Therapy*. New York: Family Service, 1961.

INDEX

VIDEOTAPES AND AUDIOTAPES

For the videotape and audiotape series *Bradshaw On: The Family* write or call:

Bradshaw Cassettes
P. O. Box 720947
Houston, Texas 77272

phone: (713) 771-1300
toll free: 800-6BRADSHAW
fax (713) 771-1362
Internet website: http//www.bradshawcassettes.com

A variety of other video and audiotapes are also available.

John Bradshaw gives workshops and lectures throughout the country in the areas of management, addiction, recovery and spirituality. For more information about lectures or workshops, write:

John Bradshaw
2412 South Boulevard
Houston, Texas 77098
or call: (713) 522-9677
fax (713) 522-2018